HOME FROM THE HILL

Hilary Hook

Foreword by
WILFRED THESIGER,
C.B.E., D.S.O.

St. Martin's Press
New York

HOME FROM THE HILL

First published in England by The Sportsman's Press, 1987

ISBN 0–312–01631–X

First U.S. Edition

10 9 8 7 6 5 4 3 2 1

Contents

FOR SIMON AND HARRY

List of Illustrations

63lb Nile perch. Namasagli, Uganda, 1968.

Partners consulting: H.H. with Major Digby Tatham Warter, D.S.O. and Hook and Tatham Warter Safaris camped in a remote part of the Serengeti.

A cheetah in the Mara and a record head, Meru National Park, 1964.

The perpetual snow peaks on Mount Kenya.

On the lawn at Kiserian in the late '70s.

Between pages 170 and 171

The house on the hill: Kiserian.

H.H. at Kiserian.

Lion cubs in the Mara.

Denis Zaphiro, with a Nile perch caught in Lake Rudolf.

With The Hon. Rosie Pearson in the Aberdare Forest, 1982.

Technical adviser for The Flame Trees of Thika. On location with Elspeth Huxley.

Home from the hill: H.H. 1987.

Acknowledgements

To all my old friends who have helped jog my flagging memory, and recently to Molly Dineen and Rosie Pearson for their help and encouragement.

Foreword

by

WILFRED THESIGER, C.B.E., D.S.O.

Hilary Hook has led an interesting and adventurous life which he describes very effectively in this book. As a child he grew up on the coast of Devon, in those days a remote area as yet unaffected by tourism. He was fascinated by the many sea birds and ravens that nested in the cliffs and acquired a lifelong interest in birds. His account of those early formative years, though brief, is very evocative. Already he was interested in Africa and read whatever he could get hold of by Gordon Cumming, Selous and the other great African hunters.

He was commissioned in 1937 and joined the Indian army. He played polo and spent his leave shooting in the mountains of Kashmir and pigsticking in the renowned Kadir country, of which sport he gives a graphic description.

After war was declared his cavalry regiment remained frustratingly unmechanised; the tanks with which they were due to be equipped were repeatedly diverted elsewhere. He transferred to the Australian forces in New Guinea, dropping his rank to private to serve in that claustrophobic jungle. I would have liked to have read more about his adventures in those harrowing operations.

In 1947 he joined the 7th Hussars and was seconded to the Sudan Defence Force in 1949; during the two years he was in Southern Sudan, an area the size of France, Belgium, Holland and Switzerland combined, he carried out long and often arduous patrols with his company, crossing immense bare plains, through forest country and over the ten thousand foot Imatong mountains. This was the primitive Africa of the past, about which he had read so avidly as a boy. I fancy those two years were the most memorable in his life.

He was then transferred first to Kordofan Province and after that to Darfur. Here the tribesmen were Moslems in contrast to the pagan tribes from which his men in Southern Sudan were recruited. He spent three happy years among these people, perhaps the most likeable in

Africa. Later he was to return to the newly independent Sudan as Military attaché.

He retired from the army in 1964 and went to live in Kenya where he spent twenty years, organizing safaris and taking his clients to the remotest and most interesting areas of that attractive country.

Hilary Hook has been fortunate. He has lived with such evident enjoyment the life he describes so successfully in this book. It has been a life which neither he, nor I, could lead today under the changed conditions of the modern world.

1

'Don't tell me,
I'd much rather not know'

EARLY YEARS: THE '20s AND '30s

———————◆·◆·◆———————

Memories of childhood stay with us fitfully like incidents in a dream which one cannot quite grasp on waking. Smells evoke even more poignant memories than sights and sounds. The sweet-sour country-man smell of a gardener as he lifted me up to peer into a hedge-sparrow's nest with four blue eggs; the waft of shag tobacco on a frosty morning and the glorious smell of blown bladder-wrack on the shore as the winter waves roar up the beach. These evoke memories of a happy childhood in Devon, but visual memories of insignificant incidents and things are more elusive.

I just remember my father who died when I was five, a tall bearded figure standing smocked at the easel in his studio, shaking with what I presumed to be rage but what I subsequently learnt to be suppressed mirth, as Nanny, the cherries on her hat bobbing with indignation, paraded me before him for picking up my cat 'Satan' by the tail. I remember the smell of lavender in high summer and the thrill of waking to a white world at Christmas-time with tracks of rabbits, weasels, and birds in the snow, and the old black barn standing stark on the hill a mile away across the valley.

My father sold our house in Devon in 1920, and casually ordering another to be built high on a hill overlooking the village, he took ship with my mother and eldest brother to his beloved Kenya for six months to travel, paint and collect bird skins. My middle brother and I were parked happily in a cottage in the village with Nanny Nunn and a nursery-maid called Gladys. There were occasional visits from a delightful maiden aunt who lived in Suffolk. Everyone was extremely kind during that long summer which still brings memories of lazy days in the apple orchard behind the cottage and walks to the sun-drenched beaches, through Devon lanes bright with fool's parsley and dog roses or shaded by high hedges. Then came a blissful morning when, scrubbed and pink, we were ushered into our parents' room where they were having early morning tea. Unknown to us they had arrived in the night and the bed was strewn with presents; black ebony elephants from Zanzibar, lucky beans from Nairobi; ivory lions and sour smelling Masai beads. And what adventures our elder brother had to tell, of days on safari; and lions roaring; of tall fierce warriors who carried him on their shoulders and the 'gully gully' man at Port Said who produced baby chickens from his nose.

Devon was a glorious county for three little boys to grow up in; all summer long we were on the seashore mackereling, swimming and boating or snaring rabbits and camping out on the wild cliffs; winter brought rambles in the fields and woods with terriers and ferrets or beating for pheasants on our neighbours' shoots, but the spring was our favourite time for it was the birds' nesting season and for that we had an overwhelming passion. We collected carefully, never taking more than one egg from a clutch and at great pains not to cause a bird to desert its nest. Our father had left a very fine collection in 'the museum', a loft built above the nursery which housed his African collections. We poured over it for hours and browsed happily through his splendid collection of bird books.

All through the Easter holidays we rambled on the cliffs or bicycled to distant woodlands and moors. The cliffs held the most fascination for us, for not only were there a great variety of sea-birds, but peregrine falcons, ravens and buzzards nested there: in those days there were five peregrine falcons' eyries within twenty miles of where we lived and we knew and visited them all. Being the youngest and smallest it was I who sat in the 'bowlin on the bight' and dangled from Berry Head or Garra Rock, with my brothers and two other friends hauling from above. Today I only have to open a drawer in our birds' egg cabinet for each egg to evoke a memory – an unmarked pure white buzzard's egg from a tall pine in the Llewellyn's woods; a raven's from Scabacombe; a cuckoo's egg taken from a Blackcap's nest in our garden and a peregrine's from Coleton cliffs where the ledge along which I was crawling collapsed and I fell sickeningly for ten feet until the rope held me swinging over the precipice and swirling rocks below. That bird cabinet is still a treasure-house of memories. In the summer we hunted butterflies and moths, but with less fervour than birds' eggs. We had a small sailing boat in Brixham harbour and summer was the time for conger eel fishing and mackereling around the big marine offshore rocks and along the rough coastline. We would disappear on bicycles after break-fast and come back after dark, fishy and sunburnt, having hunted cats with our terrier in the Brixham fish market on the way home.

Our mother was a gentle indulgent person much given to reading and her garden, and totally allergic to buff envelopes and bank state-ments; she seemed content to let us run wild and frequently said, 'Don't tell me, I'd much rather not know'. There were in fact a few small matters with which we did not wish to worry her, for instance, the acquisition of our first shotgun. It was a folding double-barrelled .410 which came into our possession through trading, I think, in fer-rets. In 'the museum', an Aladdin's cave of treasures, we discovered a large quantity of brass cartridge cases and bags of shot which my father had used in Kenya; these we loaded with homemade gunpowder and the little gun joined the sack of ferrets, nets and climbing irons on many a sporting expedition to the woods and cliffs. It also occasionally proved useful when the moon was high and pheasants were roosting, silhouetted in the tall trees out of earshot of the keeper's cottage.

One of our favourite characters was Fane, the professional rabbit catcher, a dark handsome gipsy with the face and figure of a wild west hero. He had been a welter-weight boxing champion in the army which, rumour had it, he had left for the army's good, but he was a cheerful loyal rogue wonderfully versed in gipsy skills and said to be unsteady with the village girls. Mrs Fane, who worked for my mother, was also a great favourite of ours. Once a fortnight Fane came to clean our windows and as he stood on his ladder, slowly revolving one cha-mois cloth after another, he would relate wonderful adventures of his service in foreign lands; of wild Afridi knife rushes and frontier ambu-scades; of snake charmers and opium dens. I followed him from room to room enthralled, while he perhaps sowed the first seeds which would grow into a pattern for my life. He was obsessed by boxing. 'I'll learn 'ee to box, Master 'Ilery. I'll learn 'ee to lick the big'uns at school. I'll speak to yer Mum, that I will.' And then, as he mounted his bicycle carrying his step-ladder, 'Us will be up Withycombe wood Friday with the ferrets.' 'We'll be there', I would shout after him – and we always were.

In those days the wild Devon hedgerows and woods swarmed with rabbits and Fane made a good living clearing the land of these pests; for rabbits who escaped the nets he had a good lurcher dog or two which would catch them in midfield. The sport was best on a frosty morning, when we silently put the nets in place in a selected warren, then the ferrets were loosed into the burrows; there would be a period of silent waiting and listening while the dogs, prick-eared and quivering, watched for the slightest movement; then a rumbling would announce activity underground and out of the nettles and brambles would shoot a rabbit struggling in the bag net. Another net was quickly put in its place while the rabbit was despatched and the silent watch continued until we sometimes had sixty or seventy rabbits in sacks, which Fane would then pack and send to the London poulterers by train. It was good business and the labour was willing and free. Rat ferreting was a sport which we boys enjoyed even more than rabbiting and for this Fane kept special polecat ferrets which were quick and fierce; there were frequent plagues of rats in the barns and ricks of the countryside and Fane's ferrets and expertise were in much demand from the local farmers. Armed with whippy sticks we would wait for the rats to break and then swat away with great competitive rivalry amongst dogs and boys. Every time we went out there was some new trick or bit of gipsy lore to learn from Fane.

Another boyhood hero was old Mr Cornish, who had sailed the world in clipper ships. Mrs Cornish was our cook, a kind, forceful old lady who spoilt us enormously with specially contrived 'treats' on almost every day of the week. We loved her and she took a kind motherly interest in our welfare and in what she called our 'escapades'. Sometimes old Mr Cornish would walk up from the village in the evening and sit in the kitchen with a bottle of beer on the table beside him. We boys would sit round in dressing-gowns listening to him, entranced, and watching him make beautiful seaman's knots. He was a large, benign old man, very smart in his navy blue reefer jacket with immensely broad shoulders and bright blue eyes in a brick red face and, like many Devon seamen of those days, he wore a single gold earring to ensure good sight into old age. As he wove 'turk's heads', 'monkey's paws' and 'true lovers' knots' he would yarn away about his seafaring life; tales of Rio, Shanghai and the Horn, of shipwreck off Java and piracy in the China seas. He had raced in the King's great 'J' class yacht *Britannia* and had crewed in the America's Cup many years before. He had the seaman's knack of telling a good yarn while Mrs Cornish bustled about the kitchen in her apron, clattering pots and pans and stirring saucepans. He was always a welcome visitor.

Our lives revolved entirely round the cycle of the countryside and the seaside which we got to know so well. We knew the badgers' holts in the big woods and where the foxes had cubs on the wild cliffs; we knew every hollow tree where owls might nest and the bright little rills where dippers came in the springtime. We knew the deep holes in the offshore rocks where the big conger eels lurked and the shoals out to sea where pollack took sand-worms. Spring, summer and winter each had a different call for us to which we readily responded.

Our mother was solitary, but I think contented with the simple life of her garden and her books – she took an interest in politics and charitable organisations and was very well liked in the village for her gentleness and good humour. In those palladian days there was no shortage of servants, and the kindly village people saw to it that 'the widdy up at Kings Barton house' with three little savages to look after never lacked for help. It was a happy life spent in the lush hilly Devon countryside girt by great cliffs and the glittering or angry sea, on which the red-sailed Brixham fishing trawlers plied in all weathers and, where in high summer came the 'J' class yachts; *Candida*, *Astra*, *Velsheda*, *Britannia* with King George V at the helm; *White Heather* and *Shamrock* rounding the weather mark to seaward with gunnels awash and then bursting out their spinnakers with a sound of thunder as, with spume flying, they raced for the line in Torbay, each with a big 'white bone in her teeth'.

After my brothers left school and departed into the world I was thrown on my own devices during the holidays. In the winter I went shooting wood pigeons and rabbits or walked the hedgerows and root fields for pheasants and partridges. Occasionally I was invited to more ordered shoots and sometimes I borrowed a farmer's cob and went hunting with the local harriers, but it was bad hunting country and there were no foxhounds. In the spring I pursued my passion for birds' nesting but I now only sought the rarer birds. The summer held most pleasure for me now and I spent every moment of it on the sea with my friend John Glenn and his younger brother George, sailing, fishing and camping on the coast between Brixham and Plymouth which in those days was wild, unfrequented and a paradise of nature. There were little coves and sandy bays inaccessible from the landward side where we hauled our sailing boat above the tide line and slept beside a driftwood fire which sparkled and spat with encrusted brine, and on which we cooked fresh mackerel, dabs or prawns and sometimes a rabbit or pigeon. During the day we would explore the cliffs looking for signs of peregrine falcons, or scramble round the rocks fishing for conger eel and wrasse. Sometimes a strong on-shore wind would blow up in the night and we would be unable to launch the boat in the morning –

when the sense of being marooned was a challenge to find food and make ourselves comfortable, but I think on more than one occasion after a night or two of discomfort we would leave the boat and embark on a tricky cliff climb and a long walk over the fields to a village shop for provisions and a drink of home-made Devon cider in a pub.

It was in one such cove that we finally lost our beloved little boat. We had been fishing for pollack out to sea and were so intent on our work that we didn't notice that the southern sky was darkening until suddenly George looked up and, pointing out to sea, shouted, 'Look at that!' We hurriedly hauled in the lines and ran for the coast under full sail with the wind behind us growing stronger every moment. There was only one shelter we could reach before the storm struck, and as the wind increased we hauled in the main sail and flew along under the jib; but we were too late, the gale had already struck the steep little beach, big waves were crashing onto the shingle and drawing back with a tremendous undertow. There was no alternative; we charged into the surf and leaping ashore tried to haul the loaded boat up the shingle, but the next few waves roared over us, swamping everything and dragging the little boat back to be battered and crushed in the turmoil of surf. For the next hour we struggled in lashing rain to retrieve some of the flotsam while Peter the terrier ran around enjoying the fun. With what could be saved we sought the comparative shelter of a dripping cave and watched the ruins of our favourite possession appear above the mounting waves and crash on to the shingle. After an uncomfortable night and with the aid of a salvaged rope we hauled our possessions and Peter up the cliffs next morning and set off on a long walk to telephone my mother to bring the car. Meanwhile we warmed ourselves in the stone-flagged parlour of a country inn, already discussing plans for another boat.

Whatever sage first said that schooldays are the happiest days of one's life, to my mind omitted to add, 'Of course, only during the holidays'; or perhaps that particular sage had suffered a boring home life. Frankly, I found school rather a bore and I think perhaps the reverse applied. In 1926 I went to a pleasant little preparatory school in Westgate-on-Sea, a monumental train journey from South Devon. The school, Doon House, was well run by a frightening but kindly old ex-Indian Army Colonel and his wife whose pictures, trophies and readings aloud from Kipling perhaps sowed further seeds in my young mind. Certainly the once-yearly visit to Quex Park fired my imagination and ambitions. It was the home of the famous big game hunter and collector, Major Powell Cotton, and the house was now his private museum with record trophies from all over Africa round the walls and in glass cases. Fired by this experience I read every book about big game shooting that I could find. As I lay under the blankets after 'lights out' reading Selous or Gordon Cumming by torch light, I vowed that one day I would follow in their footsteps.

Football and cricket came easily to me and, thanks to Mr Fane's instruction, I became the school boxing champion and won the miniature range rifle shooting competition. But I counted all time spent away from my beloved Devon as wasted; the Kent countryside was flat and dull and the coast was all promenades, crowded sands and low chalk cliffs where no peregrines flew. I was happy enough but my graph of happiness rose to its peak as each term drew to a close and at last the school train bore sixty happy little boys to Victoria – then, for me, a taxi across London to Paddington and a dash for a seat in the dining-car of the Torbay Limited express. Finally, much slamming of doors, a whistle above the hiss of steam, a green flag waving, and a gentle jolt. Then, as the knives and forks set up their cheerful jingle on the table, the face of old Mr Beech the guard looking down and asking in broad Devon tones of my plans for the holidays. First stop Exeter and then half an hour later the smell of the sea and the view of the white horses and the fishing smacks in Torbay.

From Doon House I went on, in 1932, to Canford in Dorset, which lies on the right bank of the River Stour near Wimborne; a beautiful place with a great area of playing fields and parkland backed by large and elegant buildings, contrived I think by some Victorian merchant prince around medieval ruins. Avenues of chestnut and lime trees line the drives which reach out in all directions; tall Wellingtonias overlook the playing fields and in the park are great oaks which may have been gazed at with admiration nearly a thousand years ago.

My house was a mile or so away from the main school buildings; it was within twenty minutes' walk of a private area of country known rather inappropriately as 'the moors', a wild tract of land comprising fir and pine wood, oak forest, bog and heather; every Sunday we were free to go there, a privilege of which surprisingly few boys took advantage. My friends and I spent every Sunday there birds' nesting, rabbiting (my ferrets had arrived in a tuck box and had been lodged with a friendly farmer) and catching snakes and other creatures for the Natural History Society. We had our own hideout in a dense clump of firs where smuggled arms, traps and other contraband were skilfully hidden, together with a frying pan and a few bottles of beer for Sunday feasts. I think our greatest triumph was the discovery on the moors of *Coronella austriaca*, the third and rarest British snake, known as the Smooth snake. We collected a number of these creatures which, although not poisonous, used to inflict sharp little bites. I wrote to the Curator of Reptiles at the London Zoo and a reply came saying that he would be delighted to accept as many specimens as we could catch, and was I 'by any chance a relation of the naturalist artist Bryan Hook who had published a paper on smooth snakes in 1899?' I replied with pride that he was my father, and our correspondence continued with further requests for other reptiles which we most delightedly supplied.

I was happy at Canford, within the confines of a rather irksome discipline which my friends and I were at constant pains to evade. I regret to say that for the first year or so we waged a constant war against authority, the enemy being the masters, the prefects and the school rules; we did so not out of a spirit of hooliganism but for the joy of the battle itself, and because both victory and defeat always caused us mirth. Our victories were few and harmless and our defeats were painful but honourable; above all we laughed enormously. Our laughter was mostly irreverent or profane, but of a quality which, I think, is given with the bright colours of youth, diverting unpleasantness and mocking authority, to fade like an old photograph with maturer years and perhaps the onset of greater compassion. I fear we were something of a nuisance.

One of the many excellent amenities of Canford was that, for the payment of three pounds a term, a boy could be taught to ride properly. There was a stable of horses, and for tuition an ex-rough-riding sergeant-major and a retired major who had been an instructor at the Weedon Cavalry School. Up to this time I had ridden by the light of nature with some scant instruction from an elusive aunt, and occasional farmers. Hunting with the Dart Vale Harriers had been a matter of scrambling and squirming through the overgrown hilly country, staying aboard by balance and agility. My mother was determined that I should be properly taught and accordingly wrote to my housemaster, and I joined the riding school. Our far-sighted and sporting headmaster had arranged with the Portman Hunt that any boy taking riding as an extra could hunt for a minimum cap. This was sheer delight and a wise move by the authorities, for any application to one's housemaster for a day's hunting had to be accompanied by an OK from one's formmaster. It was a wonderful incentive to do some work and even try and improve one's conduct. I cannot say that every one of my applications was approved but I think that probably in any of the exams that I subsequently had to pass, success may be partly due to the passion for fox-hunting which descended on me as a boy at Canford. In the summer the riders produced a bare-back vaulting team under the rough-riding sergeant-major. This was considerable fun, the standard was high, and the team performed at Olympia on the same programme as the wonderful Djuit Cossacks and the Cadre Noir.

The stables, which were a few minutes' walk from my House, were something of a social centre for the riding team in leisure moments, and a convenient place for a cigarette, a bottle of beer and a quiet game of poker. As we strolled up on a Sunday evening after chapel old Sergeant-Major Yerrill would say, 'And none of yer smoking in the 'ay loft. There's a nice fire in the tack room and if you 'ears me bang me bucket – look fly, it will be the Major on 'is rounds.'

One aspect of school life that bored me considerably was the Officers' Training Corps. I disliked parading in an uncomfortable uniform and wasting beautiful summer weather in route marches and drill. It became the practice of my friends and I to cut as many parades as possible and disappear out of bounds down the river to bathe, where a friendly farmer had been persuaded to 'see nothing'. However, I liked the little sergeant-major who trained me and his selecting me for both the Cadet pair and the school shooting eight resulted in camps at Bisley in the summer term for two years running. Sergeant-Major Edwards was a tough, leathery little man who seemed to us as ageless as a lizard. He had retired after many years service in India with the 60th Rifles and his stories of frontier fights, Pathan raids and galloping lancers, all told with a humorous and engaging Cockney accent, were heady wine for young minds; I think they added signs to the faint but already beckoning trail which lead me inevitably to the east.

As time went on the spectre of a career loomed in the not far distant future. My mother wanted me to go to Oxford and then into the Sudan Political Service but I, so far as I wanted to do anything serious, hoped to become a game warden in East Africa. The matter was shelved for several holidays until it was resolved at the drawing room fire. During the long winter evenings my mother would read aloud, which she did extremely well, making any boring holiday task that I had been given into a pleasure and giving me a taste for the classics with the minimum effort. But her taste was catholic, for she also read popular best-sellers. One day a new book called *Bengal Lancer* was sent to her and she read it to me while I lay on the carpet in front of the fire, smoking her Turkish cigarettes. From that moment, I knew what I wanted to do. The chapters on polo and pig-sticking, the wonderful description of life in an Indian Cavalry regiment and the author's concern with the mystic side of Indian life, made up my mind for me. I would join the army class, face the rigours of Sandhurst and hie away to the glamorous east to become a Bengal Lancer. Curiously enough, at about the same time the sporting artist 'Snaffles', a friend of my mother's, sent her a copy of his book *My Sketch Book in the Shiny* with a humorous letter extolling the wonders of life in India, where he had stayed with an Indian Cavalry regiment. As I leafed through the drawings in the book, I became more and more determined that this was for me. Accordingly, at the beginning of the next term I confronted the dubious eye of my housemaster with a request to join what he contemptuously called the 'canon fodder class' for Sandhurst. Six months later I found myself sitting in London with the Sandhurst examination papers in front of me, wishing I had spent more time in study and less in reading every book I could lay hands on which dealt with tiger shooting, shikar* in the Himalayas, and pigsticking. However, I managed to pass.

The impact of Sandhurst was something of a mental and physical shock to a somewhat casual young man accustomed to going his own way in his own time. It seemed that there were not enough hours in the day nor minutes in the hour to achieve everything demanded of us; we were paraded and marched at brisk light infantry pace from class to class by an awesome sergeant-major from the Brigade of Guards. He sported a bristling moustache and had the voice of a rutting stag, at the sound of which we skipped like marionettes. It seemed that in every task with which we were confronted, we were deliberately pressed for time. This was something of a challenge and called for a special effort. The sergeant-major instructors were a very remarkable body of men. Impeccably smart and efficient, they could boast that they had never yet failed to 'make a silk purse out of a sow's ear'; there was little they didn't know about instilling military habits into young men, which they did with an artful mixture of ferocity and good humour. They were the most formidable authority that I have ever encountered and I still recall them with awe not untinged with affection.

* Indian term for big game hunting; also used for bird shooting.

For the first of the three terms which constituted the Sandhurst course, there was little spare time for any kind of recreation. I made new friends and together we laughed and sweated our way through the ordeal which confronted us as juniors. The second term was somewhat easier; there was hunting with the Garth on the Sandhurst horses for which permission was easily obtainable provided one caught up in spare time with any lecture one had missed. Weekends were free and my friends and I formed a small shooting syndicate, our ferrets being kept by Jack Cox the kennel huntsman of the beagles. Our transport was a small car owned by the man that looked after the bicycle sheds and which we hired, I think, illegally.

That summer my half-brother Raymond came to England from Kenya where he had been farming, hunting and exploring since he went there in 1912. He was something of an eccentric and quite a celebrity in wildlife circles. He brought with him a dozen or so cheetahs which he had caught in the wild by the simple method of riding them down on horseback and grabbing them by the tail. Normally he sold them to Indian Maharajas for their ancient sport of hunting black buck, but these came to England to be raced on greyhound tracks. The idea was the brainchild of Kenneth Gander Dower, a sportsman author and lover of the fanciful. For a time the cheetahs were trained at Staines greyhound stadium, quite close to Sandhurst, and my friends and I spent some time there watching and helping look after them and enjoying Raymond's eccentric quirks and skills with the cheetahs. It was from Raymond that I acquired my first car, a Morris Coupé. I had bought for the princely sum of five shillings a second-hand Hardy's trout rod. It was a considerable bargain and I showed it proudly to Raymond who immediately swapped it for the car which he had been using for the cheetah project. That car served me until a week before I sailed for India, when a head-on confrontation with a granite bridge on Dartmoor finally reduced its value to the price I had paid for the fishing rod.

As the last days at Sandhurst approached I stayed up late at night with a wet towel round my head, swotting at military history, law, tactics and other subjects for which I had no aptitude; then came a week of distasteful exams and the final passing out parade – and then we were free.

For leaving seniors it was customary for discipline to relax and I recall that 'jerries' appeared on flagpoles, fire hydrants came into play and the sound of shattered glass was heard above the hubbub and laughter. An under-officer who had shown a little too much disciplinary zeal during the term and who thought it prudent to absent himself from the riot, returned late to find his room occupied by a litter of half-grown pigs which swept him off his feet and ran squealing through the corridors all night; spirits were high. We were on the threshold of becoming 'officers and gentlemen'.

2

An Officer and a Gentleman

INDIA: 1937 TO 1943

A last English Christmas, a crowded boat train and the outline of the
Isle of Wight disappearing below the horizon as our troopship rolled
down the windy channel early in 1937 – these memories I perhaps
share with the remnants of those young officers who left England for
the Indian Army in the carefree pre-war days, many never to return.
We were twenty years old, just released from the rigours of Sandhurst,
commissioned as second-lieutenants and heading for sport and adventure in the mysterious east. There would be no war and the spectre of
mechanisation in the cavalry was years away. Immediately before us
was the prospect of a Mediterranean cruise, the Suez Canal and the
Indian Ocean. I have memories of Gibraltar, Malta, Haifa and Port
Said, bum boats, gully gully men and the sparkling quality of sea and
sky. In Port Said we were held up for two days and we trotted round
the town in carriages, shopping in Simon Artz and laughing at the
Gippy pimps and panders who pursued us with dirty postcards and
promises of the delights of paradise. At night we went to the Casino
and danced with the pretty Hungarian hostesses, but I fear our atten-
tions were mostly spurned in favour of richer quarry. Then came the
Suez Canal, Port Sudan, and the stifling heat of the Red Sea, where the
soldiers on the lower deck suffered badly in crowded conditions and
the stink was abominable. Next Aden, 'like a barrick stove', with its
swimming beach and shark net, and as we cleared Cape Guardafui on
the Horn of Africa the full force of the monsoon struck us on the bows,
the great waves of the Indian Ocean making the ship buck and roll;
fewer people appeared for meals and the stink below became appalling.

At last we stood at the rail straining our eyes for the shore line of the
Indian sub-continent and the port of Karachi which was rising over the
horizon. As we watched the baggage being unloaded and the milling
crowd of coolies shouting and gesticulating below us on the squalid

dock, an officer of a British regiment said to me, 'You poor bastard. I've only got three years to do in this ghastly place – you've got a life sentence.' I must admit that this remark, and the experiences of the next few days, caused thoughts almost amounting to misgivings to form in my heat-addled mind.

After disembarking we boarded a troop train and started the slow journey through the Sind Desert to our various destinations. We lay in sidings for hours while scheduled trains passed us; the heat and dust in the crowded compartments were overpowering as we moved slowly but noisily through a landscape of unrelieved gloom, a khaki land-scape of hot sand, with nothing of interest but an occasional camel grazing on broken thorn bushes. We stopped at every little station and watched a crowd of brown humanity pushing and shouting on the plat-forms in what seemed like a pointless and depressing panic. I rather think my mind turned more to cool green thoughts of England than to the interests and pleasures that I had hoped lay ahead.

After several days the train pulled in to Allahabad station in the early morning. Here an officer was waiting to drive me out to the canton-ment and my rooms in a large shady bungalow where the bliss of a cold shower restored my sagging morale and I soon began looking forward to my coming year's attachment to the Queen's Royal Regi-ment.

Every young officer joining the Indian Army was required to spend his first year in India attached to a British regiment; during this time he was supposed to pass the first of three language exams and learn some-thing of the strange ways of the land. He had also to find himself a vacancy in an Indian regiment of his choice.

Allahabad is a large city in the middle of northern India near the junction of the Jumna and the Ganges rivers; the old city is squalid and overpopulated, but the cantonment area is spacious and well laid out with big cool bungalows, shady trees, polo grounds and a club. Out-side the city the land stretches away in an interminable sepia plain dotted here and there with patches of green which mark the mango trees of a village, or a patch of sugar cane watered from a well, round which the patient water buffalo plod, turning the wheels.

I do not remember much of that year's attachment; for the first few months of summer the heat oppressed my body and the all-pervading poverty, suffering, and barrenness of the land depressed my mind. Parades began at dawn but by midday the sun had driven every living thing into merciful shade, all save the black and white crows which cawed incessantly from the bungalow roof and the 'brain fever bird' whose mad cadence rang through the long hot afternoons while the old munchi*, his breath afire with garlic, directed my hand in the pot hooks of Urdu Script.

I started to learn polo; I shot a crocodile on the banks of the Jumna; my beloved bull terrier bitch Juno arrived from England and died, and I patrolled the stinking narrow streets of the old city with a platoon of Cockney soldiers to keep Hindu from murdering Muslim and vice versa. As the summer months drew on clouds started to gather in the brazen sky, small at first but building up until they rose bank on bank in the west. Daily they approached nearer with an occasional distant rumble; then one night they burst overhead with a cannonade of thunder and down came the rain. I remember fleeing from my bed on the lawn to the bungalow verandah and watching with delight as the continuous lightning lit up the naked figure of an elderly and portly major, his body scarlet with prickly heat, strolling blissfully about in the rain with his hand shielding a large glass of whisky and the rain dripping from his moustache.

The onset of the rains broke the tension which had built up during the blazing summer months, bringing that long-awaited fragrance of drenched requited earth after drought. The dry cracks in the land filled up; grass and flowers appeared where before had been baked soil and dust; at last the air was clean and clear. The splendour of the storm was in itself an entertainment, but after the sun was high the steaming earth made the atmosphere oppressive, and at night a million insects clustered round the lights, but at last, to my alien eyes nurtured on the Devon landscape, the sight of green horizons was balm indeed.

I had three servants, a dear old man called Shambo Nath who moved slowly but with great dignity about my room instructing his son in the duties of valeting. I think I paid him thirty rupees a month and he considered it his duty to advise me on all Indian matters for which I was very grateful. My syce† was a wizened little Muslim called Aziz Khan who smoked hashish and looked after Bijli, my polo pony, with infinite care. One day after the rains had come I saw a cobra moving in the roots of a big fig tree in the garden near my stables. I called Aziz Khan to bring me a stick and attempted to poke it out, but it evaded me.

'You should call the snake men,' said Aziz Khan. 'There are many

* Language teacher
† A groom. Indian term, also used in the Sudan.

snakes in the garden washed out of their holes by the rains. The snake men will clear the garden. I fear for Bijli when he grazes.'

'Very well, bring them,' I said. 'They will get a rupee for every snake they catch and baksheesh if they can teach me their trade.'

Next day there appeared at my bungalow two strange figures the like of which I had not yet seen in India. They wore only loin cloths and their hair was long and matted with dirt; they were smeared with ash and each carried a large cloth bag. What struck me most about these grotesque figures was the handsome cast of their features; despite their dark skins, their profiles were Grecian.

Old Shambo Nath hustled out onto the verandah to shoo them away, 'Hut jao budmash log,' he shouted at them and turning to me, 'these are bad men. Have nothing to do with them; they deal in magic, and raise spirits and dead bodies. Besides, they are thieves and their women are prostitutes. Send them away, Sahib.'

'They have come to catch snakes for me,' I said. 'They can't hurt us.'

Shambo Nath turned away muttering about the powers of evil and the red setter bitch which I was looking after rose from the verandah and, with her hackles up, disappeared inside the bungalow, a picture of dejection.

I turned to the snake men. 'You will get a rupee a snake,' I said, 'and you must leave in an hour.'

'We will take the snakes away with us, Sahib. We do not kill snakes,' said the taller man. 'You must watch from a distance or we cannot do our work.'

I sat on the verandah and watched them move slowly round the garden, occasionally pointing but saying nothing. Then they returned to me. 'There are four snakes near here, Sahib. If we catch them you will give us ten rupees and a chittee to other sahibs?' I nodded. They returned to the roots of the fig tree and squatted on the ground, having each pulled a reed pipe from the bags they carried. I saw them swaying slightly as they blew noiselessly on their pipes; every now and then they patted the ground with the palms of their hands and then paused for a moment. Suddenly one rose and walked swiftly to the base of the tree and I saw him pin a snake's head to the ground with a short stick and lift it writhing into his bag. This happened four times in the space of an hour in different parts of the garden and stable area. Finally they returned to me with two cobras, a krait and a harmless grass snake. I gave them their ten rupees and asked them to show me the secrets of their trade. For the first time a smile broke over the face of the taller man as he tucked my money into his loin cloth.

'You could never learn, Sahib,' he said, 'unless your father taught you and his father had taught him. These things are not written in books.'

'Do you ever get bitten?' I asked. The couple exchanged glances and then one untied a dirty rag and produced a small stone the size of a hazel nut with the texture of pumice. 'Yes, sometimes, but we put this on the bite and it draws the poison,' they said.

That night in the mess I told my portly major friend about the snake charmers. 'You may be quite sure,' he said, 'that they planted those snakes out there last night, and your ten rupees would have been better spent on buying me a drink, young man.'

A few miles from the city of Allahabad, near the junction of the Jumna and Ganges rivers, is a large red sandstone fort built by Akbar the Great, a Mogul emperor of India in the sixteenth century; its battlements and bastions, covering many acres, tower over the holy flood of Mother Ganges which has been sacred to Hindus for over five thousand years. A company of the Queen's Regiment was stationed in the fort to guard the wealth of the Bank of India which was held in its vaults and dungeons. When my company's turn came for this duty we marched from the cantonment in the sparkling early morning, past the city of Allahabad and over the shimmering plain for several hours towards the red battlements which rose in the distance, and then over the drawbridge and up through the elephant gates into the old fort which had once been a stronghold of one of India's ablest and wisest rulers.

That year was the year of the Magh Mela, a religious festival in which millions of devout Hindus made their pilgrimage to the junction of the two great rivers to bathe in the holy Ganges. For several miles the plain outside the fort was a seething mass of pilgrims who had made their painful journey during the previous months from all over India, to pay homage to their gods and cleanse their souls in the healing water. I had never seen or contemplated humanity in such quantity or in so many strange guises. Holy men smeared with ash on beds of nails; troops of dancers, jugglers and conjurers; sleek priests and fat babus jostling with emaciated cripples; sweetmeat sellers; prostitutes; beggars and musicians all interspersed with the vast crowd of Hindu peasant families. Several million souls had assembled to shrive themselves in holy water and enjoy the fun of the fair.

A kindly local raja had lent his elephant to Lieutenant 'Maggie' Mott and myself, the only two officers in the fort. Sitting in her howdah we moved through the crowds along the river bank in a haze of heat and dust listening to the hubbub of blaring conches, clanging gongs and cries of beggars, water carriers and traders.

Within the walls of the fort was a very ancient Hindu temple; a dark eerie place with strange voluptuous carvings, dripping walls and a pervading odour of incense and fragipani flowers. During the Magh Mela, thousands of pilgrims visited the temple. They were let in through the west gate of the fort in batches of about a hundred at a time by the guard of British soldiers and as they entered they were obliged to leave behind in custody anything that could be interpreted as an offensive weapon.

One morning I was in the office gazing out across the plain and the swarming crowds through which, a mile away, the swaying figure of 'Maggie' Mott's elephant could be seen, a flutter of colour in the howdah indicating that his attractive girl friend was with him. All at once I was aware of a growing hubbub at the west gate. I quickly dispatched a message to the guard-room and, leaping on to my bicycle, headed for the disturbance. The scene that confronted me on arrival was comical but faintly disturbing. A large crowd of pilgrims were yelling and gesticulating, but in the middle of the mob an imperturbable Cockney corporal sat smoking a pipe and reading a newspaper. As I approached he jumped to his feet, removed his pipe and saluted. 'Trouble with the wogs, sir,' he said. 'Bloke 'ere won't 'and over 'is club. I've got me orders, so I told 'im and 'is party "no temple for you, me lads, till you drop yer bloomin lathis". Now they've started squabblin' among 'emselves and threatenin' me, so I've 'ad the gate closed and the bloody hubbub is goin' on inside and outside. Wot a way to be'ave!'

On recognising the arrival of an officer, albeit a second-lieutenant, the jabbering crowd turned their attention to me and in order to try and make myself heard I stood on the corporal's chair and proceeded to try and calm the situation in my very inadequate Hindustani. I was not having much success when a sleek little rotund figure in a dhoti and smart coat pushed his way through the crowd to my side and said, 'Sir, I am barrister-at-law, Bombay, and a most influential gentleman. Let me speak.' 'For goodness' sake calm them down and say we want to get things moving again,' I said. I helped him to mount the chair and he started his peroration; slowly the shouting died and the crowd began to listen with only occasional interruptions. Carried away by his apparent success, the small learned figure started making heroic gestures. This was too much for the barrack-room chair; there was a crack, a squawk, and a second later he was rolling on the ground, plump brown suspendered legs and patent leather shoes waving about his spotless dhoti. There was a moment's silence and then the crowd started to laugh. The arrival of Maggie Mott on his elephant finally restored calm outside the walls, the gate swung open and the pilgrimage continued. A rather nasty situation had been restored by a rickety barrack-chair and basic peasant good humour. The corporal's only comment was, 'I suppose we'll be bloody charged barrack damages for the bloody chair. Well, roll on my bloody boat!'

On arrival in India I had written to the adjutant of the Royal Deccan Horse applying to join that regiment. The Royal Deccan Horse has had six different designations since being raised in 1816. They had been on constant active service all through the last century and in 1843 Lord Gough, the Commander-in-Chief, described them as 'the first irregular cavalry in the world'. They were honoured with the title 'Royal' for their services in France and Palestine in the First World War. Winston Churchill had known them and played polo with them in Secunderabad in 1897, when they were the Hyderabad Lancers. When a vacancy occurred in the very small establishment of British officers it was the custom among Indian cavalry regiments to let the younger bachelor officers decide on who should join them. This principle obviously made for harmony within the mess of a regiment; a vital factor in lonely stations and through irksome hot weathers, when tempers wore thin. At last a reply from the adjutant invited me to stay and I set off on the long dusty journey to Quetta in high hopes, but with the uneasy foreboding that I would be under the scrutiny of my fellow men.

The crisp clear air of Baluchistan, the barren hills and tall fierce-looking tribesmen presented a very different picture to what I had seen in the United Provinces; also at Quetta I encountered another way of life to that which I had known with a British infantry regiment. It was the way of life I had always hoped to find in India since my first wish to join the Indian cavalry, and everything about it appealed to me. I liked the big tough troopers and the grave dignified Viceroy's commissioned officers who wore the medals of the First World War, many of them with decorations for bravery. Finally, I liked the row upon row of shining coats and swishing tails in the horse lines – animals seen at their best towards the end of my stay when the regiment turned out for a ceremonial parade. They cantered past the inspecting general by squadrons to the strains of 'Bonny Dundee' with six hundred red and white lance pennants fluttering in the breeze and the sun shining on leather, steel and glossy horses. It was a captivating spectacle.

The days of my visit passed pleasantly. I played polo, driving to the ground each day in the regimental four in hand with matching grey horses; I went shooting, and attended various social occasions with the officers of the regiment. Then I returned by train to Allahabad to wait, in keen suspense, the news of whether or not there would be a vacancy for me in the regiment. A very long month passed before the adjutant of the Queen's came into lunch one day and said, 'Hilary, I have news for you. You are posted to the Deccan Horse. They are moving to Mardan, and you will join them there.' It was a moment of intense pleasure for which I had been hoping for several years.

Mardan was a small station some thirty miles north-east of the city of Peshawar, the ancient and picturesque destination of Afghan camel caravans coming south into India through the Khyber Pass. Since the dawn of history this lowering gorge in the mountains had admitted invasion after invasion into the sub-continent; it had seen the Aryans moving through thousands of years before Alexander the Great passed the same way, and its history was one of continual bloodshed and battle. Mardan was a shady little station, cool and delightful in winter but terribly hot in summer; it had been founded in the middle of the nineteenth century as the headquarters of the famous Corps of Guides.

On joining the Royal Deccan Horse in January 1938 I started to look for the two chargers which the government allowed me; for this I sought the advice of a good polo player in the regiment who found me two polo ponies from a home-going British cavalry regiment. I then chose two more from the polo ride and with this string of four I was assured of eight chukkas and sometimes more, three times a week. The beauty of polo in an Indian cavalry regiment was that it was virtually free; one's chargers were polo ponies and an adequate pool of troop horses were, after their initial military training, kept solely for polo and allotted to officers at the minimal charge of seven rupees, eight annas a month. The same applied to hunters or pigstickers; forage and syces were of course free.

The Deccan Horse was composed of Jats, Sikhs and Punjabi Muslims, each class with somewhat different characteristics; the Jats were solid yeomen farmers, unemotional, patient, well-disciplined and, on

the whole, easy to command. The Sikhs were volatile, smart and intensely proud of their fighting reputation but somewhat given to
intrigue and only at their best when there was hard work to do. The
Punjabi Mohammedans were dashing, humorous dandies with good
looks and the courtly manners of most devout Muslims. Mounted
parades started soon after dawn and continued until the sun was fierce,
then we would return to breakfast, a bathe in the mess swimming pool
and back to our offices for the rest of the morning. Polo was played
three days a week in the late afternoon when the stinging heat had
gone; on non-polo days I schooled my ponies and practised by the
hour, determined to acquire some merit in that prince of games.

All through the early mornings of the long hot weather I sweated
through a formidable riding course under a dour Jat Jemadar* who
had charged with the regiment in the Jordan valley during Allenby's
campaign. In the office I tried hard to absorb the strange ways of the
Indian Army and in the heat of the afternoons while my brother officers were asleep, a polite cough would sound on my bungalow verandah announcing the arrival of the munchi; then for an hour, the sacred
hour in India when all else slumbered I would try and bend my partly
paralysed mind to what the sedate old red-bearded Haji was saying
above the creak and whirr of the bungalow punkah.

Slowly the cool weather came and with it the time for manoeuvres;
the regiment paraded in full fighting order, and as they moved off to
camp each squadron gave their war cry. A trooper in the leading Sikh
squadron rose in his stirrups and turning shouted 'Jo bole so nihar' at
which the squadron roared back 'Sath siri Akal'. Then followed the
Jat war cry and lastly the fierce Muslim call on Allah; the horses fidge-
ted, and we trotted off with a jingle of saddlery for a pleasant few
weeks of cavalry training in the surrounding hills and valleys, sleeping
under the stars beside the picketed horses. During the day we patrolled
and skirmished, swimming rivers and negotiating passes in the hills;
always at midday the officers mess would arrive on a huge camel gaily
caparisoned with the regimental colours and badge; it would trot into
view to where we were waiting in the shade and with much grumbling
fold itself up to deliver iced beer and luncheon from its saddle bags.

Early one morning I was riding along with my orderly Mir Khan
when a peregrine falcon struck down a pigeon which landed at our
feet; my orderly quickly dismounted and, drawing a knife, cut the fluttering pigeon's throat while he muttered a prayer, then remounting he

* see Military and Government terms, p. 201.

hung the dead bird on his saddle bow; as we rode on, Mir Khan discoursed on falconry, a favourite sport in his Punjab village. My mind went back to days in Devon and at Canford when I was preoccupied with hawks and falcons. 'Will you bring someone from your village to Mardan to teach me?,' I asked. 'Yes, I have an old uncle, Lal Khan, who has several falcons; he used to be Biddulph Sahib's falconer, I will ask him to come.'

Accordingly a few weeks later there appeared at my bungalow a little old man with a white beard and bright hawk-like eyes. Behind was a boy carrying two beautiful peregrines and a saker falcon on a cadge*. From then on started my association with Lal Khan who, I learnt later had been one of the best professional falconers in India. I made him comfortable behind my bungalow and on the next Sunday morning we set out early on horseback with the boy walking beside us carrying the falcons; we made for one of the many duck ponds or jheels within a few miles of Mardan and as we approached it a falcon was unhooded and she soared above us with a jingle of bells; then we moved in and flushed the duck; as they rose the falcon made height and then with swish like a falling shell she dived; there was a crack and a puff of feathers as she struck the quarry and then threw up high into the sky again to return and fasten to the bird on the ground. It was a thrilling spectacle which was repeated several times that morning before the sun rose high.

Lal Khan came often that year bringing his falcons by train from Campbellpore and initiating me into the early arts of falconry; he was a delightful old man and his discourses were interspersed with much humorous philosophy.

The cold weather also brought other pleasures for our spare time of which there was a fairly generous allotment. Every Thursday was a holiday and any feast day of the four religions in the regiment was observed by the whole regiment. With autumn came the great duck and snipe migration from central Asia, filling the surrounding jheels and providing splendid sport; also the rocky hills were full of chukor, a form of hill partridge, which when driven by beaters skimmed over the ridges and disappeared downhill in the twinkling of an eye. Bird shooting expeditions always called for an early start and as we drove north along the Chitral road in the crisp chilly mornings pungent with the smoke of cattle dung fires, we would pass caravans coming south to trade in Peshawar; long strings of two-humped Bactrian camels loaded

* A square wooden frame suspended at waist height from straps over the shoulders.

with carpets, spices and silverware, their tall fierce masters strolling beside them with Afgan hounds at their heels.

As Christmas approached so did the cold weather polo tournaments; these were considered matters of some importance, each station in the Province having several grounds and most regiments producing two teams. Our regimental captain was Alec Harper who was later to play for England, and under his captaincy we won a number of tournaments.

Another sport which came with winter was hunting with the Peshawar Vale, a pack of English foxhounds with a long history in India. The country round Peshawar was cultivated and well irrigated with wide ditches and high banks; it was not unlike good Irish hunting country; our quarry was the big jackal that came out of the distant hills to forage and lie up in patches of sugar cane. If a horse or mule had to be destroyed by the Veterinary Corps in Peshawar the carcase was taken out and left for a few nights in 'fair hunting country'; we then used to drive out to the meet in the chilly dawn, mount the horses which we had sent on ahead and jog off to draw a patch of sugar cane. It was marvellous to hear the twang of a horn again and the cry of the hounds as they 'opened' on a jackal; in that clean dry air the music seemed to take on a special quality; 'jack' were plentiful and it was never long before one broke cover and made for the distant line of blue hills where probably grimy Pathan tribesmen were squatting over early morning fires, their rifles between their knees. One needed a good horse to get across the country and when scent was good on a dewy morning and a big dog 'jack' was determined to reach his refuge in the hills one could be sure of an exhilerating gallop to keep with the hounds.

War came in September and we listened to its distant rumblings on the radio, the voices of Chamberlain and Lord Haw Haw coming fitfully over the crackling ether; we had mobilised and were in high hopes of service overseas; surely we would be sent to Palestine, to Persia, to some country where cavalry was still needed. The months passed while we fretted and carried on with our normal way of life. Then one day orders came; we were to lose our horses and move back to Quetta to be mechanised. It was something of a shock. Many of the older soldiers who were considered unmechanisable would have to leave; not a single man in the regiment could drive a car and our British adjutant, an accomplished horseman and 'whip' for our four-in-hand had never in his life sat at the wheel of what he described as a 'mechanical nuisance'. There was a tremendous task ahead of us, and little time to accomplish it, but at least we now had a better chance of entering the fray.

We loaded our horses on to a train for despatch to a remount depot in the Punjab and the regiment embarked on the long journey to Quetta. I went by car with Alister Campbell, a friend in Probyn's Horse, a regiment of our brigade.

I cannot say that I remember with much pleasure the frustration of the next year or so. We trained hard in driving, maintenance, gunnery, and wireless until we considered ourselves a battleworthy mechanised regiment, but every time our hoped for equipment was on the point of arriving, it was diverted to the Middle East to stem some crisis; earlier mechanised Indian cavalry regiments were already in action; it was a time of hard work invariably rewarded by disappointment of which my only happy memories are of our yearly leaves in the hot weather.

For the first leave of those early war years, Alec Harper and I decided to go shooting in the snows of Kashmir. We travelled by train to Rawalpindi and then took a taxi for the two hundred and fifty mile journey to Srinagar; it was a hair-raising drive over a twisting mountain road with what we decided was a maniac at the wheel, but climbing out of the blazing heat of the plains into cool pine scented air was a delicious sensation. The nearer we got to Srinagar the more dramatic became the scenery with great forests of conifers, rushing torrents and a back drop of high snowy mountains; the contrasts in that one days' drive were a sheer delight.

On arrival in Srinagar we booked a house boat on the lake and next day visited the firm that had arranged to outfit our expedition; we checked the stores and tents and then, with servants and two shikaris* piled into a rickety old hired bus and set out for a two day journey by road. The way followed the valley of the Kokanag, a beautiful clear trout stream lined with willow trees; that evening as our camp was being put up we caught enough trout to feast our party.

Our plan was to take a short cut to the village of Kistwar by making a forced march with porters over the Sinthan Pass, more than twelve thousand feet high and generally snowbound; then Alec and I would separate for a fortnight's hunting and meet back in Kistwar. We hoped to secure trophies of any of Kashmir's hill game which might include red or black bear, ibex, markhor thar, gurrel or even with great luck a snow leopard.

* A shikari is a native hunter guide. The term is sometimes used for a famous old and
  bold European hunter.

We pushed on in the bus next day until the track finished at a little wooden rest house in the pinewoods where we spent the night. That evening one of our servants bound twisted grass rope shoes over our leather socks in preparation for an early start next morning; we were into our sleeping bags at dusk listening to the icy wind shaking the rafters of our little chalet; at four in the morning after a draught of bitter tea we pushed open the door and facing the great mountain which loomed darkly ahead, started what was for me the most arduous day's walking of my young life.

We reached the snowline after an hour's climb and zigzagged our way upwards to where the early light silhouetted the peaks ahead; as the new day came the snow fields above and around us glistened with the pink of dawn, and the horizons revealed range upon range of snow-clad mountains. It was a landscape of extraordinary beauty which we dared not pause to enjoy, for every moment of that day was for travel. We reached the head of the pass by midday and then dropped down through the snow to the pinewoods and the twenty mile walk to Kistwar along a stony track. Darkness came as we trudged on until at last the lights of Kistwar village were ahead and we moved into the tiny rest house and slept.

The next day Alec and I parted, each taking our shikari and servants and faced another day of strenuous travel to our shooting areas. I recall walking all morning along a narrow path up a beautiful valley; below me on the left a river roared, and around me the pine trees closed in or opened out into bare hillsides of scrub and scree; while above towered the mountains and snowfields for which I was making; by midday we reached a rope bridge which swayed perilously as we crossed over the torrent and started the long climb ahead; up and up we went until at four o'clock we came to a level place the size of a tennis court which was to be our camp for the next two weeks; we pitched the little tents and I laid out my scanty stores, then I opened the one bottle of Irish whiskey I had allowed myself for the fortnight and, pouring a generous tot into an enamel mug, added a handful of snow and sat down on a rock to admire the view, and watch the eagles and lammergeiers glide by in the valley below.

For a week I hunted along the ridges and scree of my mountain; starting at dawn with a pocket full of sandwiches and returning in the evening; my shikari, Mokta Lone, always led the way, stopping every now and then to sit down and scan the valleys and hillsides for anything that moved. His eyesight was incredible; he could see the flick of an ear or a dislodged stone falling across the valley where I saw nothing with my binoculars.

For the first few days we encountered nothing worth shooting; for an hour we had watched a small herd of ibex feeding on a hillside but there was no good head among them and each evening we had returned empty handed. Then one morning we were walking in our grass shoes across a steep slope when Mokta Lone held up his hand: 'There is something above us,' he whispered, 'the wind is wrong, we must go back.' We stealthily retraced our steps making a wide detour round the ridge, then climbing upwards we peered down into the forest below; a hundred yards away three red bears were grubbing among the bushes – Mokta Lone signalled me forward alone; with infinite care I eased my way down the steep slope until I reached a suitable place from which to shoot, then for ten minutes I held the bears in my sights as they fed towards me; suddenly a bear raised his head and looked in my direction, I fired and he went rolling down the hill with a cascade of stones; the hunt was over, nothing would move on the hill again that day.

We skinned the bear and carried the heavy pelt back to camp together with a piece of his steak; we were short of meat and I had heard that bearsteak was good. However a squeamish streak in me rebelled and that evening after a few mouthfuls I tossed the rest down the mountainside and retired to bed in a melancholy mood.

In the evenings I had many interesting chats with Mokta Lone; he was a tall middle-aged Kashmiri Muslim with the gentle courtesy of his race, his family were shikaris by tradition and he had accompanied his famous father, Mohammed Lone, on an expedition to China to hunt Giant Pandas and to the Tian Shan mountains in Russian territory to shoot world record ibex and wapiti. He talked of the days when it was fashionable for army officers to take their three-yearly six month's leave on expeditions to Central Asia and the high Karakorams to shoot the great sheep of that region, *Ovis ammon* and *Ovis poli*, also probably to indulge in a little spying at the same time, for the 'Great Game' of Kipling's *Kim* was still played on the borders and duty is the more pleasurable if tempered with sport.

One morning before dawn had lit up the mountain tops, I heard a leopard's sawing call in the distance. I rose instantly to speak to Mokta Lone but he was already at the door of my tent. 'Come at once, Sahib,' he said, 'this may be the trophy of trophies.' Both kinds of leopard frequented these mountains, but there was a good chance that this might be a snow leopard; as we climbed the hill in the icy chill the call came again from across the valley and we pressed on upwards to scan the opposite hillside; we reached the crest and lay in the snow, waiting for the light to improve and again the rasping call came from the far ridge; another ten minutes and Mokta Lone's hand reached out. 'There, by the big black rock,' he whispered; I strained my eyes but saw nothing. 'He is moving across the hill but too far – too far, now Sahib you must see him on that patch of snow.' Then into the orbit of my binoculars strolled the great marbelled cat; it was an ounce or snow leopard, not a true leopard but perhaps the most handsome of all the big cats, and a glimpse of it is rare indeed. Its thick rich fur, lowered head and long upcurved tail cast a faint shadow on the snow as the light improved and it moved across the hillside. With telescopic sights I might have taken a shot but my Rigby had open sights and the light was poor; besides, I could hardly bear to take my field glasses from the beautiful creature, which with luck would give me a better chance tomorrow or the day after. As it passed out of sight, another coughing call came to us over the shadowy valley. That morning was the highlight of my trip.

During the next few days I shot two thar and a gurrall – both species of mountain goats – then one evening I returned to find a note from Alec, 'Not a bloody thing on my mountain, let's return to the fleshpots, shooting and fishing on the way. See you Kistwar soonest. Alec.' This plan appealed to me; on our forced march to Kistwar we had passed some beautiful trout rivers and forests which held stag and black bear; besides the word 'fleshpots' had an attractive ring.

I started at dawn leaving the camp to pack and follow, and that evening Alec and I finished the last of our whiskey in the Kistwar rest house; during our leisurely return we caught trout and hunted a large black bear which evaded us; then shaved, bathed and refreshed, we proceeded to spend the rest of our leave in Srinagar in search of gentler game.

On arrival back in Quetta we learnt that another consignment of light tanks destined for us had been diverted elsewhere, and with this depressing news we settled back to the grindstone of training. Our only diversion was polo on three days a week. When we had lost our horses we had been able to buy our regimental polo ponies at a hundred rupees each; at one time I had six with which to work off my frustration.

An incident which sticks in my hazy memory of those Quetta days was an earthquake which struck the valley and surrounding hills; it was an eerie and somewhat frightening experience but not without its humorous side. I was sitting in my room after lunch with an elderly language teacher, trying sleepily to absorb some point of grammar, when a strange distant rumbling started. To my intense surprise the dignified old man opposite me sprang up and dived through the open window shouting for me to follow, using the words 'dharti kump' which I had not heard before. I ran to the door as the noise increased and saw the trees in the garden shaking and rustling as if in a high wind. Then pictures started falling from the walls and the house shook like a jelly as the rumbling passed below us like an underground train; the shock lasted for a few seconds, then there was a hush followed by dogs howling and dust rising on all sides. My language teacher had been through the disastrous Quetta earthquake a few years before and his reflexes were acute; as we stood in the garden watching the world about us wobble and heave, my teacher was saying 'each day we are learning new words, today it is dharti kump – repeat please.' For the next ten days the shocks continued intermittently and the scraping of a chair on the floor or a passing truck would bring the mess company popping out through doors and windows on to the lawn like rats out of a rick.

The war in Europe and the Middle East had been raging for over a year when our brigade moved to Karachi and morale rose a little; at least we were now at a sea port where we might receive our tanks and from where we might embark for active service. We trained in the Sind Desert and for sport raised a pack of greyhounds for coursing the numerous jackals around our camp. The duck and black partridge shooting in the cold weather was extremely good and we combined this with occasional pigsticking camps in the Indus valley sixty miles inland.

I had done a little pigsticking at Allahabad during my first year, and although the country there was not good I had considered the sport, as I still do, to be the finest in the world. Several other officers in my regiment had the same opinion and we made a resolution that, whatever the difficulties or expense, if by the next leave season we were not on active service we would send our horses to Meerut, the Mecca of pigsticking and hunt the Kadir country for a month; at least we thought this plan would give us a hostage to fortune and an imaginary German helmet surmounting a boar's head would perhaps increase our zeal for the sport.

The months passed; the war news on all fronts was bad, close friends and relations were being killed or reported as missing and still we stagnated in a backwater, only cheered by the defiant voice of Churchill on the radio or news of an occasional success at sea or in the Middle East. Was it to be Germans, Japs or pigs that year? Slowly it became apparent that it would be pigs, and we laid our plans for our 1943 leave accordingly.

Meerut is a pleasant little station in the Ganges valley some sixty miles from Delhi; each year the Ganges floods over a wide area, and this has created an extensive plain of high grass broken by water courses and interspersed with patches of jungle which harbour the famous wild boar of India. The Meerut Tent Club had been in abeyance since the outbreak of war but its shikaris and equipment were there and so presumably were the boar. We arranged with a friend in Meerut to put everything in order and then one happy day, four officers from my regiment and two from Probyn's Horse turned our backs on duty, loaded our horses on to a train at Karachi and set off with hog spears, guns, rifles and greyhounds for the Elysian fields of the Kadir, nearly nine hundred miles away.

Today, I only have to turn the pages of Alec Harper's faithfully kept Game Book to recall the details of that glorious month. Every boar we killed and the horses we rode are recorded, together with the country we hunted and the camps we made, even the name of the charming old elephant, Basant Kali, who accompanied the line of beaters with a medicine chest and cold beer on her back and was sometimes asked to flush a sulky boar from thick cover. Certainly Alec Harper's Game Book brings memories of the happiest month I ever spent in India; long days on horseback in a landscape of waving yellow grass and blue skies with a great glittering river in the distance; the thrill when a boar broke cover and the flat-out gallop to burst him before he made thick jungle; then the three short savage grunts, a gleam of tusks and the charge taken at full gallop, for woe betide the horse and rider if he is caught loitering by an angry boar.

The place names in that book conjure memories of our camps under the shady trees which filtered the moonlight as we lay on our beds discussing the next day's sport, sharpening hog spears or listening to the snorting and munching from the picketed horse lines.

*   *   *

The scene is our camp at Sherpur 'bagh'; we rise at dawn and swallow a cup of tea while our head shikari, the famous old one-armed Babu, and his two assistants are still distributing cartridge wads to the hundred beaters. Then the whole party moves off silently to the hunting area, Babu swaying along on his camel, then the 'spears', followed by the spare horses and the long file of beaters with the two assistant shikaris mounted on little country-bred ponies behind. After an hour Babu stops and makes a signal; a hundred wiry little brown men each carrying a heavy six foot pole spread out while we six 'spears' form two 'heats' of three behind the line to the right and left; Babu waves his one arm and gives an order in his high querulous voice and the line moves forward. It is fully light now, partridges are calling from all sides, a gaggle of geese pass overhead honking towards the river, and from a patch of jungle a peacock screams; the only other noise is the jingle of bits and occasional beating out of a thick bush where a wily old boar might be lying doggo. After half an hour there is a thrilling 'woof woof' in front of my heat and a black object bursts from the high grass, Alec leaps forward at full gallop in the lead with Jo and myself to right and left; for a full minute of racing pace we strive to get level with him, then Alec's arm comes up holding his spear horizontally. It is either a sow or an undersized boar – which we must not hunt; dejectedly we pull up and trot back into line. Twenty-seven inches from the withers to the lowest hair on his foreleg is the minimum height, and sows are sacred.

The advance continues, Babu changing direction from time to time by signals from the back of his camel. After another half an hour's progress there is a high pitched yell from Babu and he is trotting forward on his camel pointing to where five hundred yards ahead a red flag is waving above the grass; we are off again galloping for the flagman who is pointing and shouting at the top of his voice, 'Woh jata hai, woh jata hai – there he goes'. A boar has heard the beat coming and slipped away ahead, but the flagman has seen him; we gallop on, standing in our stirrups, searching, then there is a call from Jo who wheels right and settles down to ride; this leaves me at the back of the race for the first spear, dammit, but I have a fast horse, and the fortunes of pigsticking are fickle. A touch of whip and spur and I am after Alec and Jo hoping for a 'jink'; I hear Jo calling 'On on on,' which means he has the pig in sight and claims possession of it. Suddenly Alec and Jo disappear and a moment later my horse leaps down into a ten foot nullah* as the others are scrambling up the opposite bank and turning left. I can cut a corner here I think – Jo is close to the pig with Alec gal-

* A watercourse, dry in the hot weather.

loping on his right, at last I'm level on Jo's left; can we catch the boar before that thick patch of jhow*; the answer is no, he's dived in ahead of Jo's spear. 'Go wide,' shouts Jo, 'I'll follow him through.' I skirt the jhow and see the boar break on the other side; this leaves Jo at the back of the hunt and me in possession. I gallop flat out for the next half mile and the big heavy boar starts to tire, Alec and Jo are close behind me to left and right. I prepare to get my spear down to the boar when he jinks sharply towards Alec; they are on a collision course and this old boar has had enough of being chivvied – a series of quick grunts and he charges in; I see Alec's spear come down as he leans out of the saddle at full gallop, the point takes the boar high up behind the shoulders and he rolls over.

First spear to Alec; we dismount and loosen girths, looking for cuts on our horses' legs and discussing the hunt. Alec has examined the tusks which will be his by right and an assistant shikari rides up chattering on his pony to take charge of the meat which will be eaten tonight by our tribe of gipsy beaters. 'There is a well over there,' he says pointing, and we lead our horses away to where the other heat are drinking, and pouring cool water over each other's heads, for by now the sun is up.

Refreshed we form line again on different horses and the advance continues. This time a boar breaks on the right near the other heat, it charges a beater who leaps up his pole as it passes beneath him back through the line; the other heat is after him while we make for higher ground to watch. Bernard Loraine Smith of Probyn's Horse is in the lead on a grey horse; they hunt in a wide circle at breakneck speed, disappear behind a patch of jhow, and curl back in our direction. Suddenly Bernard is not there, only his horse's heels wave bravely above the grass for a second as the other two spears sweep past, bringing the boar back to our left. He is making for a big patch of sugar cane but Guy Nixon has caught him on his fastest polo pony; we see his spear go down as he rides over the boar and wheels again to the attack, but John Glenn, the policeman and friend of my youth, has galloped in with the *coup de grâce*, and we watch the two dismount. Bernard is limping towards us leading a lame horse.

By now the sun is high and we look for shady trees and water; Basant Kali shuffles up with her mahout clucking at her and an elephantine smile on her face. She kneels down and delivers beer packed in wet straw, also sandwiches, and our special treat for her, a bag of oranges.

* A shrubby tamarisk (*Tamarix indica*), forming a good cover for pig.

Bernard needs minor medical attention. So does his horse. Three of us ride away to the Ganges for a swim and we while away the hot afternoon chatting or sleeping in the shade; at four we are in the saddle again and hunting back towards camp. Two boar break on the way home; the other heat kills theirs, but ours is an artful old customer; after a sharp hunt we over-ride him in thick grass and he is lost for a few moments. That is enough and when we last see him he is galloping back into the bourh ganga, a tangled swamp passable only to pigs. We wish him well and ride contentedly back to camp.

*   *   *

We hunted every day, changing camps when we had covered the surrounding country; sometimes in the evening we shot partridges from Basant Kali's swaying back or coursed hares and jackals with a pack of greyhounds.

One day Alec, Jo and I were beating out the banks of a dry nullah which wound through the grassy plain; after an hour of drawing the area blank Jo said 'I wonder why this extraordinary paucity of pig'. The next second his question was answered; there was an angry snarl, as a large leopard bounded away in a streak of gold across the plain. We leaped forward at full gallop, racing to be first spear and claim the skin; for a few seconds the leopard seemed oblivious of his three pursuers, then he glanced round with blazing eyes and was away at full stretch for a line of high grass in the distance. Alec was on his fastest horse and after a few hundred yards he started drawing up to where the leopard's tail showed above the grass; another hundred yards and Alec was up to him with Jo and I to right and left, then suddenly the leopard squatted flat on the ground, Alec's spear kicked up the sand an inch from his head and we all three swept past. As we wheeled we saw the leopard now well in the lead again, streaking for cover.

Alec was shouting orders 'Hilary, get away to the left – that line of trees – Jo – wide to the right – I'll follow him through.' So saying he charged into the thorn bushes; I galloped off to the left and halted hidden behind a tree to watch what seemed to be the leopard's most likely line of retreat; I heard Alec and Jo calling to one another and the next moment the quarry was trotting towards me glancing over his shoulder as he came; here was luck indeed, perhaps after all I would have his skin. I waited motionless until he was twenty yards away, then galloped at him and again we were off at full speed. I could see by the leopard's stride that he was blown and all at once he was under my right stirrup with my spear striking the ground down through his shoulders, as I passed over him. He uttered a guttural snarl and I swung my horse to go for him again but he was on his feet and disappearing into a high patch of grass. We hunted in a wide circle and at that moment a 'spear' from the other heat trotted up from the direction of the line. 'Where is he?' he shouted excitedly. 'Just where you're standing,' I answered. 'Get galloping you bloody fool or he'll have you.' I had hardly said the words when the leopard rose out of the grass with another throaty snarl and seized the rider by the shoulder. His horse took fright and bolted, shaking the wounded leopard to the ground before he could fasten his teeth in. By this time Alec and Jo had rejoined the hunt together with other spears and confusion followed. We galloped backwards and forwards through the high grass searching but he had vanished as only a leopard can under such circumstances; we finally gave up the hunt. Bitterly disappointed, I mounted the back of Babu's camel and armed with a shot gun searched every patch of likely cover for the rest of the day, but to no avail. A day later a shikari brought in a few claws and some strips of skin; the vultures and hyenas had done their work.

I have a copy of the relevant pages of Alec's Game Book and as I turn back to them year after year, I live again that month of Kadir sunshine, recalling incidents of what, for me, was the paragon of all sports. Today I cannot kill any animal without a feeling of revulsion, but I make no apology for enjoying that fierce blood sport which now no longer exists; there were boar in plenty, and they were a dangerous pest to peasant farmers; money, meat and enjoyment accrued to the villagers who accompanied us, and the boar was a worthy cantankerous adversary who would frequently attack, unprovoked. Above all it was very rare for a wounded boar to escape although many got away unscathed, sometimes leaving us with what we at least considered to be honorable scars.

3

Into Action

1943 TO 1945

In the train that took us back to the regiment Alec and I discussed the future. We were regular officers with, presumably, a career to contemplate; there was fighting going on all over the world and up to now, as Alec put it, 'We haven't even heard a bloody door slam'. We came to a decision; if, when we got back, there still seemed little chance of active service with our regiment, we would form up to the Colonel and ask for a posting to the Chindits, a force fighting behind the Japanese lines in Burma; it would be sad to leave the regiment but our frustration was growing and we felt we had to get into the war somehow.

The news on our return was discouraging and we sought an interview with our Colonel, Tony Sanger, whose enthusiasm and drive had kept the regiment going through many disappointments; he acceded gloomily to our requests. Accordingly Alec and I prepared for our journey to Delhi to be interviewed for the Chindits. On the day before our departure the Colonel sent for me and handed me a signal. It read, 'Send an officer for front line service Australian Forces New Guinea'.

'How about it,' said Tony Sanger. 'If you go to the Chindits you may be transferred to another regiment, but if you go to New Guinea you will eventually come back here in time to go into Burma.' Delighted with the news I hurried off to pack and catch the midnight train to Bombay.

On the station I met Bernard Loraine Smith 'Where are you going?' I asked. 'To meet some pretty girls in Sydney and then New Guinea,' he replied and we climbed happily aboard the train together.

At Bombay I met my old Sandhurst friend, John Stanton, and several other officers bound for the same attachment. We boarded the SS *Mariposa*, a pre-war American luxury liner which had been converted into a troopship; she sailed next day, heading far into the Southern Ocean and relying on her speed to avoid Japanese submarines; after several days she turned east and then north until one morning Sydney harbour bridge loomed above us.

A change of life style from rough to smooth can be a special delight; during the past years we had known, for the most part, the harshness of India, the demoralising squalor of her cities and villages and the monotonous bachelor existence of the mess. Now we were suddenly transported to a fine city in cool sparkling sunshine, lapped by a glittering ocean and adorned by more beautiful girls than we had ever seen gathered in one place. Kind Australians took charge of us and for the next few days the pleasures of Sydney were ours to enjoy. Then we went north for the war in New Guinea.

We spent a few days at the base in Port Moresby, before going up into the line, and there, on Christmas Day 1943, played what I think was the only Test match of the war. Eleven Englishmen who sometime in their lives had played cricket took the field against an over age team of Australian quartermasters and storemen; the game was played with more zeal than skill and an interesting feature of its conduct was the supply of illegal whisky which appeared from the umpire's pockets between overs. England batted first and we produced the unimpressive score of seventeen runs, mostly byes let through by a rather tight Aussie wicket keeper; it seemed that defeat was imminent but the celebrations at half time were probably the downfall of the Aussie batsmen. By dint of having kept John Stanton, our only bowler, on minimum rations while we plied our hosts with their own drink it soon became apparent that we were in for an exciting finish. When their last man, a beefy old quartermaster in spectacles wove his way unsteadily to the wicket there were sixteen runs on the Australian board – one more for a draw, two for a win. The crowd was becoming noisy; for the next few balls the quartermaster played some stylish defensive air shots; barracking from the spectators increased; our wicket keeper handed the batsman a bottle of whisky, and after a generous pull, he again addressed himself to the bowler. A slow straight lob came down the pitch, the quartermaster danced towards it and with an herculean swipe smote it high into the air between the wickets; the effort cost him dear. His false teeth flew one way and his spectacles flew another; cheering reached a crescendo as the other batsman bounded towards him, but the quartermaster was on his hands and knees groping for his specs. 'Run you old bastard,' shouted his supporters. 'I can't bleeding see without me bleeding specs,' he bellowed, and then abandoning his search he set off at full speed for cover point crunching his false teeth under foot as he went. By this time several English fielders had collided under the dropping ball; one, more agile than the rest pounced on it and, racing for the wicket, struck it down as the quartermaster pounded blindly on in the wrong direction, wailing 'Jesus, me teeth.' It was a triumph for England which was celebrated late into the night.

Next morning as dawn came we looked down through the windows of a DC3 onto the terrain in which we were to fight; the great range of the Owen Stanley mountains passed beneath us with peaks rising to thirteen thousand feet, clad in mist and dense rain forest; dramatic waterfalls cascaded from the hills, and the valleys were clothed in jungle and tall kunai grass. It had been in this wild country that the Japanese had received their first wartime setback on land; they had landed on the north coast of New Guinea and marched unopposed over the mountains with the object of capturing Port Moresby and invading Australia. Taken by surprise and untrained in jungle warfare, Australian troops were rushed from the fighting in the Middle East and flung into battle on the Kokoda trail north of Port Moresby; slowly with desperate fortitude they stemmed the Japanese advance and then, suffering heavy casualties from battle and sickness, they struck back in a close contact battle of hide and seek, driving the enemy back over the mountains.

After an hour's flying we put down on a jungle strip in the Ramu valley; as we stepped from the plane a battery of twenty-five pounders was firing away at the enemy positions in the hills from whence came the distant rattle of machine gun fire and the cough of mortars.

John Stanton and I had been posted to a section of a forward battalion; we were both captains, he from the 14th/20th Hussars and I from the Indian army, but as we did not want the responsibility of command which might have been tricky with Australian Imperial Forces, we had elected to drop our rank and become private soldiers in a section under an Australian corporal, and incidently to enjoy the pay of both ranks. We were to spend a month or two with the 7th Australian Division and then fly in to meet Bernard for attachment to the 2/2nd Cavalry commandos who were operating forty miles behind the Japanese lines.

We reported to a sergeant who was sitting outside a grass hut on the air strip; after a few humorous pleasantries he pointed to the distant hills up and down which a stream of ant like figures were moving in single file. 'Follow that trail up and you'll come to your mob eventually,' he said. 'It's a longish haul.'

Loaded with knapsacks, sub-machine guns and as much ammunition as we could carry we faced the hill and toiled upwards along a knife edge ridge for hour after hour; as we climbed we met the sick and wounded being carried down on stretchers with great skill by black Papuan tribesmen. At last we reached our battalion dug in on the hillside; we sought the adjutant who directed us on to our platoon sergeant, a lean tanned man in his middle forties with a crooked smile. 'So you're the pommies we've been expecting,' he said. 'Why do you want to volunteer for this lark you silly bastards, you need yer heads examined ... Cairo – now, Cairo was different – any bugger would volunteer for Cairo ... but this bloody place, it bloody rains all bloody day, half the boys down with bloody scrub typhus, bloody awful tucker and bloody Nip snipers and mosquitoes the size of dingo pups ... not much doing at the moment but things'll jazz up soon ... that hill ahead is Shaggy Ridge, we'll be pushing the little bastards off that in a day or two ... you'll have some fun.' So saying he pointed out our slit trench and left us.

That night and on almost every night for the next few months the icy rain poured down filling the slit trench and evading all precautions to keep our one blanket dry – proper sleep was impossible but we dozed occasionally, peering into the darkness and listening; an hour before dawn the order to 'stand to' was quietly passed, we checked our weapons and manned the slit trench ready for a possible dawn attack. Light came slowly and when the sun broke through we crept into the open to get dry; the section commander came over, rolling a cigarette. 'If you guys hear a Jap mountain gun go off you've got just two seconds to get underground – they're accurate little bastards,' he said; as he spoke there came a dull detonation from the hills; every Aussie dived out of sight and seconds later came the crack of a shell exploding in the company position.

A few days after our arrival we watched the attack go in on Shaggy Ridge; our platoon was in reserve giving covering fire over the heads of the attackers; from early morning there had been gun fire from the twenty-five pounders in the valley, then bombers of the Australian Air Force, each with a 75mm gun in its nose, flew along the hillside straffing the enemy bunkers; finally as the figures of Australian soldiers appeared moving through the kunai grass on the steep slopes our platoon opened up with Vickers machine guns. In the distance we could hear the 'knock knock' of the Japanese heavy machine guns known as 'woodpeckers' and the thump of mortars; it was somewhat unreal and rather beautiful scene which might have delighted the heart of a Hollywood film director; beside us the machine gunner was pouring belt after belt into the enemy positions, his number two feeding the gun and making humorous Australian comments; all at once, with a note of pantomime farce, a flight of sulphur-crested cockatoos flapped slowly across the line of fire. For a second the gunner dropped his hands. 'Out the way you silly bastards, you'll get 'it,' he said, then putting his eye to the sights again continued firing. By evening the Japanese position was in our hands and the next day we moved down into the valley to follow up and out-flank the enemy.

For the next month or two we marched, dug, and patrolled in this forbidding country, either on the icy hilltops, or through the breathlessly hot kunai grass of the valleys, or the dark dripping gallery forests. The Australians had made themselves masters of the jungle patrol but the task of leading scout was a nerve-racking one indeed in such close country; the enemy were skilful at concealment and their ambushes carefully planned. The leading scout was therefore changed over every twenty minutes or so and he usually returned to the section with a look of relief on his face. If a Papuan native could be found to join the patrol his hearing, eyesight, and ability to read jungle signs were invaluable, but most of all it was his acute sense of smell that saved many Australian casualties, for his great twitching nostrils could detect a Japanese position with the certainty of a wild animal.

On the whole John and I were enjoying ourselves. We liked the tough humorous Aussie soldiers who taught us to pan for gold in the mountain streams and lay ambushes. Living was extremely rough but it seemed that we were on the winning side at last and we planned a sybarite leave for ourselves on the way back to India. Then tragedy struck.

On the day before we were due to meet Bernard and fly in to join the commandos we found ourselves with a weak company confronting a Japanese bunker position on a high ridge in rain forest; the company commander decided to put in a silent platoon attack on the right, while holding the enemy frontally with all the fire power he could muster; our platoon, under the platoon sergeant was ordered to attack; as noiselessly as possible we scrambled down the hill through dense forest, then we moved round to the right and formed up. The enemy position was above us and less than a hundred yards away and we hoped to close in undetected while it was being blasted with frontal

School days: (*above*) The First Eleven at Doon House, with H.H. top left
and (*below*) Bisley 1933, the Canford Shooting Eight and Cadet Pairs;
Cadet Hook bottom left.

(*left*) Allahabad, 1937: attached to the Queen's Regiment and (*above*) Jage Ram with 'Jill' at Mardan.

(*right*) Watercolour of a trumpeter in the Royal Deccan Horse c. 1939. (*Reproduced by kind permission of the National Army Museum, London*).

(*right*) Winston Churchill playing polo for the 4th Hussars against the Hyderabad Lancers about 1897 (*see page 19*).

(*above*) Quetta, 1941: Polo – Royal Deccan Horse versus Probyn's Horse and (*right*) Racing – H.H. wins on Dark Angel.

(*above*) The Royal Deccan Horse polo team, winners of the 13th/18th Hussars Cup, Risalpur 1940. *From left to right*: H.H., Freddie Wilmer, Alec Harper, Guy Nixon.

(*below*) With John Stanton on Shaggy Ridge, New Guinea, about a fortnight before he was killed.

fire; we waited silently, the platoon sergeant looking at his watch; suddenly the silence was shattered by our machine guns on the ridge above, interspersed with the stutter of sub-machine gun fire and shouts; this was our signal and we started to scramble upwards through the tangled vines and undergrowth; we had covered more than half the distance to our object. ve, mostly on hands and knees when hell broke in our midst and a mu: 'erous fire came from above; we had been detected. The sergeant urged us forward to get to grips with the bunkers but by this time men were dropping and rolling back down the hill; grenades started exploding all around and in no time any attempt to advance was greeted with a hail of bullets; a few yards in front of John and I, an Australian corporal was lying wounded along a fallen log; the Japs had caught us twenty yards too early and we were pinned. The sergeant crawled up behind a tree on our right to see what was happening; each time he raised his head the vicious crack of snipers' bullets sent the bark flying within inches of his face; he shouted to the right hand section and got the reply, 'There's a lot of blokes hit and we can't get forward'; for a moment or two he blasphemed then he shouted, 'Call it off boys, get the wounded back out,' and to the machine gunners on the ridge, 'keep boring it up 'em we've got to get to hell out of here.' I called across to him and pointed out the wounded corporal. 'Christ, it's Whitey,' he said, 'I'm going out to get him, cover me you blokes'; and as he started to struggle out of his equipment, John and I rose on each side of a tree to spray the bunkers ahead with our sub-machine guns; I fired off a magazine and jammed on another then turned quickly to see why John's gun was silent; he was lying behind our tree with blood coming from a hole in his forehead; there was another burst of sniping and the wounded corporal came sliding down the hill dead.

How we got the wounded down the hill and back up to the company position I cannot now quite recall from that nightmare half hour. John was still breathing but I knew he must die; he was a big heavy man and under his weight we stumbled and fell while snipers' bullets ripped the trees above and around us. At last we were back and contemplating the price we had paid for our disastrous attack. I spent that night with John dying in the slit trench beside me; the rain beat steadily down all night; the enemy knew they had 'put it across' us and we half expected a counter attack; we manned our trenches, straining our ears above the swish of the rain. Dawn came with an eerie silence ahead; a patrol was sent cautiously out to the left ... the Japs had gone in the night.

We buried our dead high on Kankurio ridge in the rain forest; as we dug the graves a patrol watched the surrounding jungle. I took John's signet ring and papers, someone muttered a prayer and then in a mist of misery, I turned my back on my friend.

I was due to meet Bernard that evening on an airstrip some ten miles away. As I left, the company commander said, 'Bloody sorry about your cobber, he was a right good bloke.' I nodded; compliments were never wasted by the Aussies. All that day I plodded through the mud by myself and in the evening I broke the news of John's death to Bernard.

We flew next morning for half an hour over jungles, swamps and mountains into the 2/2nd Cavalry commando base; they were a Western Australian unit who had greatly distinguished themselves by their resistance when the Japanese overran Timor island; now they were patrolling behind the enemy lines from a strong position constructed with great jungle ingenuity. Patrols went out for about a week at a time moving through swamps and along ridges and raiding occupied villages; it was tough exacting work but this time the Australians were in the ascendency and the Japs avoided contact as much as possible.

After one patrol it was here that I went down with my first and most shattering bout of malaria; for two weeks I lay on an improvised bed in the jungle, sweating or freezing and sometimes delirious. I was allergic to the new drug Atabrin, and the quantity of quinine I swallowed made my head hum with the sound of a hundred violins; when finally the fever left me I was drained and shaky.

While I was ill I could only listen to the stories of the in-coming patrols usually recounted with dry Australian humour. One patrol had approached a village known to be occupied by the Japanese; when they were a few hundred yards away they laid an ambush on either side of the narrow jungle path; a commando then walked down the path, hatless, unarmed and in full view of the village. When he was close he called out for help in English – he was clearly a lone Australian soldier lost in the jungle – heads popped up as he turned and fled back down the winding track; on reaching the ambush he leaped into the jungle and grabbed his arms. In no time the Japs were after him; when they came to where his footprints in the mud disappeared they bunched together chattering; then the commandos opened up with Brens and Owen guns from a few yards range; as one Aussie laconically remarked to me, 'It was that close you could see the meat fly out of the little bastards.'

At last the time came for Bernard and I to leave New Guinea and return to India where a battle was raging around Imphal on the Burma border. Back in Australia we resumed the rank of officers and were sent to undergo treatment for malaria in the Atherton Tablelands, rather farther away from the bright lights than we had planned. However we shared a comfortable tent in peaceful surroundings, and were looked after by an entertaining old Aussie private soldier with Australian Light Horse badges tattooed on his arms, and a Military Medal from the First World War. I think he must have been the nearest thing to an Australian batman in existence and his methods were novel; in the morning he would appear at our tent and drawl, 'Get up you lazy bastards I've got a mug of tea here.' Then he would prop himself against the tent pole rolling a cigarette and regale us with anecdotes of the First War, ranging from the brothels of Cairo to the great cavalry attack that finally broke the Turks in Palestine. He was a considerable favourite of ours, and when we offered him a handsome tip at the end of our time in Atherton, he dryly remarked, 'Thanks mate, but you'll need that for trotting yer ferrets round Sydney'.

After a week or so we were released with orders to get ourselves to Perth, then find a ship going to India. Accordingly we started the interesting exercise of hitching by air all round Australia, which caused us considerable entertainment. In Cairns we found a Short Sunderland flying boat bound for Brisbane, the captain waved us aboard and we set off south gazing down on the lagoons of the Great Barrier Reef; after an hour's flying the plane banked steeply and fled back for the shelter of Cairns harbour with a full scale typhoon on our tail. It was a hair-raising journey; we were tossed around like a feather in a gale and as we landed in mounting seas the palm trees along the shore were being torn up, and corrugated iron roofs were flying through the air. We spent that night gambling in roughish company. I won sixty pounds and we celebrated liberally, but in the morning my wallet was gone, together with all the pay I had drawn.

When we did get to Brisbane we returned to stay at the beautiful ranch called Coochin Coochin where we had spent a few days on our way up to New Guinea. It was owned by the Bell family, a mother and three daughters and they were greatly saddened by the news about John Stanton who should have been with us; he had been a great favourite of theirs. For a week we rode over lovely cattle country and enjoyed such hospitality and luxury as we had not known in years, then we moved on through Sydney and Melbourne sampling the good things of life and youth; finally we got a lift with the Air Force to Perth, where HMS *Cumberland*, a County class cruiser, was preparing to sail to Colombo.

We had a week or two in Perth and I recall a memorable day's kangaroo hunting in the bush with two Scotch deerhounds; we rode all day, occasionally racing through the scrub after the hounds and their fleeing quarry, then we feasted on kangaroo steak in a glade bright with wild flowers; in the evening as the sun sank and the kookaburras started calling, we rode home through the eucalyptus scented twilight under the southern stars.

When the *Cumberland* was ready to sail, Bernard and I went aboard with two cases of Australian champagne, a present for our regiments, then we steamed out of Fremantle and for the next ten days observed with fascination the strange and wonderful ways of the Royal Navy on active service. Half way across the Indian Ocean there was a submarine alert; we raced along at full speed, swerving and heeling over to a frightening angle as depth charges raised great plumes of water behind us and every gunner manned his sights; it was an interesting and exciting voyage in the refreshing company of sailors.

Colombo – another ship to Madras – a train on to Secunderabad, and we were back with our regiments, which by this time were equipped with Sherman tanks, trained, and ready for the coming Burma campaign. Morale was high and we toasted the future in goblets of Australian champagne.

For the next few months we trained hard, always moving north-east towards the Burma border and preparing for the big strike against the Japanese which we knew must come; Christmas Day 1944 found us in Manipur state celebrating with a duck shoot on the Logtak Lake in the crisp winter weather, then on New Year's Day we crossed a high ridge of hills and drove our tanks down into Burma for what a Japanese general was later to describe as the master stroke of the campaign.

General Slim's plan was to pass a division with a brigade of tanks with great secrecy down the thickly wooded Kabaw valley, ferry it across the Irrawaddy river and make a dash for the important town of Meiktila in the centre of Burma, thus cutting the railway and Japanese supply line to their armies in the north and dealing a deadly thrust into the vitals of their main position. It was a bold plan which depended for success on secrecy and surprise. The enemy had not foreseen its possibility, being blind to the 14th Army's ability to supply itself by air.

For day after day we wound our way down through the lovely teak forests of Burma on a single track carrying the infantry with us. At night we 'harboured' and while the infantry protected us, worked on the maintenance of our tanks, snatching what sleep we could when the job was done; at dawn we moved slowly out of harbour and on through the cold misty forests. Sometimes we crossed fast running streams where a short halt would give time for a bath, and on these occasions my orderly would disappear with a grenade, returning with a supply of fresh fish for supper. After two hundred miles the country became more open and as we sped on we started to encounter some opposition from isolated Jap positions, but the plan was to get two tank regiments across the river as quickly as possible so we bypassed minor trouble and kept going.

At last the broad slow flood of the Irrawaddy lay before us; Indian sappers rapidly put together prefabricated rafts propelled by outboard motors and as we drove our thirty ton tanks aboard we saw Pagan, the ancient capital of Burma ablaze on the far bank; overhead flew a 'cab rank' of Hurricanes and Thunderbolts with napalm bombs which we could call down on to serious opposition. The crossing took a full day and then the two regiments lay side by side on the east bank, Probyn's Horse on the right and the Royal Deccan Horse on the left, each regiment of fifty-two tanks supporting an infantry brigade.

Both the officers and men of our two regiments had long been friends. We had been brigaded together as horsed cavalry since before the war and had shared most of our sport and pastime together, but interwoven into this close friendship was always a good humoured and cooperative rivalry, natural between regiments. In the past this rivalry had mostly concerned polo or other sport, now it would concern the destruction of our much disliked adversary. We received the order to 'go'; the hunt was on; heading east, and carrying our infantry, the tanks of both regiments moved quickly into top gear.

The country in front of us was mostly good going for tanks; an arid open plain with patches of scrub intersected by dry water courses with here and there a village dominated by white pagodas. Daily as we advanced, resistance stiffened; the threat to Meiktila had become more apparent to the enemy and sharp little battles began to occur, mostly at squadron level. The tanks moved forward blasting the defensive positions with 75mm gunfire until the infantry could get in with grenades and bayonets, then the advance swept on pointing its dagger at the heart of Burma.

At last, one evening the pagodas and lakes of Meiktila came into view and we swung round to the north of the town, closing in on it from the east.

For the next five days there followed the most vicious close quarter fighting of the campaign; the Japanese resisted with fanatical zeal; every cellar or drain was a defensive bunker, every building a strong point, streets were mined and fire came from pagodas, roofs and windows; the enemy were prepared to die to a man and they were making us pay dearly; our casualties mounted. Each position had to be smashed by tank fire usually at very close range, before the infantry could advance; a series of heavy armour-piercing shots from the 75mm tank guns followed by high explosive and the survivors of the bunker would struggle out, sometimes charging the tanks with swords or explosive devices until shot down by the infantry; in the evening we would retire to our defended harbour, bury our dead, and return to the fray in the morning, probably to find the Jap positions reoccupied during the night.

At last the fighting died down and the devasted town was ours; it was a major disaster for the enemy, and our general knew that he could expect a counter-attack; prudently he kept most of his infantry as a defensive garrison and sent flying columns of armour, infantry and guns into the country to disrupt the gathering counter offensive.

Ever since my return from New Guinea I had been getting recurring bouts of malaria. Now it struck again with a vengeance accompanied by amoebic dysentery and I soon found myself lying on a stretcher beside the airfield awaiting evacuation with other casualties; after a long and extremely unpleasant wait we were put aboard a DC3 which took off amidst dropping shell fire and flew to a tented hospital in east Bengal. For a week or so I was very ill but when I was able to totter about, the doctor prescribed a bottle of Guinness a day as a welcome tonic. One morning I was sitting outside the tent with a friend savouring every sip of my precious bottle when two orderlies passed by with a body on a stretcher. This was not a particularly uncommon sight in those days, and my friend called out, 'Who is it this time?'; the reply came, 'A Major Nixon, he died of his wounds last night'. 'Wait,' I called, 'what is his regiment?' The orderly bent to read a card on the stretcher then he spoke the words I dreaded to hear, 'Major Guy Nixon, Royal Deccan Horse'. It was a sad blow; for several days my friend had lain wounded and dying amongst strangers within a few yards of my tent. As I followed slowly after the stretcher with a heavy heart my mind went back to a starlit night in the Kabaw valley a short while before, when Guy and I had sat late over a mug of rum, and I thought – so after all, Guy, you and I will not go hunting in Ireland together when this is all over – you will not ride in the first Grand National after the war, and we will not fish those west country chalk streams as we planned to do – that was just a dream – a dream shattered by a Japanese shell.*

When I was pronounced cured, I went up to the air strip and 'thumbed' a lift back to Meiktila in a supply plane; the battle had rolled on to the south but I had no difficulty in getting back to the regiment. By now the two regiments were the spearhead of the thrust on Rangoon; we shared the lead alternatively, on some days having a clear run and on others encountering stiff opposition; in their fanatical will to resist, the enemy had taken to digging fox holes on the roads and tracks in which a man would sit with a five hundred pound ariel bomb between his knees; as a tank passed over him he would strike the fuse sending everyone concerned to glory.

By now the monsoon was starting, and it was essential to reach Rangoon before it came in earnest to disrupt tank and infantry movement. Besides, there was another reason for urgency; we had heard that 15 Corps were at sea and about to invade Rangoon from the south and we, who had come so far did not want to be thwarted of our prey. But we were. When we reached Pegu some fifty miles north of Rangoon the bridges were blown and we heard that 15 Corps had landed unopposed from the sea. Before they landed they had sent bombers in; there, on the roof of the gaol was painted 'No Japs here'. Suspecting a trick, they plastered the place and returned next day to read 'Extricate digit. No Japs here'; that was proof enough.

Just as we got to Rangoon the heavy rains started with full force; we found shelter in a bombed and deserted nunnery and set about tidying up after our long drive from India. Rangoon city was shabby, dirty and looted, but it was easy to see why it had once been considered one of the most beautiful cities in the east.

We now started preparing for our next task which was to be oper-

---

* Guy had been promised some good rides by his uncle, the race horse owner Lord Stalbridge. After the war his uncle inaugurated the Pat Hore Ruthven and Guy Nixon Memorial Hunters Steeplechase which is run yearly at Wincanton in memory of Guy and his Cambridge friend who was also killed.

ation 'Zipper', the seaborne invasion of Malaya; and for the next few
weeks there was much talk of amphibious tanks and landing parties.
Then to our intense relief came the dramatic day in the middle of
August when Japan collapsed under the Atom bomb and the war was
over.

Almost at once came news that British prisoners of war were to be
flown into Rangoon from Thailand. Bobby Kennard and I jumped into
a Jeep and drove up to the airfield; our object was to try and trace a
Deccan Horse friend who had been lost in Singapore several years
before: no one knew whether he was alive or dead, and casualties in the
Japanese camps had been terrible. As we approached the airfield we
met the first grotesque party of prisoners walking towards us; they
were in rags and tatters, emaciated, blackened by the sun and sunken
eyed, but as they hobbled along they were chattering and laughing with
the bliss of sudden unexpected freedom; it was a grim but happy scene.
We drove up to the first batch of prisoners and Bobby asked, 'Anyone
here know Freddy Wilmer of the Deccan Horse?' 'Certainly,' came the
reply, 'Freddy's just coming down the road.' Overjoyed with the news
we drove on, searching the motley crowd; then we saw him, a tall
gaunt figure in sandals walking towards us with a bundle over his
shoulder. As we came up to him he lowered his bundle and said with a
shy smile, 'Well, well, how nice to see you two, and how is Belinda?'
Belinda had been Freddy's bull terrier bitch who had died when Freddy
left India three years before. 'Belinda's fine,' said Bobby, lying. 'Jump
in, we're taking you to lunch in the mess.' We fitted Freddy up with
some clothes, and that night took him to a honky tonk that had started
up in Rangoon; then, as had been our custom in the past, we lined up
six whisky and sodas on the top of the upright piano; Freddy sat down,
drained a glass, contemplated his spread ulcerated hands for a
moment; then, for the rest of the night, all the best jazz hits of the
thirties came tumbling out in skilful profusion. The next day we de-
livered him to the doctors who had been searching for him.

My thoughts now turned to much over due home leave; I was high on
the regimental leave roster and our Colonel, George Carr sent for me
and said 'There's a small steamer leaving for Calcutta almost immediately. If you can get on it good luck to you, you'll have five weeks in
England and we'll see you back in India'. I hurried away to the embar-
kation officer and managed to get a passage, then I returned to collect
my luggage and the gun that Guy had left me in his will. A round of

goodbyes and I sped for the harbour and the first leg of the journey home.

On arrival in Calcutta I went to the hospital to see Bernard who had lost his leg in the advance on Rangoon. He was still in considerable pain from his 'ghost' leg but for several nights we went out, Bernard on crutches, to what bright lights we could find and came back laughing in the small hours of the morning. My regiment had provided me with a piece of paper of fairly high priority and by dint of waving it about in various offices I found a seat on a flying boat going to England.

As we rose out of the steaming heat of Bengal and headed west, I turned my thoughts back over the past few years; a chapter had closed which I would not wish to live again; a chapter which held too many bitter memories. I recalled with what high hopes my friends and I had left England all those barren years ago and I sadly counted through the names of those who would never see England again – that was the sting of war – a sting perhaps only slightly relieved by sport, comradeship, endeavour, and occasional mirth.

Karachi, Basra, Cairo, and I think somewhere in Italy were included in our slow but comfortable journey home, then one evening the English channel was below us and we circled the tiny fields of Dorset, landing with a 'swoosh' in Poole harbour. At Waterloo I managed to find a taxi; the elderly driver regarded my jungle green uniform with interest, 'Hop in mate,' he said, 'you look nice and sunburnt, where've you come from?' 'I've been in Burma,' I said. 'Well some blokes 'ave all the luck, I 'ear the girls is smashin'. What was it some joker wrote, "if you've 'eard the east a-calling you won't never 'eed naught else"; we've 'ad it roughish 'ere you know; where d'you want to go?' 'The Cavalry Club, please,' I said.

Next morning another taxi took me through the bombed and battle-scarred streets of London to Paddington station, and as the suburbs started to slide away behind us, I felt again that sense of west-bound heart's ease that I had not known since boyhood.

My mother and a new American sister-in-law met me in Exeter and we drove the old familiar road to Brixham. We talked late into the night and I went to bed in the small hours. For a while I watched the moonlight on the old black barn across the valley and listened to the owls hooting in the elms, then I settled down on a pillow that smelled of lavender.

For the next five weeks I revelled in the comforts of home, greatly spoiled by my mother and delightful sister-in-law; I visited friends, walked the Devon woods and cliffs with Freddy Wilmer after we had spent a few days of happy debauchery in London; I tasted again English roast beef, Devonshire cream, and farmhouse cider, available even in those still Spartan days from my mother's farmer friends. Then I was summoned to somewhere in Cambridgeshire and on a bitterly cold day took off for India again in an unheated and uncomfortable bomber. However my luck was in; as we rose from the tarmac there was an unpleasant noise and one of the engines stopped abruptly. We circled back to the airfield to be told by the pilot that four Lapwing plovers had lodged in the engine and we would have to try again tomorrow. That evening I began to feel the malaria 'shakes' come on again and cursing the discomfort I foresaw ahead I went to get enough quinine pills to tide me over tomorrow's journey. The medical officer looked gravely at the thermometer which had registered a hundred and three and said 'You can't fly for at least a week, go home at once and contact your nearest doctor'. Those words probably brought my temperature sailing down and I fled for a telephone. A girl friend answered from London. 'I'm ill,' I said, 'but it's nothing that you can catch, and I'm taking you to the Four Hundred to-night.' I swallowed twice the prescribed number of quinine pills and then headed for London blessing in my heart those little Lapwing martyrs. All that night, we danced to tunes from *Oklahoma*, and in the morning, my head buzzing with quinine, and perhaps the 'tender trap' of youth, we returned together by train to our native Devon.

The fever lasted longer than usual, and before my family doctor would pronounce his first and only malaria patient fit to travel, the Christmas snow was softly falling. On my last night at home I went to bed early but before sleep came I heard a crunching of steps on the gravel drive outside, followed by children's laughter and a clearing of throats, then, born on the frosty night air came the chorus of 'God rest ye merry gentlemen'. I dressed and went down stairs to find children were stamping the snow off their boots outside and coming shyly in to where my mother was a stirring a large bowl of hot punch by the fire. Was sanity returning to the world?

4

A Time for Decisions

THE POST-WAR YEARS

The Indian army to which I returned was slowly unwinding itself from being the largest volunteer army that the world has ever seen, to a conventional peacetime force. It was a time of paper work, of discharges, pensions and gratuities and other administration. I therefore welcomed command of a wing of the Indian Armoured Corps centre where the presence of more staff officers than were needed would allow me time for other pursuits.

I arrived at Babina in the Central Province just before Christmas accompanied by Guy Nixon's old Jat orderly Jage Ram, my best pigsticker, The Busby, and my half mastiff half retriever dog, Ponto; for the next eighteen months, whenever time or growing political tension would allow, I was in the jungle.

The advent of the Jeep had not only been a major war winning factor, it was now proving to be a boon to shooting in India. Duck and snipe shoots, which used to involve long arduous journeys at the weekend, could now be reached in an hour or two, and after shooting one jheel one could move easily on to the next.

The shooting was superb. With a few friends I employed a shikari who came in every Friday with news from the surrounding countryside; we would drive off before dawn on Sunday over rough tracks, past waking villages where pi-dogs barked at us and the acrid smoke of cow dung fires hung in the chill morning air. As light came we would be at our destination and looking across the early morning mist that rose from the growing colours of the lake ahead; then we waded to our grass hides in the reeds amidst a tumult of quacking and the first shot was fired; at once it seemed that the whole surface of the lake would rise in the air in a tremendous flurry of wings and for the next half hour we would be hard at work; gradually the duck flew higher and higher, pintail, pochard and teal interspersed with wedges of greylag and whitefront geese cutting patterns in the sky until they wheeled and flew steadily off to another jheel where we would follow. Later in the morning we would drive the snipe over the mudflats or walk them up through the swamps, then, as the heat increased, and our minds turned to iced lager, we would seek a shady tree where our fat old cook was frying bacon and roasting snipe.

This was our Sunday routine, which lasted throughout the glorious cold weather while the migratory duck passed on to south India and then turned north again for their long trip back to Central Asia. For sterner game I had other plans.

Within fifty miles of Babina were splendid jungles of teak and sal* interspersed with rocky rivers and gorges, forests where tiger, panther and bear roamed; in these places I caused a constant watch to be kept, with good incentives to bring me news of tiger.

In India big game hunting was a 'do it yourself' sport. This was not a country of the professional white hunter; here, unless one knew the language and had made a study of the sport, the only available help would probably be from a skilful little Ghond or Bhil tracker who could not use a gun, and could barely speak Hindustani. There are a number of good books on Indian shikar, notably those by Colonel Stewart, Colonel Stockley, and the famous forest officer Dunbar Brander; I had studied them with care, and now with past experience of shooting in the jungle I was determined to enjoy myself while the going was still good. Tiger and other game was still as plentiful as they had been over the last hundred years, and there were government scheduled man-eaters and cattle killers to be hunted.

One evening I was working late with my adjutant when Jage Ram came into the office. 'Come at once,' he said, 'the big one has killed again, Magria Ghond has brought the news.' I returned to my bungalow where Magria Ghond, my shikari, was squatting by a lamp. He jumped up salaaming, his tiny puckish features wreathed in smiles. 'We'll talk in the car,' I said, handing him a mug of rum. 'Jump in.' Jage Ram had packed everything, and pausing only to call Ponto, we drove off south through the night which flickered with fireflies and nightjar's wings in the headlights. On the way Magria Ghond toothlessly recounted the news: 'Yes, it is the big one again – he that we have been hunting for two months and who has slipped through two beats; this time we will be lucky – it is written on the sahib's forehead. The "badmash" has killed a village water buffalo and is lying up beside it with enough meat to last him for several days. We will surely catch him this time.'

* *Shorea robusta*, second to teak as an important timber in S. Asia.

We arrived at the forest bungalow after midnight and with orders to have a hundred and twenty men ready for tomorrow, Magria Ghond faded into the night, while I lay down in a long chair and slept. At first light Magria Ghond was back and we set off to inspect the kill; an hours walking through the dew-bespangled jungle brought us to a clearing and a pool of blood; Magria Ghond pointed silently with the handle of his axe to where the buffalo had been dragged into thick bush; then for the next hour I studied the layout of the ground intently, forming a plan for the beat. On one side of the valley was a low cliff with a few dry water courses running up into it that would have to be 'stopped' in places; on the other side was broken jungle which would require closer stopping. I made my plan and we returned to the bungalow to find a hundred skinny little forest men waiting with their axes on their shoulders. Magria Ghond knew them all and went swiftly down the line selecting half the party as stops. 'This old man is getting deaf,' he said. 'He must go with the beaters – That boy has a cough. He too must be a beater where he may make as much noise as he likes – Ah! old Ram Chand has come, the best stop in the jungle; join this line, Ram Chandji.' At last the sorting was done and we moved silently in single file back to within half a mile of the kill; there we left the beaters in charge of Jage Ram while Magria Ghond and I moved round in a wide circle placing the 'stops' in selected trees; at the head of the valley a village bed was tied for me in a low tree to form a 'machan' and a field of vision quietly cleared, then Magria Ghond disappeared to my left, putting out the remaining men. I climbed into the machan and there followed an eternity of waiting until I heard the beat start with a tapping of sticks and a murmur of voices; I slipped off my safety catch to avoid all further noise or movement, and froze, straining my ears and eyes ahead. After half an hour I heard a stone roll in the valley, no louder than the irritating thumping of my heart. An animal was coming up the hill towards me; a moment later a beautiful sambhur stag stepped out of the bushes and turning gracefully to glance back, picked his way over the crest and out of sight; I wondered if the vigil would ever end, the suspense was getting unbearable – my bottom was dead, bed bugs were swarming out of the machan and feasting in my shorts, I couldn't scratch and I dared not smoke; another half hour of motionless discomfort passed then grey Langur monkeys started calling in the valley and I heard a stop away to my right gently tapping his tree; shortly afterwards a nearer stop coughed discreetly and tapped; and then, unheralded by any sound and with pantomime effect, the tiger was ten yards in front of me turning his head to look back down the valley. I quickly raised my rifle and the shot rolled him backwards out of sight; I knew that I must have killed him and after listening intently for a few moments I climbed thankfully out of the machan and walked up to where he lay; as I surveyed my magnificent victim a feeling of anticlimax came over me, and with a strangely heavy heart I called the beaters out of the trees, where they had prudently taken refuge.

During that cold weather Alec Harper arrived unexpectedly for a visit; he was on leave and going south to hunt in the rolling green Nilgiri hills of south India. I had not seen him since we parted two years before, he to go to the Chindits and I to New Guinea. Now he appeared at my bungalow as a colonel with a DSO and we found much to talk about between duck shoots and over the decanter. I was able to tell him how a few months before I had been dining in Delhi with an old mutual friend of ours, a lady possessed of a keen but sometimes muddled interest in the social scene. 'And what became of Alec Harper,' she had asked. 'Didn't you hear,' replied a fellow guest, 'he went off with one of the Chindit columns.'

'Well,' replied our hostess, 'I hear they are both very attractive girls and I hope she makes him a good little wife.'

After several days of sport and laughter Alec left, and when he called on his return journey a month later, he was indeed engaged to be married.

With the onset of spring, bird shooting finished and I concentrated on the jungles to the south, spending most weekends on the banks of the Nabudda river with my rifle and fishing rod. The rocky Nabudda narrowed in places into a fast running current, swirling into deep pools; here the Mahseer* took plug baits and spoons with an exciting rush, fighting their way down river, while my dog Ponto watched, shivering with excitement from the bank; sometimes he could bear watching the battle no longer and leapt into the flood to help his master. Then Jage Ram would seize my rifle and watch for crocodiles while I bellowed ineffectively at Ponto from the rocks.

One weekend involved me in an incident which might have had more unpleasant consequences had I not been near the river and fairly fleet of foot; Magria Ghond and I were walking amongst the rocks in

---

* A member of the carp and barbel family, the sporting fish of all Eastern rivers; record catch 213lb from the Euphrates.

the heat of the day, hoping to find a tiger from Gwalior state cooling off in the river as was their occasional habit; we rounded a bend and Magria Ghond pointed out a cave in the cliffs, the mouth of which was shaded by the branches of a tree growing below.

'Two bears live in that cave,' he said. 'They are fierce and bad, the village dare not collect fire wood near here. If you were to shoot them everyone would pray for your long life and happiness.'

'I would like that very much,' I said, 'let's have a closer look at the place.'

We crept up and having satisfied myself that the tree was climable stole quietly away. A plan was forming in my mind for next weekend's sport. During the next few days I acquired a three inch smoke candle and a six foot bamboo pole; I split the end of the bamboo, forming four fingers into which I lashed the smoke candle; I now had a javelin which I could hurl from the branches of the tree into the cave and perhaps I would be able to pick off the smoke-fuddled bears as they bolted. Thus would I earn the undying gratitude of my friends in the village.

Next Sunday, at high noon, I approached the tree and followed by Magria Ghond, mounted with infinite stealth into its branches, bearing my rifle and javelin; as we climbed up, Magria Ghond tapped my foot and held up a finger 'Hark, they sleep and snore,' he whispered. Cocking my ear I detected the sonorous drone of sleepy bears from within; success seemed certain. I hung my rifle on a branch, carefully lit the smoke candle and, waiting for it to flare, hurled it into the dark recess of the cavern; then I grabbed my rifle and awaited the outcome. Smoke started to billow from the cave but to my surprise the snoring only seemed to increase in volume; heavy sleepers these bears I thought and gripping my rifle more firmly, I peered into the smoke. All at once I was aware that Magria Ghond was on the ground and legging it for the river as fast as he could go; then the bees found me; a hundred little fiery jabs unleased my hands and in no time I was overtaking Magria Ghond and I plunged into the river, occasionally offering my nose to the fresh air. That evening I needed aspirin in abundance.

Whenever my duties would allow it, the charm of the Indian forests held me all that year; the chill sparkling winter weather of cold clear mornings, when the grass was heavy with dew in which the tracks of game showed clearly before the sun rose, and in the evenings a crackling log fire to sleep by; gradually as spring came the heat increased, until by summer the forests were tinder dry and the shrivelled teak leaves under foot made stealthy movement difficult; by midday the heat was scorching and the noonday quiet was broken only by the monotonous 'tonk tonk tonk' of the copper smith bird. Then I would lie in the shade and attempt to read, waiting for the burning sun to sink in the sky. At the end of June came a build up of clouds on the horizon and the occasional voice of thunder as the rains approached and the night sky flashed; when the deluge broke it came like a long awaited dawn and a relief from suffering, the country was clean and refreshed again but rivers rose and swamps appeared, making movement difficult.

Finally the time came for me to leave India for good; independence was imminent and the spectre of partition loomed ahead with its desperate problems. All but a very few British officers would be immediately replaced by Indians; the old Indian army would be split between India and Pa.   according to Hindu and Moslem faith and the regular British officers, like myself, would be free to seek other employment on a small gratuity or if we wished, and our seniority fitted, could apply for a posting to the British army. I found homes for The Busby and Ponto, sold my saddlery and rifles, and having bade farewell to my friends, took the train to Bombay.

As I watched the sepia landscape and the jungles of the Central province slide by the carriage window I thought, I shall always want to come back to this country, despite its frustrations and inequalities; but I am glad that I will not have to spend the rest of my working life here. For me the delight of India has been in the forests, rivers and snows and the simple country people; from the courteous brave yeomen who were our soldiers, to the little aborigines of the jungle who loved sport and laughter. But there are also dark unhappy memories which the hardest heart could never forget, memories of suffering and misery on a colossal scale, the over-crowded dirty hovels, the maimed beggars and hungry children, the starving dogs and galled gaunt tonga ponies; these are sights which I am glad to leave behind; then, as the train rolled on towards Bombay I turned my mind to the future.

I had six months in which to make up my mind what to do. I had been offered a posting to the 7th Hussars in which regiment I had several friends. Bernard Loraine Smith had recently joined them from Probyn's Horse and although the idea of post-war soldiering did not particularly attract me, at least I would be assured of good company; it was a tempting offer. I had thoughts of farming in Kenya or the post of game warden somewhere in East Africa – the future was not clear, but what matter, six months is a long time, I had money in the bank and England lay ahead.

The pleasures of the next few months in England were saddened by the terrible news that was coming from India; the land was seething with violence while it waited for partition and independence. Throughout the country Hindus were turning on Muslim minorities and vice versa, a massacre in one area was producing a counter massacre in another; stirred by hot-heads and dishonest politicians and fostered by lies and false rumours the latent savagery of an outwardly patient and placid people was erupting in a hideous manifestation of slaughter and outrage. Throughout this time the old Indian army remained staunch and loyal to their comrades of a different creed, the interchange of Hindu and Muslim troops between the Indian and Pakistan armies was going smoothly largely owing to the discipline and fortitude of the Viceroy's commissioned officers. It was natural that the Deccan Horse and Probyn's Horse should interchange their Muslims and Hindus, the Deccan Horse being allotted to India, and Probyn's Horse to Pakistan, but alas tragedy was to follow this amicable arrangement; within a short time after independence the two regiments were locked in combat, shooting down their erstwhile friends, many of whom they knew by name; a vicious war had broken out between the two countries. They were sad times.

However, turning my thoughts from these tragic happenings, I set about the business of enjoying life and attempting to fulfil some of the promises that my friends and I had made to ourselves under harsher conditions. After a visit to Devon I went off to the Marlborough downs to stay with Bobby Kennard who was exercising steeplechasers for a trainer friend of his. When a severe frost came we took the horses to the seashore at Bognor Regis and galloped the Grand National entries on the wet sands with the biting wind bringing a sea tang and seagulls rising off the beach before us as we thundered along.

One day in London during 1947 I had a telephone call from a famous old game warden called Keith Caldwell. 'Your uncle tells me that you are looking for a game warden's job in East Africa,' he said. 'If you are serious, lunch with me at White's tomorrow.' I thanked him and duly turned up next day. All through an excellent lunch Keith Caldwell talked of a game warden's life and the more he told me, the more the idea appealed. When the port came, he glowered at me over his glass and said, 'You can have the job if you like, but first I have an important personal question to ask.' I wondered apprehensively what was coming but the question was easily answered.

'How much private income can you raise?'

'None,' I replied.

Keith Caldwell pondered this while he poured out more port, then he said, 'Well in my day it was essential to have something of one's own if you were to enjoy the job, the government pay was niggardly. However think it over and give me your decision in due course.'

As I walked back to my club I called at the India Office to enquire with what gratuity or pension a grateful government would bless me if I quit the trade of a soldier – their reply was dramatically disappointing, and I strolled on plunged into indecision.

A few days later on a race course I ran into my old friend George Murray Smith. I had not seen him since before the war in which, as a 7th Hussar, he had greatly distinguished himself. We went to the bar together to swap news and I told him of my dilemma. 'Your problem is simple,' said George, 'you're joining the 7th Hussars.' I remember from my Sandhurst days that there was no argument with George's humorous and forceful banter, and the matter was resolved there and then. That evening I telephoned Keith Caldwell; 'I think you have made the right decision,' he said.

A month or two later I joined the 7th Hussars in the German town of Soltau and proceeded to enjoy their way of life at once. Shortly after joining the regiment I was detailed as a major to sit on a court in Hamburg dealing with war crimes; and there then followed five of the most interesting and distasteful weeks I can ever remember. The trial concerned Hitler's 'Terror flyers order', which he had issued at the height of the bombing of Germany when the country was being blasted by the RAF at night and by the American Air Force by day. The order laid down in effect that allied flyers who survived after being shot down over Germany were, as prisoners of war, to be denied the right of protection. It was of course contrary to the Hague convention and constituted an invitation to mob lynchings and the slaughter of bona fide prisoners of war, which in fact had occurred in a number of instances. The accused in the dock were two high ranking Germans, General Stumpff and General Schmidt, whose duty it had been to see that this order was passed on and carried out. From the beginning of the trial they both maintained that they had never promulgated or even signed the order but had deliberately blocked it at great risk of Hitler's wrath.

The court consisted of five officers: a brigadier and a colonel, a major, a squadron leader, and a flight lieutenant. It was presided over

by a judge whose duty it was to direct us purely on matters of law, evidence and procedure, leaving us as a kind of jury to decide on matters
of fact. The prosecuting council was a clever and charming barrister
from the Irish Guards and the defence was carried out by two wily
German lawyers; the interpreter's work was done brilliantly by pre-
war refugees from Nazi Germany who were totally bilingual; I could
not help feeling that there might be an opportunity for bias here, but it
was clearly up to the defence to see that no nuance could be introduced
into the interpretation which might act to their detriment.

For days the prosecution called witnesses, who lied abominably and
involved one another in stories of adultery, mistresses and the untidy-
ness of one another's private lives, which, strangely enough, was all
fairly relevant to the case; but we seemed to be getting nowhere; a
signed copy of the order had not come to light although it was clear
that it had been passed down. The generals remained adamant, they
had never signed the order of which they strongly disapproved and
without their signature it could not have been put into effect. However
we had well-confirmed reports of extremely ugly acts committed on
prisoners in the presence of the authority whose duty it was to prevent
such things happening.

The prosecution was bogging down, stalemate and boredom was
setting in, and then one Monday morning the prosecutor rose and
made a dramatic announcement – a copy of the order bearing one of
the general's signatures had come to light over the weekend. The judge
proposed that the court adjourn to allow new defence to be prepared.
This caused a considerable stir and when we reassembled a day or so
later, tension in the court ran high. We took our seats, and in the hush
that followed the prosecutor rose and addressed himself to the general
in question. 'You have consistently denied that you ever signed this
order, General,' he said. 'That is so,' came the reply. 'Then perhaps you
will explain this document,' said the prosecutor walking across the
floor with a piece of paper in his hand which could perhaps send the
general to the gallows.

I then felt a moment of admiration and pity for a man in a tight
corner; with impeccable histrionics the general screwed in his eye glass,
took the document and studied it at arm's length for a long moment,
then he tossed it contemptuously on the desk before him, dropped his
eye glass and turning to the court made, with dignity and some convic-
tion, the only possible comment available to him: 'This is a forgery,
and a bad one.' Then he sat down.

I cannot now remember how the tangle of lying, evasion and back biting by the witnesses proceeded during the next few weeks, but as the trial continued the guilt of the generals became more and more obvious, and when at last, starting from the junior member of the court we were asked to give our verdicts, we returned a unanimous verdict of guilty.

Then came the most difficult decision of all. By international law the maximum sentence for this uncivilised crime was death; the generals had known this when they promulgated the order, and foul acts had been committed under its protection. Now, because we had won the war, we were in a position to apply a law of retribution. For six years the world had gone mad and now the victors were in the unenviable position of passing a terrible judgement on those they considered responsible for this madness. It was a bad moment in history.

Even if my failing memory served me I would not wish to recall what then passed between six reasonable men behind closed doors; a death sentence must be a unanimous decision and we did not agree; for hours we talked among ourselves as dispassionately as recent history would allow but no advocacy could bring us all to the same opinion and again by the process of starting with the junior member of the court, we decided on a prison sentence.

The generals rose when we re-entered the court and stood with dignity to hear their fate. The judge read out their sentences which they acknowledged with a slight nod; when he had finished the generals thanked the court for a fair trial and turned on their heels – they were not unimpressive men.

I was heartily glad when this unpleasant episode ended. We had been investigating human nature at its worst and when our court was not sitting we sometimes listened in at another court which was concerned with the activities of wardresses and their savage dogs in a civilian concentration camp – it was not a nice tale. The utter devastation of bombed out Hamburg and the stink of death which pervaded the air amongst the desolate ruins was oppressive; besides I pined for a winding stream near Soltau where mayfly were being sucked down by fat trout, and the gentle singing of warblers would be broken only by the occasional more urgent song of the reel.

However, one memory of those five weeks still gives me pleasure; early on in the trial I became friends with the prosecuting council. He was very good company and something of a bon viveur. One day he said to me, 'Hilary, what do you know about wine?' I admitted my ignorance, but affirmed my willingness to learn.

'Well,' he said, 'I have made an interesting discovery. The Four Seasons Hotel, one of the only buildings left standing in this ghastly place, has a cellar stuffed with the very finest wines looted from all over Europe; this precious stuff is now available to you and me, at the not unreasonable tariff of one shilling a bottle regardless of vintage or vineyard. The food in the hotel is also of high quality. If you would care to join me for dinner in the evenings, which, since you are on the court and I am prosecuting is probably unethical, we will sample a different bottle every night and work our way through this splendid Aladdin's cave. It might relieve the ennui of our day time activities.' I readily agreed and for the next few weeks I was introduced to the delight of wine while my knowledgeable friend discoursed on its virtues in the language of the connoisseur; it was a happy relief after a day spent listening to the stupidities and brutality of humanity.

On the last day of the trial I was wandering through the bombed streets of Hamburg on my way to the court when I passed a small shop which sold fishing tackle; I walked into buy some trifle, and while a man went in search of it my eye caught a little book written in German; the author's name was von Lettow Vorbeck. Instantly my mind went back to pre-war days when Rudiger von Lettow Vorbeck, the son of the famous first war general* used to stay with me in Devon. When the man returned I asked him who was the author of the book. 'I am,' he said. I then enquired the whereabouts of the famous general. I was in uniform and the little party which had gathered clearly regarded me with suspicion; who was I? Did I know the general? What was my busi-

---

* Between 1914 and 1918 General von Lettow Vorbeck had contained and outmanoeuvered a British army much larger than his own in the German colony of East Africa; when he ran critically short of arms and ammunition, a Zeppelin was sent from Germany to supply him. As it passed over Khartoum it received a signal purporting to be from von Lettow Vorbeck's Headquarters, saying that the general had surrendered; sadly the Zeppelin turned north again bearing away the general's only hope of success. The signal had been sent by the British. However von Lettow Vorbeck fought on unbeaten until the Armistice in 1918 forced him to surrender with all the honours of war, and the highest respect of his enemy for his skilful and gentlemanly conduct throughout the campaign. In the thirties, Hitler had offered the general the post of ambassador to England where he had many friends, but he refused to work for the Nazis and the unattractive Ribbentrop was sent instead; from then on he was forced to live in very reduced circumstances, a victim of Hitler's spite. It is interesting to speculate whether if General von Lettow Vorbeck had accepted the post he could have diverted the subsequent disastrous course of events; it would certainly have been his wish to do so. He died in 1964, a much honoured man.

ness? I answered that I had met the great man briefly many years before, and that his son Rudiger was a pre-war friend of mine; slowly their suspicion thawed and the author picked up a telephone. 'The general is in hospital,' he said, dialling a number. There followed a conversation in rapid German in which I heard my name mentioned. As this was going on a woman said to me, 'If you speak to the general, you should know that Rudiger disappeared in Russia.' Then I was handed the telephone and a voice said, 'Hilary, I am so glad to hear from you.' We talked for a while and I said how sad I was to hear about Rudiger and that if he was a prisoner there was reason for hope; there was a pause and the general said, 'I fear I will never see my son again.' He invited me to visit him in hospital, and I continued my way to the court.

Next day I left a bottle of whisky at the shop for the general but I never made an opportunity to go and visit him. Something inside me shrank from confronting the great man in his distress. I knew that he had hated Nazism and the war between our two countries and my respect for him was such that I could not face him under the present sad circumstances. To my everlasting regret I funked the issue.

5

'The Wildest Dreams of Kew'

SOUTHERN SUDAN

———◆———

Two seasons with the Zetland hunt in Yorkshire and certain other expenses incurred within a small radius from the Cavalry Club in London, inclined my bank manager to suggest more remunerative employment than the 7th Hussars, so I applied for a four and a half year secondment to the Sudan Defence Force.

My interview with the Kaid, General 'Bolo' Whistler* in the London Sudan office was entertaining and successful. After listening to my rehearsed speech about the pleasures of bush life and my liking for service with native troops, he smiled and said, 'I suppose the fact is you're broke.'

'Yes Sir, that is the fact.'

'Well you aren't the only one and I promise you'll enjoy the Sudan and the Sudanese soldiers. Be ready to leave next month, I'll see you there – now go and talk to the Sudan agent in the next office.'

I went into the agent's office; he was elderly, amusing and more inclined to talk of his years with the Sudan Political Service than proffer advice. He finally said, 'You will be going to the Equatorial Corps in the South – very primitive indeed, they tend to eat people they don't like. I got no advice when I first went there except to take a good rifle and a mincing machine – the only meat you get is what you shoot and most of it is pretty tough. No dentists down there so mince everything twice. Good luck my boy.' And we parted.

There was a month of preparation and pleasure which probably caused more problems to my bank manager than it did to me and then on a cold October morning in 1949 I boarded an aeroplane at Blackbush with a suitcase, a shot gun and a light heart. The other passengers were mostly Sudan Civil servants, together with a missionary or two and a few Sudanese students returning from courses in England. Yvonne was the name of the hostess, she was extremely attractive. A

* The subject of a book by General Sir 'Jackie' Smyth VC.

night at a hotel in Malta and on the next day the broad silvery ribbon
of the Nile lay below us for hour after hour, until we came down at
Khartoum.

I had never been in Africa before apart from visits to Cairo and Port
Said on the way to and from India and my mind was open to the im-
pressions of a new continent.

The broad streets of Khartoum were clean, the buildings substantial
with tidy, well-watered gardens and the frontage of the river was lined
with shady trees. Everywhere the Sudanese, in white jellabahs, moved
with unhurried dignity – no pimps, panders or postcard sellers; it was a
contrast to the cities farther north. The Grand Hotel faced onto the
Blue Nile; it had an annex in one of Kitchener's gun boats moored in
the river. At the hotel I met Lieutenant-Colonel Peter Molloy the game
warden from the South who was visiting Khartoum for a conference.

'Yes,' he said, 'you will certainly want a rifle and a mincing machine
but I expect there are some other things you'd like to know about the
place.' A white robed safragi brought whisky to the verandah and as
the moon rose over the Blue Nile we talked. 'It's quite unlike service in
India,' he continued. 'Your Southern soldiers are extremely primitive
– huge jet black pagans who laugh all day and drink all night – discipline is tough and crime except for drunkenness and adultery is rare.
That is a good thing as you can't punish them, extra duties are looked
on with pleasure and if you fine them it's their wives who suffer. Your
bash shawish rules the company with a hippo hide whip – it wouldn't
do in Aldershot but it is effective in "the Bog". The country is desper-
ately harsh but full of game and you are allowed three elephants a year
on a six pound licence; it's a good way to pay your Greek grocer. There
is always a chance of little non-dangerous wars against raiders from
Ethiopia – your askaris enjoy that – it gives them a chance for a bit of
"own back" for the atrocities that the raiders commit if they get
through.'

I asked him about the other Europeans in Equatoria and the Bahr el
Ghazal Province. 'It's a closed area,' he said. 'There are only Government officials, a few missionaries and of course a small community of
Greek traders. No social life except boozing with your chums or more
likely by yourself for three months if you are lucky enough to get
posted to an out station. I should apply for that and I'll come and see
you occasionally.'

We talked late into the night and I awoke to a pearly Sudan morning
perhaps slightly wiser, certainly a good deal better informed. At nine

o'clock I visited the Sudan Defence Force* Headquarters for a briefing; a staff officer whom I had known at Sandhurst endeavoured to put me in the picture. 'I really know damn all about it,' he said. 'You're lucky – I've never been down to "the Bog", I long to get out of this bloody chair. The post boat sails for Juba in a fortnight – you catch it at Kosti, and here is a list of the stores you should buy in the meantime.' I looked aghast at the pages of type that he handed me.

'This looks like a Fortnum and Mason catalogue,' I said.

'That's about what it is, it's your complete requirements for four months as drawn up by some clown in this headquarters – down to the last pot of pepper or roll of bumph – the next consignment will come on the post boat after four months. Get it at the Armenian grocers in the square and if you can't pay see Jackson the accountant – he will give you an advance.'

I had a fortnight to spend in Khartoum, the groceries could wait – the streets of hell are lined with grocer's shops with never a gunsmith in sight – first things first, I would buy a rifle. Peter Molloy had directed me to a gunsmith and there, for the next hour I indulged myself with all the pleasure of a dowager duchess in a hat shop. I emerged triumphantly armed and munitioned and proceeded to the next item – a mincing machine; an ironmonger across the street yielded a beauty – yes, it would certainly mince a hartebeeste said the shopkeeper and I returned to the hotel feeling well pleased. Peter was there and I invited him to admire my purchases.

'It's a good rifle,' he said, 'but you won't be allowed an elephant licence on that, it's too light. You should have bought a heavier calibre.' He paused to savour this bombshell and then added, 'Not unless you can get around the licencing officer.'

'Who is he?'

'Me,' said Peter. 'And another thing, do you deal with this firm for everything?' He pointed to the name on the mincing machine – it was Husqvana, the same make as the rifle. He thought that was a happy omen and we went in to lunch.

As we were sitting down, a pretty girl walked up the steps of the hotel. Peter remarked that things were looking up.

'Would you like to meet her?' I asked.

'Of course.'

'What about my elephant licence?'

* For an explanation of military and government terms and titles in the Sudan, please see Appendix 2, page 201.

'It's a bargain,' said Peter and I went over to Yvonne and brought her to our table. She explained that she was stranded in Khartoum indefinitely while her plane had gone to Kano to collect pilgrims for Mecca. Here was luck indeed; my mind turned to the horrors of shopping which lay ahead. I didn't even understand what some of the items were. How many tins of mustard or pounds of rice would last four months – what was a cullender? Did my salvation lie in the lovely girl at our table and could some pleasure be had from the dismal chore of shopping. By the end of lunch it was settled. Peter in the meantime had decided that he should get more stores before returning south. Yvonne would do it.

'Give me the lists,' she said, 'and you can take me to the Omdurman camel market and the Gordon cabaret in the evenings.'

So it turned out that I chose camping equipment from the Government stores or visited the Defence Force Headquarters to acquaint myself with duties which lay ahead, while Yvonne shopped for Peter and I at the grocers.

On the last night of my stay in Khartoum, the three of us visited the open air cabaret for the fifth time. As the moon rose it occurred to me that it would be discreet to depart. I made excuses and walked back to the hotel alongside the glistening moonlit Nile. Peter came to my room early next morning still dressed. He wandered about chatting and finally took a piece of paper from his pocket. 'Here's my side of the bargain,' he said, 'it's your elephant licence. Yvonne and I are engaged.'

They came to see me off on the train to Kosti. Having arrived two weeks before with a suitcase and a shot gun, I was now possessed of fourteen packing cases each marked El Bimbashi, H. Hook, Equatorial Corps., Torit; dressed in the badges of a Turkish lieutenant-colonel I confidently boarded the train for Kosti. It had been an amusing two weeks. We waved to one another until the clouds of black smoke enveloped the departing train.

On the following day I arrived at Kosti and the luggage was loaded aboard an antiquated looking stern-wheel paddle steamer. I sought my cabin which was spacious, and then explored the boat. It did not take long – the first class passengers of which there were four were accommodated on the upper deck and largely surrounded by mosquito proof netting. The lower deck was overcrowded with Sudanese; on either side of the steamer were lashed barges, piled high with the firewood which fuelled the boilers. The captain and senior crew were Dongalawi Arabs from the Northern Sudan. In the evening we cast off, and with much shouting and puffing, made mid-river and headed up stream for the South. The great oily flood of the Nile curved downwards out of sight to north and south. I went to my cabin, unpacked my books and made myself as comfortable as possible for a two week voyage.

For the first few days the banks of the river were barren; fishing boats with their white clad occupants skimmed backwards and forwards under lateen sails. The farther south we travelled the more lush became the vegetation and the taller and blacker became the occupants of the fishing boats, which had changed from skilfully built sailing feluccas to dugout canoes, in which men and girls stood naked, casting their circular fishing nets with consummate grace and skill. A following wind enveloped us in smoke and the sun beat down; we prayed for a head wind but our prayers were unanswered.

My other three companions were missionaries returning to their missions from home leave: two scrawny little men and a shrivelled woman. They were not inclined to be friendly and looked askance at the whisky bottle by my side in the evenings. I had discovered their calling when two beautiful black girls standing in their dugout drifted past down stream waving and laughing. They were stark naked and my comment of approval was taken from the Song of Solomon. It was met with glum disapproval, and the information that 'the girls in our mission are beginning to wear clothes'. I had hoped to find the missionaries interesting but they were immensely dull and ate too much, so I kept to myself. In Khartoum I had bought every appropriate history and bird book available as well as Brocklehurst's *Game Animals of the Sudan* and some Arabic textbooks; with these, my field glasses and a comfortable deck chair by the rail time passed pleasantly between meals. Every few days we stopped at a cluster of mud huts on the bank to take on wood, it was always a scene of noisy confusion as the tall naked Nuer and Dinka humped logs aboard singing and laughing. One such place was Kodok on the west bank – it had once been called Fashoda but the name was changed to eliminate the memory of an incident which at the turn of the century brought Britain and France to the verge of war.* The place was small, squalid and of no value, and I thought with sadness of how the gallant French officer Major Marchand, having struggled from the west coast for two years, saw all the achievements of his party brought to nothing and, in tears, lowered the French flag and departed down the Nile.

At last we entered the Sudd, a maze of floating islands formed by

* See Winston Churchill's *The River War*, Chapter 17, 'The Fashoda Incident'.

water weed. On either hand twelve foot papyrus reeds hemmed us in –
channels led everywhere. We ploughed our way through rafts of Nile
cabbage and cut through seemingly impenetrable patches of reeds.
This was the great barrier which for thousands of years had held up ex-
ploration to the south. The Emperor Nero had sent an expedition to
penetrate to the source of the Nile but it had returned, thwarted by
these vast swamps. Other explorers had been hemmed in for months
on end and died of starvation. The source of the White Nile had
remained a secret until barely a hundred years ago.

We bumped into papyrus beds, reversed and bumped again. Sometimes we were heading north and sometimes south. At night we sought
out channels by the aid of a searchlight and in the mornings a land-
mark that we had seen on our right hand when the sun went down,
now appeared on our left. It was very confusing. There was wild life in
abundance; the heads of hippos rose in the water, gazing at us mistrust-
fully, and grunting in a deep resonant boom; herds of elephant stood
on patches of dry land lifting their trunks to take the wind before hus-
tling their calves away into the reeds; occasionally a crocodile rose to
the surface with only nostrils and eyes visible and then sank silently
into the depths again. The bird life became more interesting and
varied; fish eagles, goliath herons and ibis flew overhead, while lily
trotters, crakes and rails ran on the floating water weed. Just once I
saw, standing in the papyrus, the tall grey figure and gigantic bill of a
whale-headed stork (*Balaeniceps rex*), a morose looking solitary bird,
only found in Central African swamps. The heat and humidity were
intense, but one morning a breeze sprang up from the south cooling us
and clearing the enveloping smoke. We heard the engine revs increase
to make headway against it but after a little while the engine stopped
with a wheeze, and we drifted into the papyrus. Neither the missionaries nor I spoke Arabic so we were left to ponder future events in
silence. Exhortations and the name of Allah rose from the engine room
to the upper deck where the missionaries were conducting a prayer
meeting. I felt we were doubly insured. A few hours of deafening ham-
mering and we were on the move again – but not for long. Towards
evening a sudden quiet descended and we drifted down river in the
direction of Cairo until a friendly patch of swamp held us up. It was
a starlit night of great beauty, hippos splashed and grunted around
us and a thousand different voices called from the papyrus, the
skyline was lit with grass fires and from far away I heard for the
first time that most thrilling sound in Africa – a lion roaring.

At last, four days late, with our hooter hooting, we rounded a bend and saw our destination, Juba, on the west bank. It was a welcome but somewhat squalid sight. Another Turkish lieutenant-colonel stood on the wharf – he was rotund and jovial. 'I'm Ian Alexander,' he said, 'I hope you have enjoyed your journey.'

He turned to an enormous black soldier standing beside him in immaculate uniform with a bush hat turned up at the side.

'This is Okak Luka your orderly.' The giant smote his rifle with a thunderous clap and I held out my hand.

'You're four days late,' said Ian, 'let's go to the hotel and have a drink. Okak Luka will see to your luggage. We'll spend the night in Juba and drive out to Torit in the morning.'

We motored through the town to where on a rise overlooking the river a small single-storied hotel sweltered in the heat, but containing comforts not to be had on the river steamer. We dined that night in the open air, drinking delicious South African wine whilst Ian told me something of what to expect of life in the Equatorial Corps. Next morning I found it difficult to disentangle what had been told me from what I had dreamt in the night. It all seemed slightly unreal.

Juba was the headquarters of Equatorial province; there were a few Greek merchants, an untidy bazaar, government offices and some European bungalows for government officials. I visited the governor of the province and left my card and then we went to the Greek grocer and bought stores. We crossed the river by ferry to the east bank and set off in our truck for the ninety miles to Torit on a corrugated bumpy road. The scenery was dull to begin with – coarse five foot high grass lined the road on either side, patches of which had been burned. After fifty miles we started passing between high rocky hills on the sides of which were villages of neatly thatched mud huts – parties of naked Latuka armed with spears waved as we drove by. Smoke hung in the air from the many grass fires and by mid-day it was intensely hot. On nearing Torit we rounded a bend and saw a wall of fire with flames twenty feet high bearing rapidly down upon us. On all sides and behind us was tall dry grass. 'Here's where we do the burning hoop trick,' said Ian. 'It's quite usual but first we check for petrol leaks.'

We got out and inspected the petrol tank; it seemed dry and climbing back in we wound up the windows and charged the inferno at full speed. When we were through I said, 'What happens if you are on foot? That fire was travelling fast.'

'The only thing to do is to start your own fire and walk behind it,' he replied.

We entered Torit and drove up to Ian's bungalow which I was to share with him – his paraffin refrigerator yielded up iced beer. When we had slaked our thirst and washed, Ian took me to meet the commanding officer, Miralai Claude Reynolds Bey, in his office. A tall dark figure removed his feet from the desk, put down a copy of the *Field* and rose to greet us. 'I'm delighted you are here at last,' he said. 'What delayed you? I suppose that bloody boat broke down again.'

As we chatted I glanced round the office. Racing and sporting magazines were piled on top of official files and in the corner a black labrador bitch was curled up in her basket. 'That's Dixie,' said Claude. 'She's not awfully well – this is a bad place for dogs, there are too many tsetse fly and I can't get the right medicine.' We discussed various subjects but mostly the prospects of sport in the area. After a while Claude said, 'Well don't let me detain you, come to dinner tonight and tomorrow I will take you sand grouse shooting.' I had known sterner and more urgent military interviews and I went away suspecting what I subsequently learnt to be true, that my new boss was a man of great charm.

Torit was a small straggling township consisting of a civilian district headquarters, one Greek merchant's shop which, when given notice would produce anything available in the Sudan, and a small bazaar. There were a few bungalows for officials and a small mission. The Equatorial Corps Headquarters were a mile or two out of the town on the Geneti river – a winding sluggish stream. The position of the town had been chosen by a previous Commanding Officer of the Corps who found good buffalo hunting in the area. There were two infantry companies in Torit as well as signals, transport and all the usual clutter of a headquarters. A hundred miles to the east was another company at Kapoeta with a platoon at Loelli and an outpost at Boma far away towards the Ethiopian border. Each company had one and sometimes two officers, seconded from the British army – the noncommissioned officers and men were all recruited from the local tribes. Six hundred miles to the west was a company at Wau, the Provincial Headquarters of the Bahr el Gazal Province.

The Equatorial Corps was the only military formation in the Southern Sudan, their duties being to keep the peace in a country the size of France, Belgium, Holland and Switzerland combined and deal with raiders from across the borders. It seemed to me that the military principle 'economy of force' was applied in earnest but presumably it worked, even in a country with a turbulent history where every man carried weapons.

Ian's company, to which I was attached, consisted of a hundred and twenty riflemen and forty enlisted porters; they were preparing for the big annual event – a three month trek in the bush. On the first of January every year, each company set out on a patrol of their areas: the object was to 'show the flag' in potential trouble spots and do field training. We would return to Torit on the first of April before the rains broke, having covered about six hundred miles. Ian wanted to consult the District Commissioner John Owen on the proposed route and after a few days we went to see him. I was introduced to a large athletic figure of about forty in white uniform with bright blue eyes and curly hair; he was an Oxford scholar and rugger blue and talked in a modest but knowledgeable manner – in fact he was a very typical member of the Sudan Political service. It was obvious that he knew the tribes and his district well.

Ian asked him if there was any special area that he wanted us to patrol. He thought for a while, filling his pipe, and then said, 'You couldn't do better than to trek through the best game country. I take it that Hilary has an elephant licence.' This suited us well, it was the answer we wanted and Ian explained the route we had planned together. John Owen listened attentively with an occasional comment on water holes, local chiefs or game. Finally a smile spread over his face.

'So you will be marching over the Imatong mountains will you?' he said. 'I've always wanted to do that, it's little known country.'

'Well, we'll give you a report,' said Ian. 'Is there anything special you want to know about?'

John Owen's smile broadened, 'Yes,' he said, 'mice.'

We were somewhat taken aback but John continued in the manner of a man who is slightly shy of his own foibles. 'You see, I am collecting small rodents for a museum in Copenhagen and I've never had time to collect on the Imatong moorlands – would you have a little time?' he asked with gentle irony. 'If so I will send my skinner to meet you before you go into the hills and some prisoners from the jail to carry the traps; there are probably some unknown species up there, it's a very isolated range.'

During the next few days Ian took me round other members of the

Torit community; there was a doctor, a vet, and the delightful Greek grocer, Lolos, who was a repository of knowledge about the tribes in the area. Finally we visited an American professor called Harry Hoogstraal who was studying the incidence of malaria in the blood of elephant shrews, rat-sized jumping little creatures with long mobile snouts. He took us to see his shrews and explained that they were of interest in research, having a blood structure much like human beings.

'I suppose you will be doing a bit of hunting on this trek?' he asked me.

'Only for the pot, and of course ivory,' I said. 'We have a hundred and sixty men to provide with meat so nothing but elephant or buffalo will do.'

'Will you collect ticks and blood slides for me from anything you shoot?' he asked.

He took me to his laboratory, showed me how to take blood slides and gave me a box of equipment and three bottles of bourbon whiskey.

'This expedition seems to be getting less and less military,' said Ian as we drove home.

I had shot most of the big game of India in the slightly doubtful name of sport. I had enjoyed it greatly because it took one to remote and beautiful places from the snowpeaks of the north to the forests of Central India. It also presented one with the challenge of trying to become skilful at tracking, stalking and the interpretation of jungle signs. Above all, if one had grown up with a passionate interest in natural history, one could indulge it to the full. However, I had stood over the body of my last victim – a beautiful tiger and vowed never again to hunt big game purely for trophies or sport. Illogically, I now argued that the circumstances were different. There was no shortage of elephant or buffalo in the area, my one hundred and sixty soldiers wanted meat, and the price of ivory was good; I had an anodyne with which to anoint my conscience. I would shoot buffalo and elephant, my men would be well fed and my Greek grocer would be paid; there is no hypocrite like a happy one.

The weeks passed pleasantly with musketry, drill and company training; these normally boring activities were enlivened by the enthusiasm, humour and skill of our black askaris – their drill in bare feet was a model for the Brigade of Guards, they were excellent shots and their humour was infectious and basic. If a man fell off the back of a truck it was the best joke of the day, when the bimbashi's hat blew off in a gust of wind the company on parade shook with mirth. It was very easy to raise a laugh. Almost every man had his wife and children with him; he was only allowed to bring one wife to the barracks and these lived in the 'harimat' lines, a cluster of neatly thatched mud huts behind the company offices. On Saturday mornings the harimat lines were inspected by the company commander, the bash shawish (sergeant-major) and the buluk amin (quartermaster sergeant). The party would be escorted by the sheka or senior wife in the company. She was not necessarily the wife of a senior NCO but chosen by general acclaim of the other families. She was always a formidable lady and her word was law in the harimat. The lines and huts were spotlessly clean; the little inspection party would walk round cracking jokes, appraising babies or hearing complaints from the bare bosomed giggling Judy O'Grady's – it was all extremely comic.

On Saturday evenings, drumming started in the lines – faint at first but rising to a tremendous rhythmic thunder as the marrissa (native beer) circulated; at midnight the noise stopped abruptly. This was the weekly dance, it was a very popular event; all through the week marrissa, made from millet, had been brewed by the wives and on Saturday it disappeared to the last drop; there were always thick heads and red eyes on Sunday morning.

Christmas came and went. Other officers arrived from outstations and we sweltered over roast guinea fowl, sucking wart hog and tinned Christmas puddings. Someone produced a gramophone with carols and a Scottish officer made jugs of Athelbrose. We had a guinea fowl shoot and clay pigeon competition with tins and gramophone records thrown from a roof – we listened to the King's speech from London and drank warm champagne – it was a time of happy buffoonery which would have been much improved, and perhaps gentled, by female company. There was another revel on New Year's night and at midday on the first of January the company paraded for the long trek. Two columns of riflemen set out on either side of the track heading north. At the rear of the column came our forty porters each carrying sixty pounds of stores on their heads. These loads consisted of ammunition, medical supplies, extra rations and officers' camp equipment, food and drink. Each rifleman carried a canvas bag of rations on the top of his knapsack. Some of the askaris carried trumpets and whistles made from antelope horns and the noise as we left Torit was indescribable. The wives with their babies on their hips ran alongside ululating with high pitched yells above the blare of the trumpets, the bugler played a solo voluntary. Suddenly there was a hush and the company burst into song, one man shouted a rapid gabble of words and the company took up the refrain,

'What's it all about?' I asked Ian as we marched at the head of the column.

'I think its a sort of Equatorial "Ball of Kirrimuir", mostly about you and me,' he replied. 'It's sure to be unprintable but it's a good sign.'

After a few miles the wives and children fell away.

'Why are we setting such a cracking pace?' I asked Ian. 'Six hundred miles of this will kill me.'

'It's only for today,' he replied, 'we have got to get as far from Torit as possible and take the shine out of some of these black Casanovas or they will be sneaking back tonight for some indiscriminant farewell sport in the harimat.'

In the late afternoon we halted. The askaris piled arms, cleared the undergrowth and dragged thorn bushes into a circular 'zariba'. Ian and I chose a camp site some distance from the company under a tree; the porters quickly cleared the area with their pangas, our camp beds, chairs and tables were set up and we settled down for the night. Tents were never taken on these treks, there would be little or no rain until April and the country abounded in shady trees.

Night came, camp fires flickered, the chatter from the zariba died down and the noises of the African night took over. Lions were roaring in the distance. At four in the morning a black hand poked a mug of tea under my mosquito net, the fires flared again and the men moved briskly into formation, Ian gave an order, and we were on the march. At the head of the column an askari guide carried a stable lantern to detect puff adders, behind him came Ian and I with our orderlies and a bugler; the company and porters followed noiselessly behind. The sky was studded with more stars than I had ever seen. The pole star lay low in the sky ahead and the Southern cross blazed behind us. Occasionally a startled animal would gallop off into the darkness. We marched in silence enjoying the chill morning air. At last a flush appeared in the sky to our right and a faint cold wind sprang up; slowly the light came. The magic of an African dawn was unfolded to perfection, and as the red rim of the sun came over the horizon the company burst into song We marched northwards; the country on either side was dry burnt grassland with occasional trees; far away to the left a strip of bright green indicated a swamp and through field glasses I could see white egrets flying. Okak Luka confirmed my suspicion that hidden in that high grass were buffalo and elephant, 'Laham ketir – meat galore,' he said, grinning with anticipation. At nine thirty we halted for the rest of the day by a shady water hole; an area was cleared, we bathed and breakfasted and I wandered out with a shot gun to where I had heard guinea fowl and partridges calling.

After three days marching we approached a line of rocky hills dotted with thatched mud huts, the horns and trumpets of the company blared out and were answered from the rocks which became alive with running naked figures, drums started a rhythmic welcome. It was a Latuka village and as most of our soldiers were Latuka, we were in for a royal welcome. Camp was made a mile from the hills and when we had settled in, a reception committee approached us. A grave and dignified chief appeared surrounded by Latuka warriors in full traditional dress of beautifully made brass helmets, beads and little else but spears and knobkerries. A fat bull was prodded forward for slaughter and Ian and I were presented with chickens, eggs and milk. We sat with the chief, in deck chairs under our shade tree and gave him beer. Was all peaceful in his area? Had the rains and the millet crop been good? Did he have recruits for the company, were lions harassing the cattle? He took snuff, spat and asked for more beer. Yes, all was well thanks to the Hakuma (Government). Crops were good and he had many splendid young men wanting to join the buluk. Yes there was a herd of elephant a days march to the east and many buffalo – the company would become fat. After mutual compliments and more beer, he departed with the present of a box of twelve-bore cartridges. That evening the company feasted and drums sounded late into the night.

We spent next morning doing a field firing exercise to the delight of the village and then we inspected recruits. It was the ambition of every young warrior in the Equatorial province to become a soldier, carry a rifle and swagger about in a smart uniform; it meant cash in the pocket and an advantage among the ladies. Recruits were easily obtained. About thirty turned up and the selection committee consisting of Ian, the bash shawish and myself put them through their paces and examined them; we ran races and had a spear throwing competition. Those we selected were given a signed twelve-bore cartridge case and told to report to Torit in April for a medical examination.

Next day we marched over the hills to the east and down into a great dusty plain criss-crossed by elephant tracks and with an occasional clump of trees in the distance to indicate a water hole. Standing orders in the Equatorial Corps were extremely strict regarding water, everything depended upon its availability: the porters absolutely refused to

carry spare water, that was a woman's job. The punishment for cow-
ardice was still to be drummed out of the company carrying a pot of
water on the head as a badge of shame. Each man carried two day's
supply in his water bottles and that was all. Treks were planned from
the inaccurate cloth maps of the country; if the company marched all
day to a marked water hole which proved to be dry the orders were to
return to the last water, even if an inviting green tree-line in the
distance indicated a bubbling spring. It was the strictest rule of the line
of march; officers and men had died for ignoring it. The presence or
absence of water ruled our movements and we carefully sought local
information on the subject.

Day succeeded glorious day. We sometimes changed the routine and
marched at dawn to traverse difficult country, or conduct a few basic
military manoeuvres. There was one exercise that we practiced regularly in high grass; it was delightfully archaic and pleased Ian enormously. 'Let's play Waterloo,' he would say, giving an order to the
bugler. The alarm was sounded and the marching company broke into
the double – men rushed everywhere in apparent confusion, NCOs
shouted and the bash shawish bellowed, but it was not total confusion;
in the twinkling of an eye the company had formed square, front rank
kneeling, rear rank standing like Wellington's red coats in the corn-
fields of Waterloo; the porters had raced into the centre of the square
and lay face downwards under their loads. Ian would stride about
inside the square shouting defiance in French at an imaginary Old
Guard. Volley after volley of blank ammunition was discharged into
the high grass until the bugler sounded cease fire, then Ian would wave
his hat and shout, 'Up guards and at 'em.' The company would swiftly
form a line and, bayonets fixed, charge into the grass with horrible
yells. This little pantomime was always much enjoyed, everyone knew
it was performed for a good reason. Some years before a company of
the Equatorial Corps on the march had been ambushed in high grass
by Aliab Dinka spearmen who rushed them at close quarters. Both British officers and many askaris had been killed.

After eight days marching we came to a road where a lorry from
Torit met us with supplies. We crossed the road, changed direction
southwards and entered more wooded country. After a few more days
we came to a lake surrounded by trees. 'Just the place for a short holiday,' said Ian. 'All we want is a sailing boat, a casino and a few girls in
bikinis. I think we will spend a bit of time here.'

There was a natural campsite in the shade overlooking the lake;

while the area was being cleared I walked down to the water's edge to look for signs of game. Elephant and buffalo tracks lay in every direction, together with eland, zebra and hartebeest. There were fresh pug marks where three lions had been drinking; guinea fowl tracks were everywhere: a flight of gargeny teal rose from the reeds as I walked back to camp to report what I had seen. 'Right,' said Ian, 'get busy with your gun. I will break open the goodie box and cool the wine – tomorrow we will have a formal dinner party – who shall we ask?' The 'goodie box' was a tin trunk containing left-overs from Christmas and some bottles of excellent South African wine. Ian had consigned it to the biggest and strongest porter who had borne it on his head for the last hundred miles: tomorrow we would lighten his burden.

At dawn next morning I set off with Okak Luka in search of meat and ivory. We circled the lake looking for elephant tracks. 'Measure his boots,' Claude Reynolds had told me, 'anything of around twenty-two inches might be worth following – big boots can mean big ivory.' I had cut notches in my thumb stick. No elephants had drunk that night, but we soon came upon tracks of a lone buffalo who had wallowed in the mud; we cast round like tufting hounds. The tracks led away from the lake over a flat plain; where the grass had been burnt the tracking was easy but we were soon led into patches of high grass which the fire had not reached and the pace became slower. Okak Luka kept to the trail; a broken twig, a bruised leaf or displaced pebble led him on. Every now and again he would stoop down and pick up a handful of dust letting it filter through his fingers – the wind was in our favour. For two hours we followed a fairly straight course and then the tracks began to wander from one shaded patch to another. We were suddenly confronted with a steaming buffalo pat. Okak Luka bent down and with a thoughtful expression slowly poked his finger into it. 'Very close,' he said.

I pointed to a tree, he put down his rifle and climbed stealthily into the branches, while I kept my eyes on his face. He looked round and I saw his gaze become fixed. Slowly his huge pink tongue emerged pointing towards a tree to our right; a moment later he was beside me testing the wind again. A short whispered conversation and we crept round a barrier of bushes. The buffalo was lying under the tree, his jaw working – he looked like a big Aberdeen Angus bull. Suddenly his jaw stopped and he rose to his feet giving me an easy heart shot; I fired and he turned to gallop away but suddenly changed his mind, swung round and with his nose stuck out came for us full tilt. I got another shot into his chest and heard Okak Luka open rapid fire. The buffalo halved the distance between us and then went onto his knees; he was up again in a flash and came on swinging a leg. I was half concealed by a bush but Okak Luka stood in the open. The buffalo chose Okak Luka and plunged towards him presenting me with an easy neck shot which settled the matter. It had been a lively few seconds and I rather needed a cigarette. Okak Luka was laughing with delight at the sight of so much meat.

We had a drink from the canvas water bottle, I collected some ticks from the buffalo and took blood slides. We then tied Okak Luka's shirt to the top of a tree, opened the buffalo to bring in the vultures as a further guide, and headed back to camp. The news of a meat issue was greeted with enthusiasm; a large party of naked soldiers set out armed with pangas to cut up and bring in everything that was edible. I labelled and packed up my ticks and blood slides and then set off to shoot a duck for supper. My tick collection was growing: I already had ticks from game birds, ticks from a tortoise, ticks from snakes, ticks from askaris and ticks from bimbashis. They were all neatly labelled with the name of the host, the place and the date and they floated snugly in small test tubes of spirit. I was becoming fascinated with the beastly things, perhaps one day I would have a tick named after me – fame was the spur.

That night the company squatted round many little fires gorging themselves with meat while Ian and I sat down to a Fortnum's hamper and two bottles of Chateau La Gratitude. Ian was a good companion; he was not in the least interested in big game shooting which is essentially a one man sport and he mocked humorously at my enthusiasm. He was a witty, well read talker with an unfailing eye for the funny side of a situation and a sharp tongue for those he didn't like. He was, above all, a bon viveur; I had taken no part in the messing arrangements and we were faring extremely well. I shot for the pot and Ian made sure that the pot was good – it was a satisfactory arrangement and we enjoyed one another's company.

We spent the next few days at the waterhole doing a little training in the mornings and bathing, birdwatching or shooting in the evenings. The bird life around the lake was wonderful, the check list I was making doubled in size, and we feasted on a choice of goose, duck, guinea fowl, partridge or snipe.

One morning a tall black figure strode into our camp; he threw down his spears, held his palm towards us in the manner of a traffic policeman and said, 'Mong,' the Latuka greeting.

'Ogol,' replied Ian. 'What can I do for you?'

The man tossed down a still wet leopard skin. 'How much?' he said. 'It stole one of my goats so I killed it.'

We examined the skin but it was badly damaged and full of holes. 'No good,' said Ian.

'Then can you give me some medicine,' said the man.

'What's the matter with you, you look right enough but why are you covered in blood?'

The man grinned, jerked his head forward and his scalp fell over his face in a ghastly red mask. He turned his back revealing terrible claw marks and lacerations; the leopard had clearly disputed the possession of its skin. For the next few hours we worked on him, cleaning, syringing and sewing his scalp back on: never did he make a sound or twitch a muscle; when we had finished, the medical dresser brought a bottle of antibiotic pills. Ian studied the instructions and turned to the bash shawish.

'Tell him to eat four pills every four hours. Also tell him that according to this piece of paper it will cure his clap.'

The bash shawish took the bottle and speaking in Latuka pointed to the sun, holding up four fingers, he then pointed lower in the sky and again held up four fingers – a third time and the instructions were complete – the wounded man placed the bottle in his antelope scrotum bag, picked up his spears and strode away, his leopard skin over his arm.

We marched away to the south and after a few days again met up with the supply lorry bringing mail and rations. As it was being unloaded a large bundle of spears appeared.

'Why have you brought these,' Ian asked the driver. The bash shawish intervened.

'They say that the buffalo to the south of the mountain have got "the disease,"' he said. 'With Janabuk's permission the young men would like to hunt them when we pass through that country.'

The Latuka were traditional hunters, they would tackle any game from elephant downwards, racing through the bush and mobbing their quarry with spears. It was a team sport in which every spearman relied on the staunch behaviour of his friends. If a man went down under his shield to a charging buffalo or lion, the other spearmen would pile in on the flank until the wounded animal turned on them or died. It was greatly enjoyed and played with such skill that remarkably few bones were broken. When buffalo had 'the disease' they became sluggish and bad tempered and easier to hunt.

'You can't eat the meat if the buffalo are sick,' said Ian.

'No, but we will make many shields from the hides,' was the reply.

I badly wanted to watch a Latuka hunt, and after a discussion, we decided to ignore what would probably be a mild infringement of the game laws.

'I will attend, heavily armed with powder and shot,' I said, 'and we will limit the bag to three buffalo.'

So it was arranged. On the following Sunday about thirty naked men each armed with several spears paraded before dawn and we set off into the gathering light. Okak Luka and I carried rifles, only to be used in an emergency. The men walked silently in single file, Okak Luka and I in the rear. The sun rose, and after an hour the dew had dried from the grass. We topped a hill and looked down to a partly burnt plain in the centre of which was a patch of swamp surrounded by high reeds and grass. Men climbed trees and pointed; there was a council of war in Latuka and the party split into two, before loping off to surround the swamp. Okak Luka and I sat watching from the hill. After a long wait we saw a whorl of smoke appear from the far side of the swamp, then another and another until a horseshoe of blazing reeds and grass was burning towards us. We could hear the crackling of the fire and above it, high yodelling voices calling to one another; some waterbuck broke and galloped for safety. Suddenly the calling voices became a high babble of excitement, like a pack of hounds opening on a fox and out of the smoke lumbered three buffalo. Naked black figures were streaking across the plain from all directions; three spearmen headed the buffalo, who changed direction for a patch of unburnt cover: more figures sprang into view and the buffalo turned again, heading back for the smoke. The spearmen closed in and started hurling their spears. Dust rose as the buffalo wheeled to break through the line of their attackers. One went down on his knees bristling with spears; close by a mêlée was taking place in a cloud of dust above which a pair of black legs rose kicking at the sky – the shouting reached a crescendo. Time for modern science to intervene I thought, and grabbing our rifles we set off for the scene at full speed. But then the tumult died and we arrived to find two dead buffalo, a man on the ground and a group of happy sweaty warriors each telling the other the story of his bravery and skill. I inspected the man on the ground, he was bruised but 'walking wounded' and delighted with his part in the drama. It didn't seem to me that the buffalo were sick but after giving instructions that the meat was not to be eaten I took blood slides, collected some ticks and having congratulated all concerned set off back to camp leaving the men to bring in the skins. It had been a most entertaining Sunday morning.

During the next week's march I shot an elephant with seventy pound tusks. We managed to get the three ton supply lorry across country to where it lay; about thirty naked men, having cut out the ivory, proceeded to chop up the carcase. Little fires were lit nearby on which the working men singed and then swallowed great gobbets of meat; one man completely disappeared inside the carcase and from time to time a bloody arm appeared handing titbits to his friends outside; it was not a pretty scene. The lorry was loaded with meat and the ivory and as we departed the vultures descended. I hadn't enjoyed myself but the company were delighted and when we marched on, every man carried a good supply of biltong, and I would be the richer by a hundred pounds or more.

A few more long marches and we came to the foot of the Imatong mountains, where we made camp beside a clear running stream. Some years before a district commissioner had cut a track up through the undergrowth and forest of the steep hill side. It was now overgrown, but we found it and for the next few days everyone turned out with pangas to clear the way up to the moorland; each evening we returned to camp. During this time a truck arrived from the District Commissioner John Owen; it contained three prisoners from Torit gaol, amiable young murderers whose only crimes had been to slay a member of another tribe in fair fight or to add emphasis to some argument by wielding a knobkerry. In charge of the prisoners was John Owen's professional skinner, their luggage was three packing cases full of mouse traps.

When we had cleared the track for the porters, we set off and for two days struggled up through the forest spending uncomfortable nights on the cold mountainside. Finally we came to the moorland and marched through the long grass in the direction of the ten thousand foot peak of Mount Kinyeti. We camped in a sheltered glade and for the next few days set traps and went 'mousing'. The soldiers enjoyed it – they were quite used to the idiosyncrasies of bimbashis – if we shot buffalo and elephants for them, they would delightedly catch rats and mice for us; armed with sticks they moved through the long grass beating bushes or digging on hands and knees with pangas. A moment of great mirth occurred when a fair sized and embattled rat turned on his crouching pursuer and to everyones' delight fastened itself, squeaking to his cheek. In the evenings after baiting and setting traps I settled down with the skinner and by the light of a lantern recorded and measured the day's bag.

The time came to move on; the prisoners and the trophies were despatched with a small escort to Torit and, confident that we had contributed something to science we turned our faces to the mountain again. The march lead us over rolling grassland, and down deep wooded gulleys and across ice cold streams, but always we were climbing upwards. The country reminded me much of the highlands of New Guinea, the nights were bitterly cold and on several occasions an icy downpour drenched us to the skin. The askaris were not enjoying it, and when at last we stood on the top of Mount Kinyeti (increased in altitude by a foot high pile of elephant droppings) the bash shawish said to Ian, 'Janabuk, we must go down before sickness comes.'

That was sense, and we headed downhill towards Uganda. I was disappointed that we had to curtail our stay in the Imatongs for I had been asked to investigate the presence, and if possible shoot a specimen of any blue coloured monkey and of a giant pig which had been reported in the area some years before. A Bimbashi Gifford of the Equatorial Corps (now General John Gifford) had shot one in the early thirties and seen a very much larger specimen. The British Museum reported that it was a particularly fine specimen of bush pig (*Potamocheorus porcus*). To this day General Johnny Gifford believes that there is a separate race of enormous size, waiting for discovery in the Imatongs. I longed to confirm the presence of a pig that would dwarf those boars of classical Greek legend and just once we came upon tracks where a large pig had wallowed in the mud; however, the men did not like these cold deserted uplands and they were beginning to sneeze, so we rolled downhill through shoulder high grass and forest, eventually coming out from under the clouds into sunshine.

To the south of the Imatongs we were in Acholi country; our Acholi askaris shouted ruderies to the pretty girls as we marched along. Acholi chiefs brought fruit, milk and eggs and villages gave dances in our honour. At one village a dance was arranged on a Sunday; the drums started beating at midday in an open space near the village and people began to gather; half a mile away on a banana-clad hill, the doors of a little church opened and the congregation moved primly towards the village, their devotions at an end; the women were clad in their shape-less 'mother hubbard' church-going dresses and the men wore shorts and shirts. As the drumming increased in tempo, the girls of the party quickened their pace until they were racing down the hill waving their prayer books in the air, stopping only to step neatly out of their mother hubbards and sprint on in beads to join the happy throng who were stamping, clapping and singing to the beat of the drums. It was a pretty sight. As Ian and I watched we were joined by a smiling bland little priest, his bible in his plump black hands and his vestments somewhat out of keeping with the scene of naked gaiety before us.

'It's good to see them so happy,' he said.

We were now in a lusher greener and better watered area than Torit. We marched under shady trees and ate mangoes, paw paws and fat chickens. We patrolled along the Uganda border where I shot another elephant. We visited Lotti, an almost inpenetrable rain forest full of orchids and rare birds, and we dined with a charming Italian mission-ary who treated us to delicious home-made liqueurs. I tried to contribute a weekly buffalo for the company pot, one of which involved me in a curious incident which I have never quite understood. Okak Luka and I were hunting down a river line away from camp; it was getting late and I decided to turn back. Never put down your ferret or draw a fox cover when it is too late in the day to pursue the outcome I had been told; so it is with buffalo hunting. We turned and retraced our steps and came on a lone bull walking slowly back across the plain towards the thick bush of the riverline – he was a little farther away than I nor-mally liked and the light was poor but we wanted meat and I took a chance. He acknowledged my bullet with a stumble and disappeared into a ravine leading to the river. We followed a blood spoor with some caution as the country was thick; the tracks finally disappeared into an elephant path through a dense gallery forest. It was getting dark and inwardly cursing I turned for home. Next morning we returned to the spot and took up the trail again. After following the spoor down the narrow tunnel for a short way Okak Luka stopped and pointed: a flock of vultures were sitting in the trees ahead. 'It's dead,' he said. That was good news as we didn't want a 'rodeo' in these cramped con-ditions, and we advanced with rather less caution. All at once I was aware of a droning sound, the vultures took off and one wobbled out of the sky and fell dying at our feet, its head and neck were black with bees. At that moment a crashing of bushes ahead announced that the buffalo, or something remarkably like it, was on a return journey. We flung ourselves against the bushes, both firing as the buffalo passed, then the bees were upon us stinging with a vengeance. It was time to go and we bolted back down the tunnel, Okak Luka in the lead: an obstacle loomed ahead, Okak Luka flew it in style but it was too big for me and I took it like an Irish hunter tackling the Punchestown double, on and off. It heaved a little underfoot but the pace was too good to enquire and goaded by needles we sped on emerging breathless and swelling into the open. 'Did you tread on the meat?' asked Okak Luka, laughing, as we pulled bee stings from one another. We waited for the bees to calm down before checking that the buffalo was dead. As we walked home I tried to tell Okak Luka of another experience with bees in a far off land – but what the hell was Arabic for 'bear'. That evening the party returned loaded with meat and honey; they had found the bees' nest.

We trekked westwards along the Uganda border towards the Nile and then swung north along the foothills of the Imatong mountains until we were a day's march out of Torit. A runner was sent ahead to warn of the exact time of our arrival. We spent the last evening polishing and cleaning arms and equipment. On the morning of the first of April we had ten miles to go and morale was high; the men strode out. One mile from Torit the trumpets started, lead by the double bass of a big Kudu horn. Ululations greeted us in reply. We marched through the squealing throng of wives in the harimat lines, on to the parade ground and past Claude Reynolds on the saluting base; Ian dismissed the patrol. It was good to be back – there were certain little luxuries to contemplate, but I was sorry it was over. After long hot baths and a sleep on cool linen we dined with Claude Reynolds – that night the whisky and sodas were iced and the wine was chilled.

The next few days were concerned with the boring business of unscrambling our 'military' expedition. When this was done I visited John Owen. I gave him a brief account of what we had seen in his district and promised him a written report. We then turned to the subject of mice. Yes, there had been one mouse of great interest to his Danish professor, but tragedy had struck. The professor had written excitedly asking for another skin and skull of the same specimen – that was necessary before astonishing the 'mouse conscious' scientific world. John had one. He had gone to his cabinet and there in the corner of the drawer, plump and sleeping was a common house mouse, blissfully digesting the remains of the only other specimen of *Mus hookii* that the world has seen.

I then visited Harry Hoogstraal to hand over my ticks and blood slides. He presented me with more bourbon whiskey, cigars and shotgun cartridges. 'One day you'll get a copy of my book,' he said.*

My attachment to Number 2 Company was now finished and there was a month to spare before taking command of the company at Wau in the Bahr el Gazal Province early in 1950. I thought of returning to the Imatongs to hunt that mythical boar to his lair and do a little gold panning in the streams as I had been taught by Australian soldiers in New Guinea. However, plans were changed by a letter from my half brother, Raymond, in Kenya. I had not seen Raymond since as a cadet at Sandhurst I had helped him train his cheetahs on Staines greyhound track, but we had been in constant correspondence. Anything concerning natural history or sport interested him. He had demanded accounts from above the snowline in the Himalayas, from tiger blocks in Central India, pigsticking camps in the Kadir and the jungles of Burma; his replies were always humorous and scholarly. The letter I got in Torit was blunt and to the point. 'You are shooting with too light a rifle,' he wrote. 'One day without a doubt you will be run over. Come to Kenya and I will give you a .404.'

I longed to see Kenya and I certainly needed a heavier rifle, but there was a snag. Between yearly leaves, officers were not allowed to go outside the Sudan. It was doubtful if Claude would let me go. I thought of a plan and went to his office. He peered at me over a file.

'What can I do for you, Hilary?'

'Colonel, I have an invitation to go to Kenya and pick up a .404. I would be back in a fortnight. Hugh Woodman is driving down from Juba in a few days.'

'Not a hope, dear boy. If Khartoum got to know we'd both be in trouble, you know that.'

'That's a pity, I wanted a heavier rifle.'

There was a pause. Claude returned to his file.

'Is Dixie any better,' I said, pointing to her basket in the corner. Dixie was the biggest concern of Claude's life. He put down the paper, swung his chair towards her and started talking with all the anxiety of a worried parent.

---

* He was as good as his word. Eight years later there arrived in Hong Kong an enormous volume – *African Ixodoidia* by Professor Hoogstraal. Amongst the acknowledgements was my name. At last the bitter memory of *Mus hookii* faded.

'If only I could get this new drug she'd be well in no time – it's not even available in Khartoum. I'm very worried.'

'It's available in Nairobi.'

'So it is,' said Claude thoughtfully, and the matter was soon settled.

Returning to my bungalow I packed and drove into Juba. Dr Hugh Woodman was the province medical officer; he wanted to visit his coffee farm in Kenya. An attractive girl called Valerie Duke joined us and we set off in Hugh's rickety car from Juba, in heavy rain. All I had known of Africa apart from the Imatong mountains was heat and harshness, but as we rose into the Uganda highlands filling our lungs with cool clean air, a totally different Africa was revealed. The lush beauty of the country was a contrast to the Sudan. Kenya seemed less luxuriant than Uganda but more beautiful. After two night stops, Raymond met me at Nakuru and together in heavy rain, we skidded the hundred miles of muddy road to Nanyuki. The next few days were spent in training cheetahs, camping on Raymond's lower farm and listening to his erudite discourses on everything African. The snowclad peaks of Mount Kenya hung above us all day long; dramatic cloud formations moved through the sky and the air was like wine. It was a marvellous country. I collected and tested the rifle, took a last look at the mountains and went to Nairobi for Dixie's shopping and to meet Hugh and Valerie for the return journey.

A few days later in Torit, Claude Reynolds gazed at the parcel of drugs on his desk as if it contained the Koh-i-noor. 'You didn't run into the Kaid in Muthaiga Club?' he asked.

'No; and here is my humble penance for blackmail.'

I handed him a beautiful new collar and check lead with Dixie's name stamped on them.

'What a way to run an army,' he said. 'Come to lunch.'

There were another ten days to spend in Torit before going to Wau and I decided to have a last elephant hunt with Okak Luka. Denis Zaphiro, another bimbashi, and I discussed the likely places.

'I know a very good swamp to the north,' he said. 'It's strenuous hunting – over your knees in water most of the time but we should get an elephant there.'

We started at four o'clock in the morning in a truck and motored over a very rough track for sixty miles, coming to a village called Lafone. The old chief came to greet us. After an exchange of presents we questioned him about elephant.

'They live in the swamp,' he said.

'Yes, but the swamp is twenty miles long, where do we start?'

'My grandson will take you,' he said and beckoned a young man in the crowd.

A small party was organised consisting of our orderlies, the chief's grandson and a few others and we set off towards the swamp in single file; soon the going became rough and pitted with elephant tracks in the marshy ground. Our guide led us from one lone tree to another and climbing into the branches scanned the horizon for the tell-tale white egrets which would indicate the presence of elephants. By mid afternoon it was intensely hot and we halted under a tree on a patch of dry land. 'Let's stay here, send back for our mosquito nets and hunt tomorrow in a circle back towards the village', said Denis. I agreed and we sat smoking, pulling off leeches and chatting while the indefatigable Okak Luka made his own reconnaissances to distant clumps of trees.

After a few hours our bedding rolls appeared on the heads of naked villagers, bobbing through the swamp; but no mosquito nets. 'That means we are in for a fairly bloody night,' said Denis, 'but here is good news.' And unrolling his blanket he produced half a bottle of whisky.

As the light faded, mosquitoes came out in swarms driving us into our sleeping bags from where, turn by turn, our arms periodically emerged, passing the precious bottle.

We were on the move again by first light, wading from one island to another to climb the trees and spot for cattle egrets. After a couple of hours the guide pointed from the top of a tall tree to where a few miles away some egrets showed above the reeds. It was worth investigating and we splashed on for another mile, to a tree into which Denis climbed with his field glasses. 'It's a single elephant so probably a bull – let's try our luck,' he said.

We tossed a coin to determine who would shoot first, Denis won and we followed the guide into the swamp. Every now and then Denis pulled out his handkerchief and tested the wind by flicking a little bag of ash tied in the corner. The guide led us confidently on; sometimes we were up to our waists in water and sometimes climbing six foot anthills on dry islands to get a view of the elephant. At last Denis called a halt. 'Let's go it alone from here,' he said, motioning to the others to halt. 'We only have to make that anthill and he's ours.'

We pushed on, and for the next twenty minutes saw nothing but the reeds and the sky above; finally the reeds thinned and there was our anthill with the bull elephant forty yards beyond it. The wind was getting tricky as we waded for the anthill.

At last we reached dry land. 'I'm taking a heart shot,' whispered Denis.

We waited for the bull to turn slightly and Denis fired: my shot followed his. The bull hunched slightly and then came for the only dry land, our anthill. He came in a curve, one menacing eye on us. I heard Denis shoot again and what I had been aiming at turned into a great pillar of water; the job was done. We heard Okak Luka yodelling and firing his rifle to call up the followers, and then settled down to pick off leeches and guess the weight of the ivory. After a long delay forty naked villagers splashed towards us armed with spears. Okak Luka climbed onto the elephant and striking his rifle announced that not one ounce of meat would be taken until the ivory was on its way back to the truck. We left him in charge and set off for the long haul back to the village.

The chief brought us native beer in dirty calabashes, we gave him a mug of rum and sat under a council tree outside the village. The talk ranged through the usual topics, rain, cattle, raids, crops and recruits for the buluk.

'I would like you to take my grandson,' said the old man. 'He is tall and strong, and should carry a rifle. He must serve the Government as I have done all my life.'

'You must be a great age,' said Denis jokingly and then added, 'perhaps you knew Gordon Pasha?'

The chief considered this for a moment and then said gravely. 'No, but my father often spoke of him, he worked under "Gordoon" Pasha when he was Governor here in the south. "Gordoon" Pasha was a God, he destroyed the slave traders. My father said that "Gordoon" Pasha's eyes were like spears – no man dared tell him a lie. He was here many years, then he left us and the slavers came again but worse than before. They slew the great "Gordoon" Pasha in Khartoum and the Turks were driven from the Sudan. Then terrible years came – we lived in fear. One day from over those hills raiders came: they were not Arabs but black men like ourselves and spoke a strange language – they had guns. Before we could defend ourselves they rushed upon the village and started killing, it was a terrible day. Some escaped to the swamp, but the young men and women were herded like cattle and driven between guns towards the river. It was a long march and many died. When he reached the river we waited a long time until armed Arabs came in steam boats to take us for sale in Omdurman.'

The chief paused in thought and stared ahead. I refilled his mug with rum. 'Go on with your story, old man,' said Denis gently, 'we want to know how you are alive to tell us.'

'I was only a "wallad" then, not old enough to be a warrior. The boats were small and we suffered greatly. The dead and the sick were thrown to the crocodiles. One day we came round a bend in the river and saw a big boat with a strange flag. It had a big gun which fired at us. Our Arab guards fired back but many were killed and jumped into the river and swam. Then we heard that Kitchener Pasha had defeated the Kalifa in a great battle at Omdurman and we were free. My mother and young brother had died in the boats, but I met my father again a year later; he had escaped to the swamp taking my sister with him. They lived and my father became chief of Lafone.'

He had told his story with simple dignity and it served to remind us how recent was the turbulent history of this country. The sun was getting low when at last Okak Luka appeared with two men each carrying a tusk. He saluted and asked if he could visit some friends in the village. We were in no great hurry, it would be pleasant to wait for the cool of the evening and watch the sun go down. 'You must be back in an hour,' I said. He put his rifle in the truck and departed with a happy smile. An hour and a half went by and he hadn't appeared. We sent men to look for him but he couldn't be found. The old chief had taken his leave and the sun had set.

'Damn the fellow, why should we bloody well sit here while he pleasures all the ladies in Lafone,' said Denis, 'Let's finish the whisky and go.'

I agreed and we drove off into the night. We arrived at Torit very late but Ian's light was still burning and I went to see him. 'I'm awfully sorry,' I said, 'but we left Okak Luka in Lafone. He won't be on early morning parade – we waited for him for two hours.'

'I'll give him hell,' said Ian and we went to bed.

Next day after breakfast I went round to Ian's office to tell him the story of our hunt and apologise again for leaving Okak Luka behind. 'It may interest you to know,' said Ian, 'that Okak Luka was on early morning parade – all six foot six of him as bright as a Belisha beacon. It seems he ran the odd fifty miles by a direct track through the bush. What with the elephant hunt he must have covered a good seventy-five miles or more yesterday – and had a bit of indoor sport at half time. I think I shall promote him.'

I have often discussed this extraordinary feat with Denis who subsequently became a game warden in Kenya and has known similar
exploits of endurance in Africa which are difficult to explain. Anyway
the next time I saw Okak Luka he was wearing two stripes and he told
me he was marrying a girl from Lafone; I wished him luck and gave
him a watch.

The time came to take over the company at Wau. I packed and made a
round of visits and then went to see Claude Reynolds. He talked for a
time of people and things on the west bank. 'I'm sending you Rocky
Lambert as second in command,' he said. 'He's on leave in England at
present. You will find the fishing on the west bank is excellent, the Nile
perch run over a hundred pounds. If you haven't got the tackle cable to
Rocky to bring it from England. Also, send me a signal when the duck
are in, Dixie and I will come and inspect you.'

My luggage was piled onto a truck and with a lorry of stores for the
company following behind we started on our six hundred mile drive
over rough roads to Wau. At Juba I sent a cable to Rocky Lambert in
England for more fishing tackle, stocked up with food and drink and
drove on in the evening. The next two days driving were boring and
uncomfortable. The road was badly corrugated and led through close
bush country. We crossed several rivers flowing northwards and on the
evening of the second day, having negotiated the sunken causeway on
the Jur river, came to Wau and the company lines six miles out of the
town in the river bank. Bimbashi Budd met us.

For the next ten days I set about acquainting myself with my new
surroundings. We went into Wau and met the Governor, a charming
scholar called Richard Owen, and other civilian officials. We peered at
ledgers and into stores, handed over confidential documents and secret
emergency schemes and visited the platoon at Aweil a hundred miles to
the north.

At last Bimbashi Budd packed and departed and I stood alone on the
verandah of the bungalow contemplating the future. The prospects
were pleasing. The bungalow was large, comfortable, and for some
reason not in keeping with the normal government practice, well situated. It stood on a bluff above the Jur river and every evening green
pigeon flighted overhead from the fig trees on the river bank. What I
had seen of the Company had impressed me. The bash shawish was obviously good, there was an efficient and delightful African under officer called Rinaldo, who would shoulder most of the administration,

the fishing and duck shooting was the best in the Sudan and the pleasures of another long trek in new country lay ahead. I gazed at the river for a while then put my tackle together and went fishing.

The men of my company were either Dinka or Zande but there were a few from other tribes. The Dinka were tall black Nilotic cattle owners. They had a formidable reputation as warriors but like the cattle owning Masai in Kenya, they were not particularly amenable to discipline. The Zande from the Sudan Congo divide were squat brown ugly little men with filed teeth and the stigma of cannibalism on their reputation. They were intelligent, humorous and probably owing to the feudal nature of their tribal society, good disciplinarians. The bash shawish, Sambiri Belal, came from a smaller tribe and therefore probably could not be accused of sectarianism. He was not popular but greatly respected and said to be an artist with the hippo hide whip which he carried. No one had ever seen him smile. After a week or two the rain came in earnest. The days were cool and clear but at night the thunder, and rain beating on the corrugated iron room proved a sleep-defying cacophony of sound and fury. There was plenty to occupy my solitude for the next two months and the occasional visit from friends was all the more enjoyable.

One day the game warden's truck drew up at the bungalow and out stepped Peter and Yvonne Molloy. The course of true love apparently had run smooth, they had been married shortly before and we had a delightful reunion from which the Greek grocer in Wau profited greatly. Yvonne was determined to become a proficient bush girl, Peter and I taught her to fish and the first steps of rifle shooting with my .22. We had much to talk about and their visit was all too short.*

I had acquired two ponies from the veterinary department, one for Rocky Lambert and one for myself. In the evenings I rode up and down the river with a rod. My pony soon learnt to wade into the river while I cast from his back into pools which could not be reached from the bank. Tiger fish are perhaps one of the most sporting and active fish in the world; they have a mouthful of vicious teeth and are usually able to throw out a triple hook, but once they are properly hooked they put up a splendid athletic performance leaping all over the pool; most success was to be had with a large salmon fly which would get behind their teeth and hold. Nile perch are dour fighters but great fun in a fast running river; the record for the Jur river was a hundred and thirty pounds

---

* Peter Molloy's *The Cry of the Fish Eagle* describes the life of a game warden and his wife in the Southern Sudan. Yvonne certainly did become a proficient bush girl.

and I keenly awaited Rocky Lambert's advent with stronger tackle.

On Saturday nights I usually went into Wau to dine with one of the few Sudan Political officials; this was always an enjoyable event. The Sudan Political Service had always been a most highly prized accolade for those who wished to serve in 'heathen' lands; the mantle of the Indian Civil service had fallen upon it at the beginning of the century and only men of the highest scholastic and athletic attainments from the universities were accepted. The Sudan had well been described as 'a country of blacks governed by blues' and it was in this company that my Saturday nights were spent. My hosts were all men of charm, intelligence and generosity, but some were prone to a certain ascetic forbearance with the decanter, not amounting to stinginess but alien to my usual habit. When dining in this company, my orderly would thoughtfully put a little bottle of 'comfort' in the car for the drive home towards the Saturday night drumming from the harimat lines.

The Latuka and Lango drums on the East bank were mostly made of skin but here the Zande drums were skilfully hollowed logs with a slit running along the top upon which the dummer beat out a syncopated rythmn with two clubs. On a still night or with a favourable wind the drumming could be heard from a great distance. It was said that the Zande could pass simple messages by this method; I rather doubted this and decided to put it to the test. One day when the company was shooting on the range two miles away I kept back a good Zande drummer on some pretext and said to him, 'Tell the men to stop firing and parade for pay.' I drove off to the range with under officer Rinaldo and as we arrived the men were lining up with pay books in their hands. 'The Zande heard the order on the drums,' said the bash shawish and another seemingly unlikely African legend was confirmed.

At last Rocky Lambert arrived back from leave and we delightedly unpacked the new fishing tackle. From then on whenever time, a generous thief in Africa, allowed, we were on the river. At weekends we went to distant pools which had never been fished before. The sport was excellent, bringing a constant supply of fish for ourselves and our friends in Wau. Bait for Nile perch has to be absolutely fresh so the requirements for a fishing expedition were a local fisherman with his circular throwing net, and a bag full of grain. On arrival at a likely pool the fisherman would throw grain into the shallows and cast his net, bringing in herring-sized fish called kawara. These were killed and fixed to a large hook so that they twisted with the current when reeled in. They were irresistible to Nile perch which took them with a tremendous tug and usually set off down stream with determination.

On our first expedition together, Rocky was fishing at the head of a pool. He hooked a big fish and it forged down river, impossible to check and heading for Khartoum.

'I can't stop him and I'm down to the backing,' shouted Rocky. His rod was bent double and still the bow wave in the distance forged on, out of the pool and into the next run.

'Are there crocs in this river?' he bellowed.

'It's lifting with them.'

'Well, please stand by with your gun.' So saying he leaped into the flood and struggled half submerged to the tail of the pool, where he pursued on foot and landed an eighty pounder. It was exciting fishing, and added interest was provided by the presence of hippo in the big pools. They snorted and threatened and when snagged, it usually meant loss of valuable tackle.

In October the duck migration appeared at Aweil. Every year thousands of duck which bred in Central Europe and Asia would fly south up the Nile valley and spread out into feeding grounds in the swamps and waterways which fed the Nile. Aweil was in the middle of the south westerly limit of this migration. In March the duck returned northwards. I sent a signal to Torit: 'Reynolds Bey. For information Dixie. Duck are in.' The reply came:

'Prepare for administrative inspection next week.' I informed the bash shawish.

After a few days Claude arrived with Dixie, some delicacies from Juba and a bundle of *Fields* for Rocky and me. He carried out a two day inspection and then swore in the new recruits. This was an amusing ceremony; the young men were paraded before Claude who walked down the line with the senior NCO of each tribe.

'Who is this chap, he looks like a giraffe,' said Claude. There was a gust of laughter and the recruit's sponsor stepped forward.

'He is the grandson of Nyangdu who died in the Aliab raid when Stigand Bey was killed. He is a good boy.'

Claude moved on. 'And this – now he looks like a bush baby.' Further laughter while the Zande NCO explained that he was the son of Chief Yubo.

'Chief Yubo is like an old goat. We will raise another company if he keeps going.'

There was more laughter. After the inspection the recruits were sworn in. The oath was administered to each man in turn as he held a naked bayonet in front of his face and repeated what the bash shawish said. When it was finished a huge pink tongue appeared, licking the bayonet from end to end. The recruit then about turned and rejoined the remainder. Claude presented a bull to the company and that evening we attended the dance and feast given in his honour.

The next day we drove north to Aweil with Dixie curled in the back of the truck. We stayed with the District Commissioner and the following morning Claude inspected the outpost. The rest of the weekend was ours. Twenty miles to the west of Aweil, a series of water courses drained northwards into the Lol river. They were swarming with migratory duck, mostly garganey and widgeon. As Claude and I walked towards our cover in the reeds that evening they rose in thousands and started to flight up and down the river bed. We took up our positions and started shooting; in the distance I could see Dixie splashing backwards and forwards between the river and Claude, retrieving the duck: she was obviously enjoying herself.

In front of me two small jet black Dinka boys scampered through the swamp enjoying themselves equally, and squeaking with competitive delight as they raced for the fallen duck. Slowly the light faded and we peered into the western sky from where a whicker of wings would announce the arrival of another flight. Then, unexpectedly, a great full moon sailed up, the light improved every minute and more duck came in. The moon lit up the reeds and the shining black bodies floundering about in front. An idea struck me: on the day that I left the army I would buy the blackest of black labrador puppies and call him Dinka of Aweil and that is just what I eventually did.

We shot again next morning in a different place surrounded by naked Dinka men and girls. They had never seen a dog like Dixie before, much less one that would bring in birds and do everything its master told it to. Dixie stole the show with obvious enjoyment, she retrieved beautifully, obeyed hand signals and then carried Claude's hat about and jumped over sticks. The Dinka were delighted and showed it by doubling up with mirth and calling 'Dixie, Dixie'. We drove the hundred miles back with enough duck to feed ourselves and the households in Wau. On the way Claude said,

'You're damn lucky, there's nothing like this on the east bank and aren't some of those Dinka girls lovely.'

That was certainly true, they were the prettiest girls in the Sudan.

'I thought you were missing rather a lot of duck this morning,' I replied.

'Yes,' said Claude. 'There were too many people about and shooting is so much a matter of concentration.'

That night we dined off baked Nile perch and Canard á l'Orange. Dixie had a bit of both.

After a round of visits in Wau and a day's fishing Claude departed for Torit with an icebox full of duck and fish and, I suppose, the easy conscience of one who has performed his military duties. He would return with Dixie before Christmas, 'To see what plans you have for a trek and another go at the duck.'

Rocky had a house a few hundred yards from mine and we usually had a drink together in the evenings. He was a delightful companion and an ideal second-in-command. We were the same age but he had enlisted in the ranks sometime before the war, risen to be a senior NCO and had got his commission in battle. The men liked him for his sense of humour and toughness and so did I. He was a knowledgeable country man and keen sportsman.

At about this time I received a crie de coeur from Raymond in Kenya. His home had been raided and his rifles stolen; they had not been under lock and key and this was a serious offence. Would I please send him a police certificate that I was in possession of his .404. This was embarrassing as I had 'forgotten' to declare the rifle when I returned to the Sudan and it was not on my licence; this was also a serious offence. I wanted to talk to the Governor of the Province, Richard Owen (no relation to John), about our forthcoming trek. I made an appointment and went to see him. When I had confessed he gravely reached for his law manuals and announced that the maximum penalty for arms smuggling was only twenty years.

'It ought to be more,' he said, and we turned to the subject of my annual trek.

'Where would you like me to take the company this year?' I asked.

'On the contrary, where would you like to go?'

This was the answer I wanted and I traced a circle on the map. 'I would like to follow the Jur river north,' I said, 'through Gogrial to the Lol river and then westwards to Aweil and on to Nyamlell. From Nyamlell we could take a look at the country south of the Bahr el Arab river, march to Ashana, and then go south to Chakchak.'

'So far so good,' said Richard Owen. 'Then what?'

'From Chakchak I want to walk up the Chel river to where it crosses the Wau to Raga road, and then back into Wau.'

'That looks like a very good bimabashi's sporting tour,' he said. 'I wish I could come with you. Come again in a few days; in the meantime I'll do some research.'

A week later Richard Owen sent for me. 'Here is your rifle permit,' he said. 'Now let's return to the subject of the trek.' He approved my plans and talked of places, native personalities I should meet on the way and what to look out for. He knew his province well. We followed my proposed route on the map until it came to Chakchak on the Chel river. 'I've never been there,' he said, 'but there is something I would like you to enquire about. Old Chief Chakchak might be able to help. Years ago I heard a story about an English bimbashi who was stationed at Wau in the early part of the century – it was when Darfur Province was an independent state ruled by the black Sultan Ali Dinar – it was only incorporated into the Sudan in 1917. The country then was still in a very wild state and Rizegat Arab horsemen used to raid over the border for slaves and ivory. This bimbashi was with his company on the Bahr el Gazal river. While he was out shooting with his bash shawish they were ambushed by the Rizegat, tied behind horses and marched northward into captivity. After a few days they came to a plain of very high elephant grass. By this time they were no longer tied but guarded with rifles and the ten foot long spears of the Rizegat Arabs. Bimbashi Greenwood saw his chance and somehow explained it to his bash shawish. He gave a signal and they both dashed off into the grass, zigzagging and changing direction. After running hard for several minutes Greenwood lay down in the thick grass, covering himself as well as he could. He heard in the distance his bash shawish being hunted and then the Rizegat searching all round him with their spears. When darkness fell the Arabs left and he made his way southwards. After several days he reached Chakchak village and collapsed. The chief sent runners to Wau and his daughter nursed Greenwood back to health. She was said to have been a very beautiful girl, and I believe there was a bit of a romance, which of course was pleasant for Greenwood after an unpleasant experience. I wonder if there is much truth in the story – try and find out.

'There is another matter which may interest you. On going through the province records I find that no white men has ever patrolled the Chel river before – I believe it's uninhabited except for a few honey hunters and a mass of tsetse fly. The honey hunters come from a small tribe in the west called Shatt. I would like a report in due course, also Peter Molloy would be interested in what game you see, particularly if you come across rhino or giant eland.'

When I returned to the company I despatched an askari to bring in a Shatt honey hunter who knew the Chel river area. The distance from Chakchak village southwards to the Wau to Raga road was about a hundred miles on the map: it would be perhaps a hundred and twenty as we walked along the river. Each askari carried eight days' rations in a canvas bag on the top of his knapsack, but I wanted to spend two weeks exploring the river line. Everything depended on the presence of game and a bit of hunting luck. One elephant or a couple of big fat buffalo would do, otherwise we would be hungry. After a week my askari returned, accompanied by two squat anthropoid-looking men. They stuck their spears point upwards in the ground and squatted grunting in front of Rocky and I.

'You are Shatt honey hunters?'

They nodded and spat.

'Do you know the Chel river from Chakchak to the road which goes from Wau to Raga?'

'We know it well.'

I started drawing in the dust and asking questions to which they replied intelligently, drawing their own map of the river on the ground. 'Are there elephant and buffalo along the river?' I asked.

'Many elephant and buffalo like cattle,' they replied.

I gave them money and then cut a bank note in two, handing them one half. 'Meet me at Chief Chakchak's village after sixty days and I will give you the other half of this – we will mend it by magic and you will guide the buluk up the Chel river. If what you say is true you will be fat with meat and collect much honey.' They departed grinning.

Plans for our trek went ahead. In the evenings Rocky and I poured over our fishing tackle, constructing unbreakable traces and irresistible lures. Claude Reynolds and Dixie visited us again for a duck shoot. One weekend Rocky and I went down the river in a collapsible boat fishing the pools and runs on the way. We had an amusing and somewhat anxious time avoiding schools of hippo. One big lone bull covered with fighting scars refused to let us pass – he almost paid dearly for his truculence but we spared him and dragged the boat round. We slept on the river bank and continued fishing down river next day to a village where we had arranged for a truck to meet us in the evening. We arrived with the boat loaded with fish and were greeted by the villagers with great hospitality. They plied us with fruit and tea as we sat waiting for the truck. After a while I noticed that everyone who came to shake hands appeared to have some part of their anatomy missing; the chief had no fingers on one hand and several people had no toes. I remarked on this to the chief who replied cheerfully. 'Yes, we are all lepers in this village, it's a government leper colony. Have some more tea.' I was rather glad when the truck arrived – we gave the village all the fish we had caught and drove home to rather more than normally diligent baths.

Guests came for Christmas – an extremely amusing District Commissioner from Gogrial called Ranald Boyle arrived on Christmas Eve. He came in the post boat, landing just below my bungalow and announced himself with a toot on the boat's siren. I walked down to meet him and became involved in yet another fracas with bees. As his luggage was being unloaded the boat swung round and the superstructure became caught in the branches of a large tree where one of my askaris, had, unknown to me, put a native beehive. In a second the air was filled with the angry drone that was all too familiar to me. I bolted for the bungalow followed by Ranald. We had a drink and sat wondering what to do about the luggage. Inspired and perhaps emboldened by a second drink, Ranald formed a plan.

'A pantomime horse,' he said. 'It's perfectly simple. We put on bush hats, get under your mosquito net and advance in step upon the scene of the disaster. It's essential to keep in step, but since you are a cavalry man and I was in the Navy a special effort may be required.'

'One more drink and I'm your back legs,' I said.

Laughing feebly we climbed under the mosquito net and set off down the steep path, Ranald calling the step. The boat was a scene of confusion; some of the Sudanese had jumped into the water and the poor old Arab helmsman had thrown his jellabah over his head and stuck gallantly to the wheel, his bottom exposed to attack. Ranald started laughing and fell out of step. I trod on his heels, tripped and in a moment the inside of the mosquito net was full of angry bees. 'Abandon ship and back to base,' shouted Ranald.

We struggled free and made for the bungalow pursued by the enemy. After a while a siren announced that the post boat was on its way again, and I sent for the bash shawish.

'Please find the askari who put that bee's nest in the tree and tell him to bring the luggage and mosquito net he will find there.'

'Your Arabic's getting better,' said Ranald.

Peter and Yvonne Molloy arrived that evening and we spent a most enjoyable Christmas, picnicking, fishing and visiting friends in Wau.

On the first of January the company paraded and the scenes of last year were re-enacted. Having inspected the parade with Rocky and the bash shawish I gave the order to march and leaving under officer Rinaldo to hold an empty fort, a hundred and twenty riflemen and forty porters moved off in two long lines, Rocky and I in the lead and the bash shawish at the rear followed by two syces leading our ponies and Rocky's little pi-dog Dina yapping around the column. The families ran ululating along beside the company. After a while I passed back the order 'march at ease'. The Kudu horns blazed out, the men started singing and we were off on another three month's trek in the bush.

We headed north along the Jur river, into Dinka country. To our right a few trees showed the line of the Jur river, to our left and in front of us was a vast plain, known as a 'toich'. Here and there a few neatly thatched huts stood on stilts and mobs of cattle herded by tall naked Dinka spearmen moved slowly on the horizon. Small herds of graceful antelope called kob grazed in the shimmering distance, lifting their heads to watch us pass. We marched on until midday when the heat had become intense and then turned in towards the trees on the river bank and made camp. After several days' marching we arrived at Gogrial where Rocky and I stayed with Ranald Boyle and the chief presented the company with a bull. We had a wonderful last day's fishing in the Jur river which curved away to the east, then turning our backs on it, marched at midnight for twenty-five miles towards the Lol river which ran across our front to the north.

The night was bitterly cold, stars blazed with almost unnatural brilliance in the dry air, lighting up the flat landscape. We marched in silence on the Pole star with our backs to the southern cross which hung low in the sky behind. The only sound was the 'chuff chuff' of soldiers' feet in the grass or a whinny from one of the ponies. We halted occasionally to rest the porters; as dawn broke, the tree line of the Lol river appeared in the far distance and the company burst into song. The sun was high when we reached the river, it was a clear running shallow stream a hundred yards across with sandy beaches and shady trees; having piled arms we all plunged in and drank our fill. For the next few days we trekked west along the river until we came to a village of the Twij Dinka on the south bank.

News had gone ahead of us and as we approached the village, drumming started which was answered by our Kudu horns and bugles. A dance in our honour was in full swing. After we had made camp a mile from the village the Dinka soldiers stripped and ran to join the revels.

The other tribes' turn would come when we passed through their country later on. When Rocky and I had finished our supper we walked over to the sound of the drums. On the outskirts of the village was a cleared space and here the village maidens clad only in a string of beads* round their neat waists were clapping and singing as they advanced and retreated with decorous grace. The young bloods, amongst whom I recognised several soldiers, were shouting and stamping in time – their arms held high to represent the horns of a bull – the noise and the skill of the drumming and rhythmic stamping made one's senses reel. We watched for a time and strolled back to camp.

'I reckon that's got the edge on Queen Charlotte's Ball,' said Rocky. 'At least the boys and girls are left in no doubt of what to expect.'

The distant drumming lulled us to sleep under the stars; at dawn we waded the river and marched away to the west again for five hours. I thought it best to put a fair distance between the company Romeos and the attractive little black Juliets of the night before; also a long march would work off the effects of the local brew of marrissa.

The next few weeks were spent in patrolling the country to the north, between the Lol and Bahr el Arab rivers. We seldom spent more than a night at any one place, we visited villages, sent patrols up waterways and scouted for elephant. Game was scarce in the area and we had to rely for meat on the occasional present of a bull; there were a number of hartebeeste, kob and waterbuck to be seen but none of these would feed the whole company and I disliked shooting them. Rocky and I lived well on fresh fish, guinea fowl and duck of which there was an unlimited supply. Shade was rather hard to find on these great plains; we usually marched before dawn and started looking for trees to camp under at about nine o'clock. When we found a suitable place the soldiers cut the grass, our tables and chairs were laid out in the shade and after a large breakfast Rocky and I went fishing or bathing. The evening was the best time to hunt for the pot because guinea fowl and partridges started calling on their way to roost. Rocky and I used to ride out on our ponies and shoot from the saddle. We never rode the ponies on the line of march, they were slow walkers and lagged behind the column unless constantly legged on, which was a tiresome exercise, but they were useful for hunting.

One day Rocky and I decided to try our ponies paces against a kob,

* It was here that we saw for the first time the beads which Major Marchand of Fashoda fame had distributed during his march from the west coast in 1897. They were distinctive and highly prized by the Dinka.

of which a herd were always to be seen grazing on the skyline. Rocky had had to listen to my tales of pigsticking in India and he felt inclined to give it a try. We borrowed Dinka spears and advanced over the plain towards a herd of kob which contained one big buck. 'Wait till he trots off then we go for him flat out', I said. 'First spear gets the horns.' We zigzagged slowly and obliquely from down wind towards the herd hoping that the kob who had never seen horses before would think we were some new kind of Dinka cattle. When we were two hundred yards away some of the females lifted their heads and gazed in our direction; the buck continued to graze. We moved on at a slow walk, closing the distance between us and the buck to a hundred yards, crouching behind our ponies' necks, and trying to look as unpredatory as possible. Seventy, sixty, fifty yards and the buck's head came up – he stared for a few seconds then turned and moved away.

'I think now's the time,' I whispered. 'Get ready – go' and we jumped forward at the gallop. Taken by surprise we were almost upon him before he decided to take the matter seriously and sprang away a few yards from us. He moved with effortless grace keeping an even distance ahead, at what appeared to be only a brisk canter. Rocky and I were racing neck and neck as fast as our ponies would go; every few seconds the buck rose in a beautiful capriole, kicking up his back legs and showing his white belly; just once I got my spear down to him but he moved contemptuously away scarcely bothering to increase speed – clearly he was enjoying himself; we pressed him as hard as we could for about half a mile in a wide circle, and then suddenly I was flying through the air with my head tucked in waiting for the bump. I got to my feet and looked around but I couldn't see Rocky, until a voice beside me started using strong language. There he was, extricating himself from one of the many cavernous warthog burrows which surrounded us.

'So much for your Kadir Cup' he said. 'Let's look at the ponies. You wouldn't have caught that chap on a Derby winner with wings. Anyway I'm very glad we didn't, he was a lovely sight.'

In the distance we could see our quarry, head down, grazing peacefully amongst his harem again. The ponies were unhurt and we led them back over the plain towards our askaris who were coming out to watch the fun.

'And let's have no more pigsticking tales,' said Rocky limping ahead of his pony. 'It would be easier galloping over the points at Crewe than over this country.'

I had to agree with him, and we never tried the game again.

For several more days we moved over this great plain seeking what shade was available. Before going to sleep we always pulled our beds well away from under the shade tree; this insured a much more restful night's sleep owing to the quality of the air, and it was a delight to lie and look up at the blazing canopy of stars, listening to the noises of the African night and watching the moon sail up over the flickering embers of the camp fire.

The nights out on these wide toiches were very cold and our blankets and faces were drenched with dew in the mornings. Once a week the supply lorry from Wau arrived at a prearranged rendezvous bringing mail and rations and taking letters back to post. One day, as had happened in Equatoria, I noticed that spears were being unloaded.

'What are the men going to hunt?', I asked the bash shawish. 'There are no buffalo in the area.'

'Baraboose,' he said, and seeing that I looked puzzled went on to describe what I identified to be cane rats.

'There are many in the reeds along the river bank and they are good to eat – the men would like a hunt.'

'Very well, we'll have the opening meet on Sunday,' I said, feeling rather relieved that the quarry was not to be the lions we had heard roaring every night, and recalling our near disastrous buffalo hunt with Latuka soldiers. Rocky was delighted when I told him.

'Ratting,' he said, 'I love it and what fun for Dina – she's had no sport on this trek so far.'

Neither Rocky nor I had ever seen a cane rat and we didn't quite know what to expect when next Sunday we set off behind the hunt to watch. We arrived at a patch of reeds and the men surrounded it. Two men ran up wind with lighted brands of grass and fired the reeds which blazed towards us. After a short wait, brown beaver-like creatures started scampering out of the reeds closely pursued by the soldiers jabbing with their spears. Dina joined the hunt darting here and there among the shouting men. The scene brought back childhood memories of Devon when the last patch of a cornfield was being harvested and the rabbits began to break. When the patch of reeds had burned out the bag of six cane rats were slung on spear shafts and the party moved on to the next 'cover'. I inspected one of the dead creatures. Its body was about two feet long and covered with brown spiny hair, it had a short rat-like tail and weighed about fifteen pounds.

'It doesn't look edible to me,' I said.

'Well, I believe your wrong,' replied Rocky. 'They are reported to be delicious. We'll have one "jugged" tonight.'

We moved from one patch of reeds to the next and the bag grew – the men were enjoying themselves greatly. Rocky and I fell behind and sat on the river bank smoking and listening to the hunt going on in the distance. Suddenly Rocky lifted his hand. 'Listen,' he said, 'that's not cane rats, that's "riot".' The shouting and laughter had changed note and doubled in intensity. Above the hubbub came the cry of 'Nimr, nimr' and the angry snarl of a leopard. 'Somebody will get chewed up, quick, tell them to leave it alone,' I said. We grabbed our shotguns and raced off towards the tumult. As we got nearer we saw that the hunt was really 'up' and our distant shouts to desist were being taken as encouragement to close in for the kill. A large leopard broke out of the smoke ahead and galloped for another patch of reeds through a shower of spears. The men on the flank had seen him coming and in seconds the reeds were ablaze and he broke again. 'There will be a lovely stitching job if we don't stop them,' said Rocky as we strove to catch up the hunt. We could hear the yaps of Rocky's little pi-dog in full pursuit of she knew not what. At last we got among them and our orders started having effect. The men rested on their spears laughing, breathless and thwarted.

But the drama was not over. Dina the pi-dog was deaf to orders and unnoticed by us had dived into the reeds. There was a roar and a squeal and out popped Dina at full speed, making for her master with the leopard in pursuit swatting at her. There was a brief scuffle, a dozen spears flew through the air and the leopard rolled over.

'That was a good Sunday's ratting,' said Rocky as we walked home. 'Shall we toss for the skin.'

'You can have it, I liked that leopard.'

'How shall we have the baraboose done tonight, roast or stewed?'

'Duck for me, please,' I said.

'Well Dina has leopard, perhaps it will make her fierce, she's had a lucky escape. What bloody spoil sports we are.'

That evening a puff adder appeared in the light of our camp and I called to a Dinka askari to bring me a panga to kill it – they were the snakes we disliked most for being sluggish, they were easily trodden on in the dark and their bite was a serious affair. The askari looked embarrassed and hesitated.

'Get on with it – hurry, bring me something to kill it with,' I said.

'I cannot do that, Janabuk,' he replied. 'He is my grandfather.'

'What about that damned leopard today,' I said, 'I suppose he was your uncle.' And seizing a stick I despatched the snake. I then called for the bash shawish, our adviser on all strange customs and over a bottle of beer questioned him about the boy's grandfather. It emerged that each sect of the Dinka tribe had a different totem into which the spirits of their ancestors had passed. This boy's tribal totems were puff adders and under no circumstances would he kill one.

'In his country,' said the bash shawish, 'the huts are full of puff adders, they are fed and handled and nobody ever gets bitten.'

'It's another case of "the wildest dreams of Kew"*,' said Rocky.

We followed the river westwards for another two days and came to a Dinka village at a place called Nyamlell, which means the stone of good eating. A rocky hill on the south bank overlooked a large pool in the river. Twenty or more dugout canoes were fishing, each had two occupants, one to paddle and one to cast the circular fishing net. It was a scene of great beauty. The tall naked boys and girls, thin lithe figures mirrored in the water, cast and retrieved their nets with the grace of a ballet movement; in the shallows young men wading in a line threw their spears at random in front and retrieved them with an occasional glittering fish on the end. Several hippos rose and snorted in the deep water and thousands of white egrets, their delicate form reflected in the water, criss-crossed the river.

We camped on the hill and sat resting in the shade; village girls brought us eggs, fish and fresh milk. The chief came in the evening; he was a tall, smiling middle-aged man with a wooden leg and an air of authority. We gave him a bottle of beer and discussed the usual topics: cattle, crops, tribal squabbles and recruits. Finally I said, 'Who dared steal the leg of a great man like you?'

He laughed. 'I was not a great man then,' he said, 'I was a wallad [boy] and the thief was a girinti [hippo]. We were spearing fish in the pool below. The biggest fish lie under the bellies of the girinti and my spear hit him in his fat backside so he stole my leg. That is why men call me Abu rigle [the father of the leg].' What could be called 'banana peel' humour is very popular in Africa and everyone laughed.

Again we marched westwards along the Lol river through Malwal Dinka country, and after fifty miles came to an attractive lake and game in great quantity. The lake had at one time been the bed of the Lol river; it was about two miles long and a hundred yards wide; the banks were shaded by large trees and on the surrounding plain grazed herds of kob, roan antelope and Lelwel hartebeeste. We camped on the

* From Kipling's *In the Neolithic Age*.

General Paul von Lettow Vorbeck, 1914 (*see page 59*).

(*below*) General's inspection at Juba, 1949. *From left to right*: Miralai Claude Reynolds Bey, commanding the Equatorial Corps of the Sudan Defence Force; Governor Jim Tierney, provincial governor of the Equatorial Province; The Kaid, General 'Bolo' Whistler, commanding the whole Sudan Defence Force; Bimbashi H. Hook, company commander in Equatorial Corps.

Exploring the Chel river, Bahr el Gazal Province, 1951 (*see Chapter 5*).

The company's meat ration trek near Torit. Okak Luka is on the left of the bottom picture.

(*left*) The bodyguard, 50 strong, of Sheik Ibrahim Musa, Nazir of the Rizegat. They are wearing crusader chain mail and are armed with traditional Baggara spears. (*centre*) Seven or eight thousand armed and mounted Rizegat march past Governor Henderson of Darfur Province, led by the flag of the Western Arab Corps. (*below*) Servants of the Nazir beating copper drums.

Saristal: (*above*) Bringing in the cattle killer and (*right*) Caledon Alexander with his tracker. (*below*) H.H. The Maharaja Bahadur Bundi, M.C., Bundi State (*see page 158*).

lake shore and Rocky and I strolled out to bag a duck or two for supper; we soon became aware that the lake was teeming with croco-diles; everywhere we could see the two telltale bumps rising in the water to regard us.

'Here's where we make our fortunes' said Rocky. 'Croc skins and musk glands fetch a good price in Omdurman, and the company can gorge themselves; they haven't had meat for a time.'

I ordered a few days rest, and next morning Rocky and I set off in different directions in high hopes. I took an army rifle and a hundred rounds of ammunition and after twenty minutes walk along the bank came to an overhanging tree in which an obliging vulture had built a large nest of sticks – a perfect shooting platform. I climbed into the branches and settled myself on the nest from where I could get a good view of the rising crocs.

The only good shots for crocodile are the brain or a neck shot which are difficult from ground level, but from my vantage point I soon had several dead crocodiles floating on the lake below me. We retrieved them with the aid of an abandoned dugout canoe and set about taking off the belly skins and cutting out the musk glands from under the neck: these glands which are about the size of a small walnut are dried and used in the manufacture of scent.

The company were delighted at the sight of so much meat but some of the soldiers whose totem was a crocodile were mildly disapproving. The fishing was excellent and Rocky planned a feast of spurwing goose, Nile perch and guinea fowl, preceded by a plate of roast croc. Being of the 'try anything once' school Rocky professed contempt for my rather conservative tastes.

'I'll skip the croc course,' I said.

'You don't know what you're missing,' he replied, tucking into the flaccid white meat in front of him. 'This is really excellent, why are you so fastidious?'

'For one reason,' I said. 'That is the croc in whose stomach they found a black toe and a copper bracelet.'

He stared at me, his jaw moving more slowly. 'Cut me a bit of that goose,' he said, putting his plate on the ground for Dina to finish. I think that was the last time that Rocky ever suggested such delicacies as elephant's trunk, roast puff adder or boiled tortoise.

Next morning I climbed again into my bird's nest and was preparing myself for a morning's sniping when I noticed movement out on the plain, and mounting into the higher branches I saw a pack of ten wild dogs pursuing a kob; they ran in a wide circle, the kob fifty yards ahead, looking beautiful, at full gallop, and the dogs in a straggling line behind. As the kob changed direction, the tail-end dogs cut the corner and took up the running; this happened twice and then suddenly the whole hunt was coming in my direction; the kob's lead shortened to fifteen yards as it made for the lake and leapt from the bank with a great splash; it rose, swimming strongly and the dogs halted staring and whining. I watched transfixed and rather horrified as the kob's head neared the opposite bank, and then the inevitable happened – from two different directions torpedo-like tracks of crocodiles bore down on the wretched creature – there was a short turmoil in the water and a bubbling bleat as the head disappeared. It was a grisly little drama, and after watching the dogs trot off into the distance I turned with a more unreasonable zeal to my task of croc shooting.

Wild dogs (*Lycaon pictus*) are interesting creatures; they are about as large as Alsatians but more slenderly built, with massive jaws and short muzzles: their colour is a curious marbled mixture of large black, white and rufous patches; they have big round ears and a white tip to their tails. A unique species, they differ from the true dogs by having only four toes to each foot. The size of the pack varies from a few individuals to as many as thirty or forty; they are remorseless killers, hunting their quarry by sight and cooperating intelligently as I had seen that morning. I believe they have rarely been known to attack man but it is a somewhat eerie experience to be surrounded by an inquisitive pack of wild dog uttering deep harsh barks and jumping up in the grass to look. This has happened to me twice, once in Africa and once in India, when I was encircled by a pack of Indian wild dogs (*Cuon dukhuensis*) a different species, known as dholes. On each occasion they looked menacing and I recall wishing I had read my natural history books more diligently. Do they 'never' attack man or was the word 'rarely' used? Anyway I felt justified in putting a few bullets amongst them to insure against my innaccurate memory.

After a pleasant few days we turned southeastwards and marched for Chakchak, the Kreish village, fifty miles away on the Chel river, where we hoped to find the guides for the next part of our journey.

On arrival in Chakchak we found the guides and under officer Rinaldo with the lorry and a bundle of mail; to my chagrin it was all for Rocky except for one letter; the rest of mine had gone astray – a disaster in the bush.

'Well,' said Rocky with some irony, 'it must be an important one, what does it say?' I opened it to find a circular from a house of doubtful virtue in London somewhat euphemistically called a night club. The letter announced the sad death of the proprietress, Milly, but ended on the more cheerful note that 'it is business as usual, and Freddie the barman will be here to greet you'.

I was determined to investigate Richard Owen's story of Bimbashi Greenwood's escape, and I asked Chief Chakchak who had met us on arrival to come again next evening for a drink. He was a fat old man with grizzled hair: as he sat down the canvas chair creaked ominously. I poured him a tin mug of rum, which he sniffed, sipped, and then swallowed in three great gulps. A slow smile spread over his face and he rubbed his tummy with pleasure. I refilled the mug.

'How many years have you been Chief of Chakchak?' I asked.

He belched, held out both hands and looking thoughtful started counting the segments of his fingers with the thumb of each hand. 'For more than thirty years, Janabuk,' he said. 'And my father was chief before that. I'm an old man now but by God this mug makes me feel young again, it contains the embers of a fire.'

'Do you remember,' I asked cautiously, 'very many years ago when even you were a small boy, an English bimbashi came to your village alone and wounded. He had escaped from the Rizegat Arabs of Darfur. Your people found him in the land beyond the Lol river and brought him here.'

The chief gazed thoughtfully into the fire pretending not to notice another tinkle of the rum bottle on his enamel mug. Then he turned to an old man squatting beside his chair; they spoke in their language for a time, nodding their heads and pointing north.

Yes, he remembered the happening, he was a young boy and his father was Chief Chakchak. 'The bimbashi was wounded and ill, he stayed here for many days and then returned to Wau, he sent presents, and a patrol went to punish the Rizegat but I don't know what happened after that.'

I didn't reply for a while, letting him toy with his memory, then I asked, 'Who looked after the bimbashi and nursed his wounds, wasn't there a girl?'

'Yes,' he said. 'That was my sister, Yatong, she was older than me — she wanted to follow the bimbashi to Wau but my father forbade her and she tried to die in the river.' He turned and gave an order to one of his men who slipped away into the darkness. We sat talking in the fire-

light and I changed the subject to our journey up the Chel river asking
what game we might see. At last I rose and thanked him but he signalled me to sit down.

'Wait,' he said and a little while later into the circle of firelight came
a shrivelled old crone weighed down with beads and supported on the
arm of a young man. I called for a chair but she waved it away and
squatted beside her brother gazing into the fire.

'This is my sister, who looked after the English bimbashi, she was
young and beautiful in those days but now she is old and ugly and her
grandchildren take care of her.'

He turned and talked to his sister for a full minute. Never lifting her
eyes from the fire, she nodded and nodded: at last rummaging in her
scanty clothing she handed her brother a dirty rag. The chief untied it
and passed me a flat silver and enamel snuff box of the type used in the
past to carry quinine pills. By the light of the fire I could just discern the
worn outline of a coat of arms on the back. After studying it for a
minute I handed it back to the old lady. She never lifted her head but
slowly repacking the snuff box in the folds of the clothes, rose and leaning on her grandson left the firelight followed by the chief and his
retinue.

Rocky and I sat late over the fire that night speculating on the past. I
felt I would have an interesting and rather melancholy story to tell
Richard Owen when we got back to Wau.*

Next morning we were on the move as dawn came up. The guides
had told us of a water hole to the southeast where game came to drink;
we wanted meat and I planned to shoot a buffalo, camp by the water
hole and march westwards to the river next day. From what the guides
told us we should reach the water hole at midday; it was clear crystal
water bubbling from the ground, they said, 'ze firdos – like paradise',
and there would be honey for everyone. The sun rose and we
found ourselves marching over a flat plain of burnt black cotton
soil.

Here and there we came upon elephant tracks leading towards the
river and as it got hotter, giraffe, kob and hartebeeste appeared in a
mirage on the horizon. After four hours marching it was unpleasantly
hot and nothing in the distance suggested a paradise of shade and gushing springs. I questioned the guides again only to be told that another
mile would bring us in sight of our haven. After two more hours of
growing ill temper and some anxiety, a smudge appeared on the hor-

* See Appendix 1, 'Escape in the Grass', p. 195.

izon which slowly revealed itself as a patch of trees. Morale improved, the men strode out and started to sing. At last we entered a grove of dead, skeleton-like trees providing a minimum of shade, in the middle of which was a patch of almost dry mud fouled by baboons, and swarming with bees.

'Is this your spring of paradise,' snarled the bash shawish to the guides. 'It's a dried up swamp of hell and your brothers have made it disgusting. Do you see what I carry in my hand – by God you will feel it if you lie to the bimbashi.'

'There was water here two years ago,' replied one of the guides. 'My brother told me so – he came here to collect honey.'

'That is why you dogs have lead us here,' roared the bash shawish. 'To collect honey and watch the buluk die of thirst.' And turning to me he lifted his hippo hide whip.

'May I give them their baksheesh now, Janabuk?' he said.

'I think we will wait and see if their information improves,' I replied. 'How much have the men got left in their water bottles?'

'Very little,' he answered.

'Right, we march again an hour after midnight due west for the river. In the meantime get some men digging for water.'

It was my fault for relying on 'native intelligence' in which happy fantasy usually takes precedence over unhappy fact. It was by no means the first time I had been caught out and I was therefore angrier with myself than with the guides.

The rest of that day and half the night was uncomfortable in the extreme. Rocky and I gave our water for the ponies and Dina and opened a bottle of beer – digging failed to provide anything but damp mud from which we squeezed through our handkerchiefs a few drops of foul-tasting water: we were glad to be on the move again at one o'clock in the morning. By marching towards the river I was techni-cally disobeying the standing order of the Equatorial Corps requiring me to return to the last water at Chakchak; however, unless the river took a big curve away from us – and this was not shown by the dotted line on the map, I calculated that five hours marching would bring us to the water.

The men of my company mostly came from well watered country and were less inured to thirst than the Latuka of the east bank. The pre-vious days' march had been long and hot, and only the wisest men had a mouthful of water left in their bottles. We marched in silent discom-fort with the Pole star on our right hand, over ground deeply pitted with elephant tracks in the dried out swamps into which the porters stumbled with their loads. The pace was slow and painful. The light came slowly and we strained our eyes for a river line ahead. The sun rose behind us revealing nothing but a boundless plain. There was no song to greet the morning and I cursed my stupidity, the Shatt guides and the rough going. Another hour passed and still no welcoming tree line appeared ahead. High in the sky a flight of sand grouse passed over, they would be making for the nearest water and I adjusted the line of march accordingly. We trudged on in thirsty silence and at last Rocky spoke.

'There is a little pub on Dartmoor,' he said, 'where iced draught cider costs threepence a glass – I wonder if . . .' the rest of his ill-timed humour was cut short by loud whinnying from the two ponies. 'That sounds like good news,' said Rocky changing the subject. The whinny-ing was repeated and the men of the company started to murmur. Ten minutes later we topped a slight rise and there below us a few hundred yards away ran a glittering stream. The syces slipped the saddles and bridles from the struggling ponies who, followed by Dina, galloped forward and plunged in. The company increased its pace to a shamb-ling trot until a bellow from the bash shawish halted them.

'Who gave the order to double?' he croaked. 'Halt. Form threes and dress by the right.' He checked the dressing and strolled down the line glaring. 'Ground arms, you miserable female baboons. Is there no discipline in this buluk?'

'I wish the old bugger would get a move on,' muttered Rocky. 'I'd rather like a little drink.'

After glowering at the company for a moment the bash shawish marched up and saluted. 'Permission for the buluk to fall out?' he asked. I nodded. In a few seconds the men were out of their clothes and running to drink.

The bash shawish turned his back on the river and walked off to inspect the porter's piled loads. I called to him and as he came I noticed that his mouth hung open and his tongue protruded. 'Come and drink at once,' I said. He saluted, turned on his heel and having with great de-liberation undressed and folded his clothes, marched smartly down to the river. I learnt later that he had given the last of his water to a Zande porter who was nearly at the end of his endurance.

'I am not an over fastidious man' said Rocky 'but let's choose a place upstream of our happy soldiers.' As we lay in the cool clear stream drinking and absorbing moisture through every pore of our dehydrated bodies, we discussed the last twenty-four hours and decided we had run it a bit too close. 'Another hour with the sun getting higher and we'd have been in trouble,' said Rocky. 'I doubt that booze helps much in these circumstances – let's stick to the river from now on and to hell with mythical water holes.' I agreed and apologised for my faulty judgement.

Up-stream, we could see shady trees which had been hidden from us on the march by rising ground; we made camp and rested for the remainder of that day. Having checked that nobody was seriously the worse for our thirsty march we made a leisurely start up river next morning. The river twisted in places but we decided only to cut the most obvious corners, it was shady marching and signs of game began to appear on the river's edge. As we went southwards the country became more wooded and the prospects for meat improved: the camp sites on the river bank were delightful and we were in no hurry – morale was high.

I had planned an order of march which I thought would give us the best chance of bagging an elephant or a buffalo for the company. Rocky and I walked half a mile ahead with a guide, a bugler, and a flag on a long pole. The main body followed as silently as possible. If we saw game ahead the flag would be waved, the company would halt and await the outcome of our hunt until summoned forward by the bugle. We marched like this for several days and although the tracks of elephant and buffalo were frequent we saw nothing which would spin out our rations for fourteen days. I began to be perturbed. We wanted meat and we wanted it badly. Each evening Rocky and I went hunting in different directions only to return empty-handed with tales of steaming elephant dung and fresh tracks of buffalo. If we didn't get meat soon we would have to force march to the road where the supply lorry was waiting. That would be a bore and a disappointment. At last one early morning our chance came. We were walking through lightly wooded country, the company following silently behind. As we came over a slight rise the Shatt guide held up his hand and pointed. Two bull buffalo were grazing a few hundred yards ahead. The bugler crept back and waved the flag while Rocky and I formed a plan. 'We must get down wind to that anthill,' I whispered. 'I think we can get a shot from there.'

We crawled through the grass on hands and knees in a wide circle, testing the wind every few minutes; the buffalo continued to graze placidly. Another fifty yards and our larder would be filled; we crept forward. Suddenly something moved in the grass behind and up trotted Dina, wagging her tail. She had slipped her collar and tracked Rocky through the grass. 'Good Dina, good Dina,' hissed Rocky, 'come to master, there's a good bitch.' But Dina knew the signs and wasn't going to miss a hunt; ears pricked, she started jumping up in the grass to look. Rocky lunged forward to grab her but she had seen the buffalo and was after them yapping at the top of her voice. I rolled on to my back and lit a cigarette hoping that dignified silence would serve as a tacit rebuke. Rocky stood up gazing after the disappearing trio and using every expletive ever heard in a barrack room. When the bugler arrived I said, 'Go back and tell the company what's happened. I'm going to wait for two hours and then follow up the buffalo. We will want you as a tracker.' At that moment Dina returned panting, wagging and well pleased with herself. 'Take this little dog and if she escapes again the company will eat her – and the man who let's her go,' I added.

We lay in the shade finding little to talk about, and after two hours set off after the buffalo. The sun was getting high and I calculated that if the apparition of Dina, and Rocky's language, had not made too deep an impression on our quarry, they would soon lie up. After a mile we came to where the tracks slowed down to a walk and turned towards the river; half an hour later we saw two black shapes ahead lying in the shade of a tree and again we made a plan. 'We will stalk to that tree,' I said. 'Wait for me to shoot first. I'm going to try and knock out the one on the left with a neck shot and you take the one on the right as he gets up. The bugler stays here. Watch their jaws – if they stop chewing be ready to shoot from anywhere.'

We crept forward watching for any sign of alertness and got into position on either side of the tree. I nodded to Rocky and his shot followed mine by a split second. There was a short struggle, we each fired a second shot and the two buffalo lay still. The bugler ran up and climbed a tall tree.

'Sound Dinners,' said Rocky and for the first time ever, the call of 'Come to the cookhouse door boys,' rang out over the Chel river. A short while later we heard a deep happy chant in the distance growing louder as the company approached.

'I wonder what they're singing,' said Rocky. 'A sort of African version of "Boiled beef and carrots" I expect, anyway the larder is stocked, there's tongue for us and titbits for Dina.'

'I hoped we weren't mentioning Dina for the rest of today,' I said.

The company arrived and a hundred and sixty black faces smiled as they set about cutting up the meat, even the bash shawish grimly nodded his approval. We made camp a hundred yards away and Rocky and I walked down to the river for a swim; as we lay in the water a herd of ten giant eland came down to drink forty yards away. It was both Rocky's and my first sight of these rare magnificent antelope and we watched them under ideal conditions. They were no more massively built than the common eland but their wide spiral horns and sandy blue coats striped with white distinguished them as the more handsome race. The bull was the size of a large ox and he waded into the river dipping his muzzle and dewlap into the water to drink; his cows followed nervously a few yards behind. Rocky and I watched spellbound, only our faces above water. Here was a scene that many a hunter might have dreamt of – the 'blue ribbon' of Sudan game drinking quietly at close quarters and we in what seemed to be perfect camouflage. Just once the big bull lifted his dripping muzzle and stared intently down stream towards us for half a minute, then, apparently satisfied, dropped his head again to drink. When they had finished they waded across the river and disappeared over the far bank. 'I don't think I have ever been taken for a crocodile before,' said Rocky. 'That was the finest game sight I have ever seen.'

We camped for two nights and while the men made biltong and feasted, Rocky and I went in search of the giant eland with an antiquated camera. We didn't see them again that day but we had an interesting time with the Shatt honey hunter who came with us carrying a gourd. As we were walking along a game path through scattered trees the Shatt stopped and cocked his head on one side. 'Do you hear that bird?' he said. 'He is calling us to honey.'

From the tree overhead came a sound as if someone was rattling a half empty box of matches, it was a fussy urgent note; a grey bird rather larger than a sparrow with two white tail feathers flew out to the next tree and continued its chatter. 'We will follow and he will guide us to the bees,' said the Shatt.

The bird flew on from tree to tree chattering as it went and sometimes waiting for us to catch up. After half a mile its note changed, becoming more urgent, and the Shatt pointed to where bees were flying in and out of a hole in a hollow tree. Rocky and I removed ourselves to a safe distance and watched the honey hunter cut a bunch of grass, light it and having thrust the burning brand into the hole, start hacking

at the tree. After half an hour's work and more burning brands, he had
enlarged the hole into which he thrust his arm, scooping out handfuls
of comb. The bees buzzed furiously around him but he appeared none
the worse when he walked over to Rocky and I with some of the comb.
We strained it through a handkerchief and ate the honey with relish.
When the Shatt had filled his gourd he left a large slab of comb in the
fork of the tree. 'That is for the bird,' he said. 'If you forget to leave him
some or if you are greedy and take it all he will lead you to a snake or a
lion next time.'

We sat in the shade smoking and eating honey while the Shatt rega-
led us with the skills of his business and legends of the honeyguide. His
discourse was an interesting blend of natural history and fantasy which
are often difficult to separate in Africa. There are eleven species of
honeyguide in the world whose family name is appropriately enough
Indicatoridae, two in Asia and nine in Africa. Some of these, notably
the black-throated honeyguide have developed the art of leading men
or honey badgers to bees' nests. This must be an inherited instinct and
not taught as the birds have the same breeding habits as cuckoos and
probably never see their own parents. They have a tough skin and a
special membrane over the eyes to protect them from stings, also a
musky odour which may be a form of insect repellent. They do not eat
the bees but feed on the wax for which they have a unique digestive
system. The Arabic name for them is kareima, which might be trans-
lated as the 'generous' or 'precious little one'. Many of these facts came
out in the colourful legends which the Shatt guide told us that day.

The country was changing slightly as we marched up river. We were
now climbing low rolling hills and winding our way through sparse
forests. Beside and below us ran the sparkling Chel river, fifty yards
across and almost everywhere fordable. We headed due south welcoming each occasion for crossing the cool winding stream. The only
annoyance were the tsetse flies. In some places they swarmed out of the
bushes, biting through shirts and shorts and raising livid bumps where
they bit. The bash shawish even had a solution for this problem.

'Boy,' he shouted to a young Zande soldier. 'Take your shirt off and
march between the Bimbashis.' And turning to me said. 'The flies
prefer a black skin – they will all settle on him and you will not be
bothered.'

'That,' remarked Rocky, 'is a little joke that would produce some interesting "resolutions" at the United Nations.'

'Thank you, bash shawish,' I replied. 'I don't mind the flies, we have as good in England in the hot weather.'

Rocky went on chuckling at the bash shawish's suggestion.

'Put it in your book – *Tips for Empire builders*,' he said shaking with mirth. 'We ought to do it just to get a photograph to send to Sir Stafford Cripps. My God he's the hell of a good sergeant-major.'

A minute or two later I turned round and saw a young soldier marching behind us with his shirt over his arm and a grin on his face.

'Awamir ya bash shawish – bash shawish's orders,' he said.

'Put your shirt on and get back into the ranks you bloody young fool,' I said, swatting at the beastly flies. By this time the whole company were dissolved with such mirth that I called a halt. We lit grass fires and rested down wind in the smoke, letting the swarm of tsetse disperse.

It was no wonder that this bit of country was uninhabited. Tsetse not only transmit disease in cattle but also sleeping sickness in man, both killers. The disease had spread to the Southern Sudan at the beginning of the century from the Congo and French Equatorial Africa where between 1911 and 1921 the population was reduced to a third of its normal size – from nine million to three million people. Only the dedication and energy of Sudan government doctors working under conditions of great hardship and danger had prevented the same tragedy occurring in the Sudan. There is another interesting matter concerning this blood-sucking insect, which resembles a European horsefly. The Arabs under Amr ibn al Asi had conquered Egypt in AD 640 and for the next few hundred years moved southwards in search of slaves, ivory and grazing for their stock. They conquered, absorbed and converted to Islam the people they encountered but when they reached what is now the Bahr el Ghazal and Equatorial Provinces their camels and horses started dying mysteriously and they ventured no further. It is interesting to speculate whether, had it not been for the tsetse fly, that Jan van Riebeck landing at the Cape in 1652 might have encountered 'grave white turbaned merchants' of Arab descent rather than a few primitive bushmen.

Early one morning the bash shawish reported to me that an askari had been bitten by a snake during the night. I went over to see him; he was lying on his bed of cut grass shaking with fever, his eyes rolled upwards with only the whites showing. The bash shawish showed me the small puncture marks on the man's calf around which his friends had made a dozen little vertical cuts which oozed. It seemed to me that the man was very ill, he was ice cold and sweating. The bash shawish was not worried; he showed me the dead snake which proved to be a rhombic night adder (*Causus rhombeatus*), not a very deadly species and assured me that the man would be marching tomorrow. I produced what medicines I thought might help and saw to it that the man was made as comfortable as possible. The only precaution I ever took against snake bite was to carry in my hat band a razor blade and a phial of potassium permanganate. My soldiers who knew more about snake bite than I did scornfully rejected my suggestion of tourniquets and other Western devices. I did not altogether despise witch doctory and mumbo jumbo which probably has its affiliations with the psychiatrist couches of Harley Street. My only fear was the extraordinary African ability to voluntarily give up the ghost when ill; this is, of course, balanced by their ability to endure terrible wounds with stoic good humour. I mentioned this to the bash shawish who grimly remarked, 'Don't worry, Janabuk, I have given the boy his orders, he will march tomorrow.'

'Then tell him I have marked him for promotion,' I said, 'if he is better tonight I will give him a mug of bimbashi's rum and a wakil onbashi's stripe when we get back to Wau.'

By nightfall the soldier was much better but his leg was swollen and it was clear that he wouldn't be able to march. I gave him his mug of rum and we set off next morning with porters carrying him on an improvised stretcher.

We marched in the usual formation with Rocky and I and our Shatt guide in the lead looking out for game. It was pleasant to walk through the drenching dew beside the bright river, wondering what we would see round each bend or from the top of every low hill. Rocky and I walked in silence, each busy with our own thoughts. We had been going for an hour when suddenly a shot rang out behind us, then I heard the bash shawish's whistle and a gabble of orders followed by another shot. 'My God! it's an ambush,' said Rocky. 'What the hell is going on?' We ran back and as the company came into sight I saw they were hurriedly forming square, but what the devil were the porters doing? They had abandoned their loads and taken to the trees. Then the cause of the trouble became apparent – two rhinos were galloping around in the bushes making token charges and snorting. As we arrived the rhinos made off on an erratic zigzag course, their tails held high. The company were in hollow square and every man convulsed with mirth pointing at the porters who were climbing out of the trees with as much dignity as they could muster under the circumstances. I disapproved of the riflemen's favourite sport of teasing the porters but on this occasion they gave their humour full rein. 'Who gave you leave to go home?' they shouted. 'How's your brother up there, is he still stealing the maize cobs?' Soon order was restored and everyone was enjoying the joke until Rocky and I discovered the only serious casualty – our last bottle of whisky had not survived the jolt. The snake-bitten askari had been dumped in the thorn bushes and had leaped into a tree – he elected to march for the rest of the day, and by evening had quite recovered.

A few more days marching, a buffalo hunt and the sight of another herd of giant eland, and we reached the Wau to Raga road where Rinaldo and the supply lorry met us. We rested for a day and then turned eastwards for the dusty hundred mile march to Wau.

On the day after our arrival back in Wau I went to report to Richard Owen. I gave him a verbal account of our patrol and promised him a written report and the maps which we had made of the Chel valley. He listened with interest to the sad little saga of Chakchak and then said, 'I fear I misinformed you on one point, you are not the first white men to explore the Chel river, a Commander Fell of the Royal Navy went down it in a boat in 1904. The navy usually get there first.'

On reading through my mail in the office I learnt that I had been promoted and after three months leave in England would return as a Kaimakam and a Bey to the Camel Corps in Kordofan Province. My feelings were mixed, I did not want to leave the Equatorial Corps, I liked the cheerful black pagan soldiers and like many other 'Southern' officers I had come to associate myself with them. It was impossible not to detect the disdain with which some of the Northern Arabs treated the naked Southerners and I resented having to change my loyalties. However my orders were clear beginning with 'On return from leave in the UK, you will report' etc., and ending with a congratulatory message on becoming a Bey.

Before I left the Bahr el Ghazal Province I was determined to see more of the south, so leaving Rocky and Rinaldo to unwind the patrol I took a few Zande soldiers and set off in a truck to Zande-land and the Congo border. We motored a few hundred miles southward camping on the way and fishing for Nile perch in the Sue river amongst a school of hippos. I took a tent as the rains were due and indeed they broke with majestic force on our first night in camp; the thunder, crashing of

trees in the gale, and lashing rain obliterated all other sound; the lightning turned night into day, surrounding us in a holocaust of flame. The
Zande soldiers did not like it; deaths by lightning are not infrequent in
the Sudan, they took mouthfuls of water and spitting on the ground
muttered incantations. I finally got some sleep and dawn came, still
and cool with only the sound of each new gushing rivulet and the song
of birds.

We motored on to Source Yubo on the Congo border where the
Yubo river bubbles out of a rock and sets out on its long journey to the
Nile and the Mediterranean. A few yards away a small stream called
the Suni rises, to flow into the Welle river and the Congo, reaching the
Atlantic Ocean some three thousand miles from the Nile Delta. Source
Yubo was a pretty little settlement which had been founded for the
study and prevention of sleeping sickness and it was now a leper
colony with a few dedicated overworked doctors; there were neat
flower beds, vegetable gardens and training workshops for smithying,
brickmaking and carpentry. I dined with an erudite Scots doctor who
knew much about the Azande tribe and although he liked them, he was
under no illusions as to some of their less attractive customs and
habits. Until the British administration, the Azande, some of whom
lived in the Congo, had been ruled by the Avungra tribe who had
conquered them in the distant past and treated them with ruthless
cruelty, inflicting terrible mutilations which were still evident as one
walked round the bazaar. They were a tribe still steeped in magic and
witchcraft and riddled with disease despite the prodigious efforts of the
Sudan Medical Service. Most of the other tribes disliked them for their
filed teeth, their knowledge of poisons and their dark forest-haunting
ways. They had been given the half contemptuous name of Nyam
Nyam which suggested an addiction to cannibalism. I had found my
Zande soldiers quick witted and hard working but somewhat given to
intrigue.

I called on the local chief and then motored eastwards along the
border through wooded well watered country of considerable beauty
with splendid views to the south into the Congo. The Game Department in Khartoum had made me an honorary game warden and asked
me to report on certain game in the far south, so I decided to take a few
days hunting in the forest with my Zande orderly. I sought local advice
and found an attractive camp site. My object was to try and locate four
creatures, the Western bongo, the giant forest hog, the West African
sitatunga and the yellow backed duiker. I would not shoot but only

report the presence of these animals if I found them; some of them were thought to be extinct in the area, owing to hunting by the increased native population.

The case of the bongo is curiously ironic. This beautiful forest antelope has a bright rufous coat with a dozen or so vertical white stripes. There is a belief in some parts of Africa that the eating of any striped animal induces leprosy. Before the Zande came under a civilized administration at the beginning of this century the bongo enjoyed a certain degree of immunity from hunting for this reason, leprosy being a terrible scourge among the Zande. With the advent of the first British administrators and doctors this myth had largely disappeared and the bongo's life became more hazardous. They were hunted with poisoned arrows, caught in pitfall traps, and driven into nets by the strange little Zande hunting dogs (now known at Crufts by the name of Basenji), who pursued them through the dense forest, each wearing a wooden bell to mark their progress. The bongo therefore became something of a rarity in the Zande area. However, with independence and the subsequent sad happenings in the Southern Sudan, the old superstitions seem to have crept back for today the bongo is reported to be reasonably common again in that area and its flesh is treated with suspicion.

For several days I hunted through the gallery forests and swamps starting at dawn when the tree tops resounded with birdsong, and dew-spangled spider's webs stretched across the game trails. A half-naked gnomelike tracker led the way, his eyes on the ground, I followed and my Zande orderly padded barefoot behind me with my rifle. Tracking was easy after a night's rain and I watched the skill of my Zande gnome, comparing him favourably with those greatest of all experts, the Ghonds of Central India. Now and again he bent down to touch the rim of a hoof print or a dropping in order to gauge how fresh it was, occasionally he pointed with his spear to a broken spider's web or a crushed leaf with wet sap or saliva on it. Beautiful butterflies flitted around us and orchids hung from the trees; the onset of the rain had freshened the forest, filled the waterholes and produced colours everywhere, especially in the sky where great blue and white clouds built up at midday to the accompaniment of rolling thunder.

We usually hunted in a wide circle from camp, stopping at noon to share a tin of bully beef and rest, keeping an eye on the sky for threatening rain. On the second day I decided to take the lead and I signalled to the gnome to drop behind me; he grinned and shook his head pointing to the ground. 'What is his objection?' I asked my Zande orderly who was looking sheepish. 'Janabuk,' he replied, 'it would not do for the honorary game warden to fall into one of the traps that the Game Department have forbidden here. This man not only knows where the pits are – he dug them.' I saw the point of this argument, particularly when a few hours later our guide pointed to an innocent looking place on the game trail and on tossing a stick revealed a deep dark cavern, skilfully covered with twigs, banana leaves and earth and provided with spikes at the bottom. From then on I followed our guide's footsteps more zealously.

After a few days hunting in this Garden of Eden we had glimpsed both bongo and giant forest hog. The latter is a monstrous black hairy pig weighing up to about 600 pounds: it was discovered as late as 1904 by the famous soldier naturalist Colonel Meinertzhagen whilst serving with the King's African Rifles, and was named in his honour *Hylochoerus meinertzhageni*. It is very much feared by the natives and when an old boar which we had been tracking suddenly appeared in our path and swung round to regard us with a fixed piggy stare our Zande gnome swung himself into the branches of a tree with the agility of his forbears, at the same time my orderly tapped my shoulder and gently but firmly exchanged my field glasses for my rifle. We stood frozen for several seconds until the vision of gigantic black balls bade us farewell, as he trotted away with a savage grunt. I couldn't help wondering what effect the appearance of such a Goliath pig would have had from the back of a horse in the Meerut Kadir. Years later, in the Aberdare mountains in Kenya, I was to watch a leopard treed by four angry giant forest hogs, grunting and squealing as they surrounded the tree. The leopard caught sight of my car and, faced with a choice between humans and hogs, decided on the latter: with a flying leap over the hogs' heads, he took to the bush, hotly pursued by his piggy adversaries.

We saw the bongo from a concealed position overlooking a forest pool where we had found tracks; this method of 'still hunting' is delightful and rewarding, one often sees a great deal more of undisturbed bird and animal life than when one is on the move, and with two pairs of bright African eyes looking out I could read a book or lie on my back scanning the trees for birds and watching the clouds drive by through a pattern of branches. The bongo came suddenly and silently into the clearing, two females; their coats gleaming foxy red in the midday sun, their flanks a dazzle of stripes, they moved delicately down to drink and then were gone again, fading into the forest without a rustle, their white tipped horns laid along their backs.

One evening I returned to find a witch doctor in my camp; it appeared that my cook was having wife trouble and had sent for him to cast a few spells; I walked over to the kitchen tent to see what was going on and a creature of surpassing ugliness looked up at me from beside the fire; it had red ferret eyes, grey hair matted with filth, and on its face an expression of pantomime malevolence; laid out on the ground were some unattractive looking dried up objects. 'Get this bloody little man out of here,' I said, 'and if he appears again I will take him to the D.C. and the police bash shawish will thrash him.' Witchcraft was not in itself illegal, it was too deeply instilled in these tribes. Indeed some witchcraft produced beneficial results, but malevolent witchcraft was proclaimed antisocial and was punishable by law; it held too strong an influence in the dark recesses of these primitive minds. I was fairly certain that the horrid little creature in my camp was up to mischief and probably over-charging for his services. My orderly spoke rapidly but politely to him in Zande while the witch doctor fixed me with a stare of implacable hatred. For a time he remained squatting, then getting the trappings of his trade together he rose and limped, muttering down the jungle track. As the bushes closed behind him, there was a gasp of horror from my servants and a clicking of tongues but this was quickly followed by the usual African reaction to a nasty moment, gusts of good-natured laughter.

We saw quantities of commoner game, including elephant and buffalo and on most nights lions roared on the plains in the distance, but we found no trace of either the Western sitatunga or the yellow backed duiker; however, I had greatly increased my check list of birds. Time was running out and I decided to return to Wau and write my report for the Game Department before handing over to Rocky.

Two days hard driving brought me to my bungalow on the bank of the Jur river. After a much needed bath I sent a note to Rocky and we sat on the verandah watching the moon rise, a whisky decanter between us. 'What's the news?' I asked.

'I've booked you on the weekly aeroplane to Khartoum next Friday,' he said, 'and then it's three months of England, home and beauty for you. And don't forget that Freddie the barman will be there to greet you,' he added. 'I believe you can brush up on your camel riding in Regents Park.'

I reached for the decanter and refilled our glasses. And so I thought, my sojourn in the south has come to an end – I wonder how I shall enjoy the harsh northern deserts, Arab askaris and somewhat more conventional methods of soldiering; I was apprehensive, and sad at the thought of leaving the south; I also hoped that I would find other companions as congenial and humorous as Rocky; however, this was no time for melancholy and as the level of the decanter fell, I turned my thoughts to the gliding chalk stream in Wiltshire where mayfly would be popping, and a beat on the Blackwater in Ireland where I had an assignation. The prospect was pleasing, and as if to encourage my hopes for those bright waters, a hippo started grunting and splashing in the pool below.

As I was packing in the evening of the next day, a truck drew up at my bungalow and out stepped Denis Zaphiro: he was just the man I wanted to see. I had heard rumours of trouble on the Ethiopian border where Denis was patrolling; and now I would get the tale at first hand.

'I've lots to tell you,' he said, 'but first things first, I need a bath.'

'It looks as if you've been having one,' I replied, contemplating his bedraggled appearance.

'I've just spent an hour up to my waist in the Jur river, trying to get my truck back on to the causeway and all because of three naked Dinka girls.'

'That's an old trap, I suppose you had one eye on the girls and one on the causeway.'

'No – both eyes on the girls and trusting to luck; as you well know, I am not only an artist but a student of Greek mythology; the vision of three black Aphrodites rising from the waves of the Jur river was more important to me than sticking slavishly to the causeway, I just had bad luck. Anyway the girls nearly drowned giggling and I finally made them help push me out.'

An hour later when we were settled on the verandah I asked for news.

'I've handed over No 5 Company,' he said, 'and am leaving the army in a week's time. I've got a job as Game Warden in Kenya.'

I congratulated him: 'It's what you always wanted,' I said. 'Now tell me about your patrol.'

Denis had been patrolling near the Illemi triangle in an area which touches on Uganda, the Southern Sudan, Ethiopia and North Kenya. It is a wild harsh stretch of country and wild and harsh are the cattle-owning tribes who dispute the grazing in that savage bit of Africa. The

Nyangatom from Ethiopia, the Topotha from the Southern Sudan and the Turkana from Kenya make raid and counter raid upon one another; cattle thefts, murder, rape and mutilation are the national sport. If a tribe is punished by being disarmed, they are the next target for their joyful neighbours.

In those days indignant protests passed between District Commissioners of Kenya, the Sudan, and Uganda who had, perhaps, shared the same digs at Oxford. Bimbashis from the Southern Sudan met majors from the King's African Rifles at border stations, to argue the cause of their tribes and recall their Sandhurst days together. It was a confusing situation bedevilled by the non-cooperation of Ethiopia and the fact that the raiders from that country had a plentiful supply of Italian rifles.

After a dry year the grazing was poor, and Denis had been ordered to keep the Nyangatom from moving their cattle into Topotha country; this would have provoked bloody clashes between the two tribes. 'I got word,' said Denis, 'that the Nyangatom were moving in, so I quickly collected a patrol of two platoons which was all I could spare, and made a forced march into that hellish bit of country, where I met a party of Nyangatom elders coming to beg for grazing. They were dignified men, as cattle owners mostly are, and although my sympathies were on their side my orders were clear: they must get their men back across the Ethiopian border, or I would bring more troops, and drive them and their cattle out. It was a heart-rending decision. I gave them three days to clear the area which was more than enough, and then I followed them somewhat cautiously as I knew they were well armed with rifles. We picked up the tracks of about a hundred men, sneaking back into the Sudan, which eventually led us into thick scrub country, crossed by sandy river beds.

'My advance guard were crossing one of these river beds when they were ambushed from the far bank, and I had a sharp little battle on my hands. Three of my askaris were killed but we put in a platoon attack and drove the Nyangatom out of cover – they bolted eastwards leaving a few corpses. We followed them and after a four hour pursuit I called a halt, I was sickened by the death of my askaris, and for that matter by the Nyangatom casualties. They were brave men fighting for their cattle as they had done for centuries, I regretted the whole thing but it had to be – I suppose you had a much more enjoyable patrol.'

'I certainly did,' I said.

The next few days were spent in packing, handing over to Rocky, and a round of farewell visits in Wau. Promotions had to be decided upon and reports written. I relied very much on Rinaldo and the bash shawish in these matters, their judgement was unerring and they showed no favouritism for their own tribes. I enjoyed our long talks together. Rinaldo was conscientious, and intelligent, also a devout Catholic, I hoped he would go far; men like him were needed in the south.

On my last day the bash shawish asked to see me. I gave him a chair in the office and called for tea; he refused a cigarette and sat very upright staring ahead. I waited, and finally he spoke; 'Mabruk ya sath el bey – Congratulations, your excellency the Bey,' he said, with the ghost of a smile. 'So you are leaving us.'

I nodded. 'Inshallah, wa lakin ana hazeen giddan – If God wills, but I am sorry to be doing so,' I replied.

He remained silent for a long time and the smile left his face, then he spoke again. 'There is talk that all "El Ingliz" will one day leave us.'

'Yes, there is talk – one day you will govern yourselves, it is right that this should happen.'

He shook his head. 'We will not govern ourselves, we will be governed by Northerners from Khartoum. They do not understand us or like us.'

'That is not true,' I said. 'What of our Northern Sudanese officers here in the Equatorial Corps. What of Bimbashi Zein? What of Bimbashi Khalil? What of Sagh Talat? They are every bit as fit to govern or command as we Ingliz and more so, as they are also Sudanese.'

'That is true,' he replied, 'they are officers of the Sudan Defence Force. You Ingliz trained them, but there are many whose hearts are not so good, they call us "abid" (slaves) and despise our nakedness and our customs.'

'Do you not want to rule yourselves?' I asked.

'Yes, one day, but the time is not yet, the young men you have educated are conceited and dishonest and the old chiefs think only of their tribes. They are no match for the Northerners. The time is not yet – my father told me terrible things that happened before the Ingliz came.'

'We are soldiers not politicians,' I said. 'We must obey the orders we receive.'

'I know that, Janabuk, but I tell you this. On the day that the Ingliz leave us there will be bloodshed and more bloodshed. You will hear of

it in Ingilterra and be sad, they will never govern us from Khartoum –
never.'

He rose, saluted and left, and next day as I flew North over the green
maze of the Nile Sudd I brooded sadly on his words 'bloodshed and
more bloodshed'. The old man was seldom wrong.*

* Twelve years later, in the early 1960s, I met him secretly in a hut on the Congo
  border. His son had been killed and he was a sad broken old man with a terrible tale
  to tell. He bore no grudge except against his soldiers who had joined the revolt, but
  over and over again he said, 'I told you, Sath el Bey, I told you.'

6

Hot Desert Days, Chilly Nights

NORTHERN SUDAN

Khartoum was a refreshing sight in the sparkling spring sunshine of 1951, the pink of the desert blended with the azure sky; the glittering river slid past Gordon's Palace and the great shade trees planted by Kitchener; it felt to me like civilization again, and the Grand Hotel was the height of luxury. I went to see the Kaid, El Ferik Scoones Pasha, who commanded the Sudan Defence Force, a man of great charm; he had been a young officer in the Western Arab Corps many years before, and there was little he did not know about Sudanese affairs. During the war he had been my brigadier in Burma and I was delighted to see him again as my general.

He congratulated me on my appointment to the Camel Corps and asked about the south; we talked for a while and then he said, 'I think before we inflict you on the Camel Corps, you had better have a verbal Arabic exam. Will you fix it up with Abboud Bey, and if you are free, come to dinner tonight.' I thanked him and left.

That night after dinner I found myself talking to Bill Luce* who had risen to the top of the Sudan Political Service, he was a scholar and administrator of enormous ability, who subsequently became one of Britain's last great proconsuls. He had once served in the south and our talk rather naturally turned to that subject. I told him something of what my bash shawish had said to me. He nodded sadly in confirmation of a matter of which he knew far more than I. 'Yes,' he said, 'independence will come long before the problem can be resolved, if indeed it ever can be solved. The history of the place is all too recent. We can only hope that good sense will prevail on both sides.'

I could see that it was a matter which concerned him deeply.

(Years later I dined with him when he was a governor in another land and he told me about his own sad part in the negotiations between north and south. 'I fear,' he said, 'that our forebodings on that night

---

* Later Sir William Luce, Governor of Aden and then Political Resident in the Gulf.

long ago were fully realised.' After a pause he added, 'You know, they shot your under officer Rinaldo. I tried to prevent it but I had no authority then. There were wrongs on both sides.'

The news of Rinaldo's death was a sad blow, he had been a loyal friend, and had he lived he would have been a valuable man in the south.)

Next morning I went for my Arabic exam to Kaimakam Abboud Bey's office. He was a rotund smiling little man, the senior Sudanese Staff officer in the Defence Force. He had long service and combined great courtliness with bubbling good humour.* After the usual pleasantries and coffee he said, 'and now please tell me in Arabic all about the three month's patrol you have just done.' I took a deep breath and launched into the language I had been using for nearly two years in the south – at least it was fairly fluent but some of the words didn't sound quite right even to my ear. Abboud Bey cocked his head like a puzzled terrier, he nodded and smiled, and soon I saw that his shoulders were shaking with suppressed mirth; with infinite politeness he bade me desist and, wiping his eyes, called for more coffee. 'I fear you will need a teacher when you come back to El Obeid,' he said. 'I will see that you get a good one.' I had been talking the terrible patois called Mongallese Arabic which is used in the south as a lingua franca among a welter of tribal languages, and is as comic or offensive to an Arab ear as pidgin might be to a professor of English. I apologised for abusing his language, he laughed good-humouredly and wished me an enjoyable leave.

I looked down as the plane circled over Blackbush aerodrome, and saw again with delight the tiny green fields and blossoming hedges of an English country side in spring. The bus took me to London and I made for the Cavalry Club and went in to see my friend Thompson, the barman.

'Good God!' said a voice from the end of the bar, 'We heard you'd been eaten' – my leave had begun.

Three months of idleness and self indulgence is a pleasant prospect, particularly with no responsibilities and a reasonably healthy bank balance. I cannot now exactly remember how the time passed but I recall long lazy days fishing on the Avon in Wiltshire with the sedge warblers singing in the rushes and the fat trout rising: sunny days on

---

* After a military coup in 1958 he became General Ibrahim Abboud, President of the Sudan and in 1964 paid a State Visit to England (see p. 172).

the Cowdray polo grounds in the company of the Harpers, and a
stretch of glittering salmon river in Ireland, with an Irish ghillie whose
reminiscences were sadly as unintelligible to me as mine had been to
Abboud Bey. Neither did I ignore the delights of London, where the
tunes from *South Pacific* were now being played in the Four Hundred
Club. The time passed very pleasantly; I was thirty-four years old, my
bank manager was friendly and the sun shone through that leisurely
idyllic summer.

My first act on arriving back in Khartoum was to seek an interview
with the Kaid, General Scoones; I was somewhat apprehensive as to
what the outcome might be. The general gave me a chair and asked
about my leave. We chatted for a while and then I took a deep breath.

'General,' I said, 'I know the regulations of the Sudan Defence Force
regarding wives but...'

The general rose from his chair and held up his hand. 'Say no more,
Hilary – so you want to get married. It is high time you did, and as for
regulations, they are for the observance of fools and the guidance of
wise men. But tell me how you have persuaded any girl to marry you;
I'm amazed.'

'That is the catch,' I replied. 'I am taking the precaution of asking
you first.'

'This is the sort of joke Ella will enjoy enormously,' he said. 'Let's go
and tell her.' And off we went to break the news to the general's wife.

And so it transpired that, a month or so later, I flew to Kenya and
was married in the little church in Nanyuki, returning to El Obeid with
a wife and good resolutions for the future.

El Obeid lies some two hundred miles south-west of Khartoum. It is
the straggling capital town of Kordofan Province, an area larger than
Britain and Ireland combined. It contained the headquarters of the
Camel Corps which comprised several Arab and Nuba companies
stationed in Kordofan Province and one in Atbara on the Nile, north of
Khartoum. The country surrounding El Obeid is semi-desert becoming
harsher and more arid towards the north. To the south the country
changes from dry scrub ranges of rocky hills called the Nuba mountains; it was from this area that the Camel Corps obtained its soldiers
for the Nuba companies – stocky, muscular men of Negro origin who
many years ago had been driven into the hills by the Baggara Arabs,
but never subdued or administered until after the battle of Omdurman.

For the first few weeks of my new appointment, I set about acquainting myself with a rather different way of life than that which had pertained in the 'Bog'. I got to know the Sudanese officers, charming courteous men, some with considerably longer service than myself. I visited outposts, read through files and during the long hot afternoons, when my mind prayed for sleep, I struggled with the intricacies of conventional Arabic. My teacher was a schoolmaster and religious teacher; he came to my bungalow, riding his donkey, at three o'clock every afternoon, and for the next hour attempted to repair the dreadful patois with which I had conducted my life in the Bog. 'No, that is not quite right,' he would say politely. 'Can you not hear the difference between these two sounds?' And, working his throat like a lizard, he would produce from somewhere two noises which sounded to me as identical as the monotonous cawing of the crows on the tin roof. He was patient and humorous and had listened to many a tone deaf English bimbashi demolishing the language of which he was so justly proud.

After one particularly painful session he said with a smile. 'Do not be discouraged, Sart el Bey, one of my best pupils once said to me in despair, "it seems, Hadratuk, that there are three distinct meanings for every Arabic word, one is the conventional meaning, two is the exact opposite, and three of course is another word for a camel".' We used to have tea together at four o'clock and after a courteous leave-taking he would ride away while I changed and made for the polo ground.

The Camel Corps had long been mechanised but it still kept camels for patrolling in areas which were unsuitable for wheels; I was keen to go on a patrol and after the first few weeks of settling in I consulted the Commanding Officer, Pat Cousens, and made the necessary plans. The camels were sent ahead and three days later I drove out in a truck to meet them forty miles away; the truck departed, and surrounded by smiling Camel Corps soldiers I gingerly climbed on top of my burbling mount; we then set off over a land of desert, scrub and rolling sand dunes.

My memories of that patrol are that it was hot and uncomfortable during the day and very cold at night. We started before first light each day and, led by an askari guide, the swaying line of mounted men moved forward at the walk, silhouetted in starlight; the only sound was the soft footfall of the camels and the squeak of leather. As soon as a glimmering of light appeared and a cold wind stirred, we broke into a trot, welcoming the desert sunrise and the glow of warmth on our numbed fingers. By ten o'clock we had usually reached a water hole or campsite where we off-loaded and sought the shade, while the camels browsed on the unhospitable looking thorn trees. The evening 'shid' began at three when the heat was still like a furnace, but after two hour's riding the sting went out of the day and towards evening when the shadows lengthened on the sand we halted and made camp.

One day I shot a redfronted gazelle for the pot. From the back of his camel my orderly had seen a herd grazing a mile away. We halted the column and I moved cautiously round the sand dunes, crawling the last hundred yards through a carpet of devil thorn. I picked out a buck and before I fired whispered to my orderly, 'Allahu akbar – God is most great'; this would make the meat lawful or 'hilal' even if its throat was cut after death. The moment the shot sounded my orderly raced forward drawing the knife which the Arabs carried strapped under their left arm. Muttering a prayer he cut the throat of the still kicking animal and bore it back in triumph to the couched line of camels. We returned, covered with devil thorn, the spiky burrs called 'heskenit' which are the curse of Kordofan, but we feasted well that night.

We headed west but after a few days turned towards the south and entered a country of thin scrub, dotted here and there with enormous baobab trees. These trees (*Adansonia digitata*) are known in Arabic as 'tebeldi'; their girth is sometimes more than seventy feet, and they seem to defy most of the laws of botany; their huge trunks are surmounted by straggling bare branches looking like roots and making a stark, somewhat eerie silhouette in the sky.

The tebeldi was once, so Arab legend tells, the most beautiful tree in the Garden of Eden, but the devil in a fit of jealousy uprooted it and planted it upside down. It provides rope, spice and medicine for the Arabs, but its most useful function in this part of the world is for water storage. The Arabs hollow out the trunk and, during the rains fill it with water; some trees hold several thousand gallons for use in the dry weather. Each tree is owned and named by a family or a village. During the campaign against the Sultan of Darfur, Ali Dinar, in 1916, Colonel Kelly Bey bought and hired trees on the advance route to El Fasher to supply his two thousand troops with water. However much the trees are shorn, hollowed or ring barked they seem to live on placidly for thousands of years, their presence making this inhospitable land habitable by man.

In the evenings I squatted with the askaris round camel dung fires, eating Arab food and listening to their humorous or sad legends and their chatter about camels and past tribal fights.

I learned a good deal about the stars during those nights. My Arab shawish was something of an expert and took trouble to teach me; from his instruction I learnt the Arab names for the stars that have found their way into the English language. I came to know that the bright star in Orion known in English as Betelguex came from the Arabic 'bet el aguz', the house of the old woman; that Fomalhaut was 'fam el hot', the mouth of the fish, and that Rigel, the forefoot of the giant Orion was from 'rigl', the foot. During the day I learnt something of the grumbling obdurate ways of camels and how to tie their loads, hobble and picket them. I learnt how to clear muddy water in a calabash by stirring it with the white bark of a certain tree, and I learnt, or tried to learn something of the extraordinary Arab skill of tracking in the sand.

'Two men and a woman have passed this way with a donkey an hour ago' the guide would say. 'They are followed by a dog. Here they have stopped and the older man has mounted the donkey, they are tired and move slowly.' The signs in the sand were barely visible to me, but an hour later when we caught up with the scene described, the askaris would laugh at my delight. It seemed a different and more baffling art than jungle tracking and I failed to master it.

During the hot afternoon rests I read the only book I had brought – it was James Elroy Flecker's grim play *Hassan* which seemed appropriate enough reading for the trip. As I lay swatting at the beastly camel flies I learnt by heart most of the hauntingly beautiful poetry in that play; the verses remain with me today evoking memories of hot desert days, chilly nights, and flickering dung fires of that camel patrol.

Polo was an important part of life in the Camel Corps; the Sudanese officers were very keen, they played with a dash which might perhaps have brought the whistle rather frequently to the lips of a Cowdray Park umpire, but we took the view that the rules were for guidance and should not be too zealously applied to the detriment of the fun. Our team consisted of Pat Cousens the Captain, who was a good, well-mounted and experienced player, Sagh Hassan el Atta, a big muscular man who had the eye of an eagle, Bimbashi Mohommed Osman, white haired, small and frail but a skilful player and a beautiful horseman, and myself. We played three times a week on the landing ground outside El Obeid; the surface was hard baked gravel, suitable for aeroplanes but an uninviting surface on which to fall at full gallop. Ponies cost about fifteen pounds each and there was a good supply of them.

We played teams from Khartoum and from the Western Arab Corps in Darfur but our greatest triumph was a visit to Wad Medani where we met the European team of the Gezira cotton growing syndicate in the final of a tournament. The last minute of that game was fraught with tension – with the score level, our jovial giant Hassan el Atta suddenly pounced on the ball and careered down the field; he was a formidable sight with arms and legs flapping and much daylight between his gigantic bottom and the saddle; suddenly his pony crossed its legs. Hassan somersaulted along the ground with a shattering thud; but he was up in a second and hauling his pony bodily to its feet. With a cry of 'Ya ibn humar – you son of a donkey', he leaped into the saddle again and hatless, without stirrups and spitting out teeth, bore down once again on our opponents' goal. Then, with a prodigious stroke which again swept his mount from under him, he sent the ball sailing between the posts and from a sitting position in the middle of the ground he acknowledged the shouts of the Sudanese crowd acclaiming a popular Camel Corps victory.

There was a lake called Keilak some two hundred miles south of El Obeid and in November when the migratory duck were due to arrive I decided to make a tour of the Nuba mountains, visiting outlying companies of the Camel Corps, choosing Nuba recruits and having a duck shoot to alleviate the burden of duty. A new bimbashi called Andrew Athill had recently joined the Camel Corps. He was from the Norfolk Regiment, an excellent shot and a witty companion; he also wanted to see the Nuba mountains so we set off together in my Bedford truck to combine duty with pleasure, a fairly easy feat in the Sudan Defence Force. The weather had become cool and we bowled comfortably along the sandy roads southwards for sixty or seventy miles until we entered the Nuba mountains. This was an area of isolated rocky hills, some with vast grotesquely balancing boulders, and deep caves. Perched on the sides of the hills were clusters of neat well thatched mud huts; these were Nuba villages. Big shady trees grew in profusion amongst the rocks and dotted everywhere were the bright pink flowers of a stunted bignonia, known locally as poison trees.

The Nuba are an interesting people whose negroid origins are lost in history; they had taken to the hills when the Arabs moved south and had resisted the Turk's and subsequently the Khalifa's fierce rule. They had caused trouble under the British Administration until quite recently, but after several hard fought patrols by the Camel Corps they had been brought under government control. Well armed with primitive rifles they had been difficult to dislodge from caves and rocky heights where hidden stores of grain and permanent wells allowed them to sustain long sieges.

The Nuba had their own language but dialects differed with the sub-tribes from one rocky massif to another; they mostly went naked, the young men with fine athletic figures and some of the girls with shapes which would have been the envy of a Dior model. The bodies of a few of the men and most of the women were adorned with a complicated pattern of cicatrization, designed one presumes to attract in the absence of silk and satin. Personally I thought the effect was disappointing if not repellent.

A favourite sport among the Nuba was wrestling at which they were experts. We watched an inter village contest on a cleared space at the bottom of a jebel.* It was carefully refereed by elders and excitement ran high; the sweating grunting contestants grappled in the ring, using every throw and trick known to wrestlers, striving to catch the eye of the recruiting shawish who accompanied us. Another sport was knife fighting; 'the knife' was a circular band of sharpened iron, fitting like a bracelet on the wrist; this sport was somewhat frowned upon by the authorities and although we never saw it performed the evidence of its popularity was there in many vicious scars.

We spent a few days with the Nuba and then motored south for Lake Keilak. On the way we camped in a glade of trees under a great black rock which towered above us for over a thousand feet. As our beds were being made and supper cooked Andrew and I sat in deck chairs savouring that most satisfying moment of the dusty Sudan day – a long cold whisky and soda from a tin mug. We were gazing upwards at the great rock silhouetted against the rising moon when a bent old Nuba entered the circle of firelight and squatted down to warm his hands. After a while he started to chat, asking us who we were and where we came from.

'Walahi! So you are the Bey of the Hajana,' he said smiling and nodding at the information. 'That is good. My son was in the Hajana and his son is now serving with the company in Atbara. I fought against the Hajana many years ago, they fought well and defeated us so I sent my son and my grandson to serve the Hukuma. When the Hajana pressed us hard we climbed into the jebels and fought from our caves where they could not follow but the Hajana won in the end.'

* hill or mountain.

'When you were hiding in the hills where did you find water?' I asked.

'We had wells and water storage in many of the highest jebels and baboons will show a thirsty man where to find water,' he replied. 'Even at the top of this great rock there is a well so deep that if you drop a stone you hear no sound of its fall. I do not know if it was made by man or by Allah, but when I was a boy I climbed and saw it.'

'Very well,' I said, 'bring me a guide tomorrow morning at dawn and the bimbashi and I will climb and look.'

He slowly shook his head: 'No guide will take you up there,' and then, looking rather abashed, 'it's too difficult and dangerous, and there is an afrit (spirit) at the top; the afrit is a great black and white bird who strikes men off the edge of the cliff and they die on the rocks below.'

Next morning I searched the cliff face with binoculars and into my vision sailed a pair of beautiful Vereaux eagles; as they circled and turned, hunting along the face of the precipice, the light struck their dazzling black and white plumage. It is well known that these magnificent birds will attack a man who climbs too close to their eyrie; they will also dislodge animals from a cliff face in order to feed on the shattered carcase below. The mystery of the evil spirit was solved, but the mystery of the bottomless well remains, probably to this day.

We motored on towards the south and as we approached Lake Keilak in the evening, swiftly moving smudges in the sky told us that the migratory duck were there. Leaving camp to be made but taking our orderlies we walked down to the lake and waded in; the duck swirled above us like bees. We made for clumps of reeds a few hundred yards apart and started to shoot. The birds came over as fast as we could load and we soon had a bag of european teal, gargeny, widgeon, shoveler, and pintail, lying in the reeds around us. Before it was too dark I stopped shooting, and began to wade around picking up duck. Seeing a movement near me in the reeds which I took to be a wounded duck, I waded over and plunged my arm in, to seize a cold writhing object. The next moment something like the Loch Ness monster reared up and I sat back into the lake to watch a twelve foot python wriggle away through the reeds. Andrew was delighted with the incident. 'No presence of mind – you should have shot it,' he said. 'We could have had python steak, and made at least six ladies handbags.'

'I wasn't thinking of ladies handbags at that moment, my gun was at the bottom of the lake, and anyway I would rather eat duck.'

As we sat by the fire that evening stripping and oiling my drowned gun, we heard my orderly, amidst much laughter, enacting the whole comic scene to the circle of brown faces on which the cook's fire flickered.

We shot again at first light and then motored thirty miles to the town of Kadugli where I had an outpost to inspect and people to see. We distributed duck amongst the Sudanese officers and government officials and having performed a few duties set off south again next morning, heading for the Bahr el Ghazal river a hundred and fifty miles away.

The rough road wound interminably on through flat featureless bush country; at midday the heat was abominable; a following wind enveloped us in clouds of red dust every time we slowed down to negotiate a washout, and it was not until after dark that we arrived at the District Commissioner's little house at Bentiu on the river.

After hot baths and a comfortable night we rose early and prepared for the road again. Before we left our host said, 'There are some Fellata from West Africa catching crocodiles somewhere along the river; it might interest you to visit them and, since you are an honorary game warden, see that they are not up to mischief with the game laws.' We thanked him and drove away to the west over roads even rougher than the day before. After progressing very slowly for several hours we came in sight of the Bahr el Arab river on our left and saw a lorry parked under some trees. We went to investigate and found the party of Fellata mentioned by the District Commissioner; they were skinning several crocodiles and the stench was somewhat unsavoury but they were a friendly lot, and invited us to have coffee. A few spoke Arabic, but amongst themselves they conversed in Hausa. As we drank minted bitter coffee from tiny cups they told us about their activities. They were Muslim pilgrims from Nigeria travelling to Mecca, a journey which would take a year or even two.

On the way they were earning money by their own particular skill of crocodile catching; the skins would be sold in Omdurman and the party, richer by several hundred pounds would proceed another step forward towards that great moment in their lives – the sight of the holy city. Would we care to join them in a hunt tonight before the moon rose? In the meantime here was a present of some meat, carefully cut from the tail of a tender young croc. We thanked them and moved well upwind to a clump of trees on the river bank where our camp was set out in shade and comfort. We lay and read through the afternoon and at dusk walked over to the Fellata camp to watch preparations for the hunt. There were two fifteen foot dugout canoes pulled up on the bank and in each was a harpoon, an axe, a torch and a coil of rope. The harpoon was three feet long with a barb two inches wide; at its base was a bundle of 'ambatch', sticks to act as a float, and this was attached to the harpoon by a wire rope fifteen feet long wound loosely round the shaft. When it was dark the canoes were launched; Andrew and I each boarded one, sitting amidships in an inch of stinking bilge; the paddler sat at the back and a man knelt in the bows armed with the harpoon and a torch. Andrew's canoe disappeared upstream into the darkness and mine floated silently down. It was a pitch black night and as the powerful but noiseless paddle strokes propelled us forward, the man in the bows swung his torch beam over the water. After going for twenty minutes two bright red eyes appeared thirty yards ahead, just breaking surface in the beam of light; the man in the bows softly clicked his tongue and the canoe surged forward. The eyes ahead remained steadily in the beam as the distance closed. Holding his torch well forward the harpooner slowly raised the weapon above his head and remained motionless. Two more strokes from the paddler and the canoe glided on unaided. Ten yards, five yards, and still the eyes burnt like coals in the beam; at a yard's range the harpooner struck down, driving the barb into the soft neck skin of the croc. Then all was pandemonium; there was a moaning grunt and a swirl of water, the canoe rocked perilously and the croc departed with the telltale ambatch float unwinding behind him in the light of the torch; the float skittered along the surface of the water, coming to rest fifty yards away; quietly the canoe crept up again and slipping a noose over the float, we made for the bank; then silently the three of us stepped ashore and the tug of war began; the croc played bravely but was soon lashing and grunting on the beach until a blow on the head with the axe finished the matter.

Leaving the carcase on the bank we moved on down river killing several more crocs, although a number evaded us by sinking silently into the depths as the canoe approached. At one point the river broadened into quite a large lake; the harpooner swung his torch around but no eyes were visible. He put down his torch and harpoon and cupping his hands produced a series of eerie grunts and bellows; these were immediately answered from different directions and when he shone the torch again several pairs of eyes were lit up. It was possible to gauge the size of the quarry by the distance between the eyes and if there was any choice we chose those which were widest apart. After a couple of hours

The 7th Queen's Own Hussars win the inter-regimental Polo Tournament, 1958. *From left to right*: Captain Billy Richardson, Captain Mike Fraser, Major Hilary Hook, Lt. Colonel Tim Lewellen Palmer.

63lb Nile perch. Namasagli, Uganda, 1968.

Partners consulting: H.H. with Major Digby Tatham Warter, D.S.O. and (*below*) Hook and Tatham Warter Safaris camped in a remote part of the Serengeti. The guest tents are in the background.

A cheetah in the Mara and (*below*) a record head, photographed by Jonny
Baxendale in Meru National Park, 1964.

The perpetual snow peaks on Mount Kenya, photographed from Kiserian, and (*below*) On the lawn at Kiserian in the late '70s. Nyeri hill in the background.

we had a bag of six crocs, two small ones in the canoe on which I sat to keep my bottom out of the bloodstained bilge, and four large ones, each over ten feet long, left on the bank to be collected later. Then the moon rose and the Fellata pronounced further hunting useless; we paddled back up stream to camp, discussing the evening's sport and I learned something of crocodiles and their ways. I noticed that the jaws of the crocs in the boat were tied with twine; the Fellata told me that this completely pacifies a croc and renders him harmless; it was perhaps as well because on the way back my cushion started to grunt and heave until it received another quietening blow on the head.

Andrew was waiting in the Fellata camp and we walked back to bed under the moon, swapping stories of much the same adventures.

For a few days we moved north towards El Obeid, using the network of roads and tracks through the Nuba mountains to visit outposts and British and Sudanese officials; we distributed the duck from our ice boxes and on the last day drove into El Obeid after a long dusty journey from Dilling.

Duties and recreation continued in and around El Obeid pleasantly enough; musketry competitions, manoeuvres, tours of inspection and polo tournaments followed one another in the sparkling winter weather. My Arabic improved somewhat and just before Christmas I flew to Khartoum to confront Abboud Bey again in an oral exam which I passed.

In the spring of 1952 I was unexpectedly transferred to Darfur as second in Command of the Western Arab Corps. I was sad to leave the Camel Corps but very much welcomed a chance to see the west of this huge country.

Darfur province has an interesting recent history. It covers an area the size of France, the north being mostly desert and the south turning to scrub and thorn forest; to the south-west the Mara mountains rise in a 10,000 ft massif. Before the Mahdi's rebellion Rudolf von Slatin Pasha had been appointed by General Gordon as the Governor of Darfur, but he was captured and made a prisoner and slave of the Khalifa for twelve years, until he finally escaped to write that great saga *Fire and Sword in the Sudan*. After the reconquest of the Sudan in 1898 the government, with enough on its plate, allowed Darfur to remain semi-independent under their Sultan, paying a token yearly tribute in recognition that the province had once been part of the Sudan. When

Turkey entered the 1914 war on the side of Germany she made every possible effort to raise sympathetic revolts in Muslim countries living under British rule. Letters were intercepted between Turkey and the Darfur Sultan, Ali Dinar, proving that arms were being smuggled into the country by the Sunusi in the north. Sultan Ali Dinar then experienced a lapse from good manners, and instead of paying the trifling annual tribute, he sent to the Sudan government a deputation armed with spears and throwing sticks on which were inscribed ruderies and threats; these arrived with a covering letter addressed to 'The Governor of Hell and Flames.' It was a declaration of hostility, supported by Turkey and could not be ignored. The challenge was accepted and in 1916 Lieutenant-Colonel Kelly set out from El Obeid for the three hundred and fifty mile approach march to El Fasher across burning desert; his force consisted of two thousand Egyptian and Sudanese troops including the Camel Corps. Overhead flew Lieutenant (later Marshal of the Royal Air Force Sir John) Slessor to report the enemies' movements. The going was extremely heavy and the summer heat intense but after many long marches Kelly's force encountered Ali Dinar's army of four thousand men drawn up twelve miles north of El Fasher; Ali Dinar's warriors attacked in a wild Dervish rush of fanatical bravery; Kelly's troops remained steady and after a short fierce struggle the battle was over, leaving many enemy dead and allowing the advance on the 'palace' in Fasher to continue. Amongst the few casualties on the winning side was Lieutenant Slessor who, while flying over the palace received a bullet in his bottom from a 'dead eye' sniper who had never before seen an aeroplane. Sultan Ali Dinar retreated to the mountains in the south, shadowed by Major Huddleston (later Major-General Huddleston, Governor General of the Sudan) with a company of the Camel Corps. Huddleston's orders were to watch and contain the remainder of Ali Dinar's army until another force could be gathered together to deal with it. With such vast distances involved, things moved slowly. Huddleston was an impetuous dashing officer, he waited several months and then against orders, and dryly remarking 'this is either a DSO or the sack', he struck. Leading his company of Camel Corps in a dawn attack he dispersed the enemy, killing the Sultan and capturing a quantity of arms, ammunition and ivory, together with large herds of cattle. Peace descended on Darfur which then came under the Sudan government from Khartoum. Huddleston got his DSO.

We arrived at El Fasher by air to be met by the Commander of the Western Arab Corps, Miralai Powell Bey, a large jovial officer of the Royal Marines who had served some years before as a bimbashi in the Camel Corps. After looking at our little house perched on a hill a mile out of the town we lunched with the Powells and proceeded to settle in. That evening at a drinks party I met the other Sudanese and British officers and officials in El Fasher. To my delight I met again Mohammed Osman who had been the best player in our Camel Corps polo team; he was now a Kaimakam and the Senior Sudanese officer in the Western Arab Corps; a man of particular charm, good humour and wisdom, he would be of enormous help in advice on Sudanese matters, also a great asset on the polo ground.

El Fasher was the capital town of the province; it owed its existence to a lake or fula which had permanent water, becoming shallow at the end of the dry season but filling again in the rains. The town, which consisted of Arab houses and shops and one Greek grocer to supply all our needs, was on the north of the fula; government buildings, the Western Arab Corps fort and Ali Dinar's palace were to the south, together with the officers' and officials' bungalows. Just outside the town were the polo grounds and air field. Ali Dinar's palace was lived in by Governor Henderson and his family; it was by no means a palace by Arabian Nights' standards but a large rambling wooden structure built haphazardly of great beams and tree trunks; a few hundred yards away a stark dead tree cut the skyline serving to remind many of the older inhabitants of El Fasher of the grisly corpses which had swayed from its branches when Sultan Ali Dinar was out of humour. Near the tree, perhaps in its erstwhile shade, was a patch of ground where slaves used to be buried up to their waists in the sand to recuperate from castration. He had been a naughty man, the Sultan, hated and feared by most of his Arab tribes.

Several companies of troops were stationed in the fort and there was a mounted infantry company at Nyala a hundred and twenty miles to the south. This was commanded by Bimbashi John Clarke, a tall Life Guardsman. The askaris, who were recruited from Darfur province, were Baggara Arabs; the word Baggara means 'cattle owners', and it includes a number of different tribes. They had been the mainstay of the Khalifa's army in his many campaigns and at the battle of Omdurman, where they had distinguished themselves greatly by their reckless courage.

Every Baggara could ride and the tribes possessed thousands of horses; my old cook trotted up to the bungalow on his broken-down horse every morning. When not riding horses they rode bulls and a Baggara family on the move was an entertaining sight; the men rode in front each carrying an eight foot Dervish spear, and behind followed the women and children piled with their belongings on slow plodding bulls.

For the first few weeks in El Fasher I went through the usual process of taking over a new job and getting to know the personalities involved. I chose new polo ponies, employed new servants and ord-erlies, and then set out to pay a visit to John Clarke's mounted com-pany in Nyala.

The long sandy drive south was fairly uneventful; occasional herds of gazelle appeared in the distance and the further south we went the more wooded the country became. In the heat of the day my truck de-veloped petrol trouble and for several miles we progressed in jerks, my driver assuring me that all would be well when he found what he sought. I was somewhat puzzled but finally we came to a patch of culti-vation, the driver jumped out, and returned a moment later with half a water melon which, with invocations to Allah, he squashed down on the carburettor; we then proceeded with no further trouble, my driver expounding to me on various other magic virtues of the water melon. I later learnt that this bit of Arab ingenuity was normal practice in Darfur for overheating engines.

Nyala was a pretty little town with shady trees; apart from John Clarke and his mounted company there was a British District Com-missioner, Jack Wilson and Ann, his wife; a veterinary officer and some Sudanese officials; enough in fact for an occasional dinner party without much variation. I drew up at John's bungalow in the late after-noon and after a bath and a rest went out with him to look at the various animals he kept. Amongst other creatures were a tame cheetah, a pangolin, and a large cock ostrich, with a baleful look in its eye. I was inclined to give it a rather wide berth, but John gave an order and one of his askaris appeared; two men held the ostrich while the askari leaped nimbly on top, folding the wings over his legs; the bird was then released and set off at great speed into the distance, dodging and swerv-ing between the trees in a manner which would have unseated most rough riders. The mounted askari's only aid was a thin 'Charlie Cha-plin' walking stick which he crooked round the bird's neck to control its air supply. It was a skilful performance and an extremely comic sight which I photographed and subsequently sent to my regiment as a

Christmas card, with the comment that I had a hundred and twenty such mounted men for use on lightning raids.

Next morning John took me round his company and the horse lines; everything shone with Household Brigade efficiency, the ponies were sleek and fat, the saddlery in perfect condition, and the men spotlessly turned out. 'I will show you the trick ride tomorrow,' he said as we returned to lunch, an afternoon rest, and a game of polo in the evening.

That night we dined with Jack and Ann Wilson, a delightful couple. He had been one of the best oarsmen of his time at Cambridge, from where he had joined the Sudan Political Service and become something of a legend. During the war he had served in a remote area of Nuer country in the Upper Nile where a half-mad litigant in a 'cattle case' drove a spear through him; he was carried on a long journey to the river where he lay waiting for a steamer or, as he put it, the after life. Eventually a steamer arrived belonging to the Egyptian Irrigation department but on hearing that there had been a spot of bother it immediately raised all steam and bolted over the horizon in panic, leaving Jack to wait the arrival of better Samaritans. Shortly afterwards Jack and another member of the Sudan Political Service, Ran Laurie, had won the Gold Medal for coxwainless pairs at the first Olympic games after the war – a fairly remarkable story which Jack told with humour and modesty.

In John Clarke's company office I read the official report of the Nyala rising in the 1920s in which District Commisioner McNeill, and Bimbashi Chown had been killed. It appears that a fanatical religious leader had appeared in Southern Darfur, claiming to be Jesus, the Prophet of God. It may seem strange that a Muslim should make such a claim, but it is part of Sunni orthodox belief that one day a Mahdi will appear who will be the prerunner to the Second Coming of Jesus and make way for the Millennium, striking down all who are not of 'the true faith'.

McNeil in Nyala had only forty armed police at the time and not realising the urgency of the matter merely sent a report on the troublesome prophet's activities with a comment that he thought he could contain the situation. The Governor in El Fasher suspected it might be a bit more serious and despatched sixty mounted infantry. Then an urgent second letter came saying that Nyala was about to be attacked by five or six thousand fanatics. Bimbashi Chown, the only British officer available in El Fasher, hastily put a second party of mounted infantry together and out-stripping them caught up with the first;

urging them forward, taking a fresh horse, he again outstripped the party on his hundred and twenty mile ride, arriving an hour before the fanatical attack started. McNeil and Chown died fighting and the situation became critical. Only the gallantry of a Sudanese officer of the mounted infantry and the cupidity of the fanatics saved the day. Instead of completing the annihilation of the enemy their holy purpose was diverted by the thought of loot and they turned their attention to the bazaar (a situation not altogether uncommon in war).

This brief respite gave the only Sudanese officer left a chance to rally his men and reoccupy the government buildings; in the fierce fighting which ensued the false prophet was wounded. This lessened the zeal of his followers who had been given to understand that government bullets would turn to water. As the second party of mounted infantry arrived on the scene the tide of the battle began to turn and eventually the situation came under control. While these events were taking place the Camel Corps in El Obeid had been alerted; they trotted into El Fasher ten days later having force marched for over four hundred miles, but by then order had been restored in the province.

During this crisis there had occurred some strange and inexplicable events; the deaths of Chown and McNeill and certain other incidents had been accurately reported by rumour in the 'suk' (market) of El Fasher long before tidings could have been brought by human agency. Officials were puzzled by this but to the Fur the explanation was simple, the news was brought by 'were', hyenas galloping through the night – a strong belief in Darfur.

Early next morning we went to watch the trick ride practising on the open plain near the horse lines. A display was to be given at the Rizegat horse show later in the year at which the Nazir (head) of the tribe and thousands of horsemen would parade before the Governor of the Province, Bill Henderson, and the Commander of the Western Arab Corps. I had seen many military trick rides before, including an excellent one produced by my own Indian Cavalry regiment; but John's mounted infantry display exceeded them all in skill and daring; in fact it almost matched the brilliant Cossack show I had once seen at Olympia. The riders careered past us at full gallop picking up coloured handkerchiefs from the ground, and performing circus acrobatics in the saddle; it was a splendid exhibition of dash and horsemanship.

After a few days at Nyala I drove north again for forty miles and then turned west towards Jebel Marra the great mountain massif of

Western Darfur which was ever visible against the sky. The country soon became more forested and the rough road wound upwards crossing innumerable dry watercourses; once a pair of cheetah galloped across the road ahead, disappearing into the long grass; more exotic birds were to be seen and baboons barked at us from the tree tops. We bumped on for hour after hour, climbing into the dark hills ahead which revealed landscapes of increasing beauty; below us the plains stretched away in a shimmering heat haze but as we mounted higher the air became clearer and cooler. At dusk we came to a tiny rest house which was our destination for the night. I sat on the verandah watching the moon rise over the distant peaks while supper was cooked and an aged caretaker lit a much needed fire inside.

Next morning I set out at dawn with an askari and after several hours climbing reached a grassy plateau which was the summit of Jebel Marra, ten thousand feet high. We rested for an hour admiring the view and watching the fantailed ravens and swifts circle below us, then we began the slow descent, so often a more testing exercise than a plodding uphill climb; every so often I had to sit down and rest my wobbling knees, but the views were dramatic and my lungs were filled with cool elixir. During one rest my orderly put out his hand for my field glasses. After studying the opposite hillside for a moment he handed them back and pointed; moving through the trees across the valley was a magnificent bull kudu; as he walked into patches of sunshine the light struck on his white flank stripes and the ivory tips of his great horns. He was going obliquely away from us and after a few moments I put my fingers in my mouth and whistled, a trick I had learnt whilst hunting in India; he stopped for a moment and turning, pointed his great bell ears towards us, then with consummate grace bounded slowly up the hillside and away out of sight. That night I slept well after a supper of freshly picked mushrooms and a roast guinea fowl which I had shot the day before. When dawn came, touching the surrounding peaks with light, we turned our backs on Jebel Marra and motored down hill in the chill morning air.

After driving for an hour we forked away to the west along the base of the mountain, heading for the town of Zalingei. The country was heavily wooded and the track again led us up and down over dry water courses which had cut into the mountain side. We arrived at Zalingi at about five o'clock and after settling into the rest house, I went round to see the District Commissioner, Sheik Ali Abu Sinn, a middle-aged man of great charm and intelligence who had joined the administration many years before, when his father had been paramount Sheik of the Shukria tribe.* He welcomed me with the usual Arab courtesy and gave me a basket of fruit from his garden to which I was able to return a brace of guinea fowl. That night I dined with Sheik Ali on his verandah under the soft light of a hissing lamp around which a thousand insects buzzed. He was a delightful and interesting host and although he did not drink himself he saw to it that my glass was never empty; the conversation ranged widely but it was mostly about his district that I sought information and Sheik Ali provided this with great erudition and humour; he talked of the Fur people, their history and ethnic origin and their attitude to Islam which they had adopted from the Arabs many years before, and which as a conventional Muslim caused him some amusement. He also told me much about Boustead Bey his fabulous predecessor† who had ruled the district for many years, maintaining an unbeaten polo team which consisted of the Emir's brother, the local Health assistant, Boustead Bey and his cook.

Next morning I had a walk round the small township of Zalingei and a look at the Beau Geste style fort, then I took my leave of Sheik Ali, crossed the Wadi Azum, a sandy three hundred yard wide river which in the rains becomes a raging impassable torrent, and headed northwest through forests of large haraz trees for the outpost of El Geneina on the western boundary of the Sudan. A hundred and fifty mile drive over a sandy track brought me to the little fort and comfortable bungalow of the British DC. At my destination I learnt that we had an invitation to lunch next day with the French officer in charge of the outpost at Adré just over the border of what was then French Equatorial Africa. It turned out to be an enjoyable affair; a guard of colourfully arrayed black French soldiers met us at the border post. I was formally invited to inspect them and then with a flourish of bugles we drove to the Capitaine's bungalow for a superb lunch and a variety of wines, returning in the heat of the afternoon, torpid and drowsy. After an early morning ride round El Geneina next day I headed east for the long drive back to El Fasher, spending a night in the bush and arriving just in time for polo in the afternoon of the next day.

Both the Fur and the Baggara Arabs are very keen hunters; they pursue

---

* He subsequently went on to become Governor of Darfur succeeding the last British Governor there and then he died suddenly of heart trouble – a very sad loss to his country and his friends.
† Colonel Hugh Boutstead who wrote *The Wind of Morning*.

any sporting activity particularly if it is mounted, with enormous verve and dash; the English hunting cry of 'tally-ho' is said to have returned to England with the crusaders, adopted from the Arabic 'tala – come on', when quarry is sighted. Whenever possible sport plays an important part in the Arab way of life.

Many of the inhabitants of El Fasher had dogs and in the rains they used to wander out into the surrounding scrub armed with throwing sticks to knock over any wild thing that moved; these throwing sticks (known as 'trombash') were a relic of prehistory and the old conventional weapon of the Fur people. They were shaped like an Australian boomerang but had no pretensions such as returning to the hand of the thrower; they were however incredibly accurate in the hands of an expert, twirling through the air just above the ground with a low trajectory they could strike down hares, guinea fowl and even gazelle, giving the hunting dogs time to move in. I decided to capitalise on this local sport and get the matter somewhat better organised and so the Fasher Hunt was inaugurated.

Every man in Fasher who had a dog was invited to join, and on Sunday mornings during the rainy season Bimbashi Michael Clarke used to set off at dawn for the suk in a lorry to collect the pack; on arrival he blew a few sharp twangs on his hunting horn. Men armed with throwing sticks would then tumble out of the mud houses and climb on to the lorry with their dogs snarling and snapping in a happy turmoil; an askari was posted at the tailboard to see that no dogless but aspiring sportsmen climbed in; but in the confusion it was almost impossible to prevent small boys from clambering onto the bonnet and the roof, or hiding in corners. The pandemonium only died when the lorry was fully loaded, and arguments over dog ownership had been settled. The party then drove out over the sandy plain to some pre-arranged tree eight or ten miles from the town, where the horses had been sent and Sudanese officers had assembled for the sport. A long line of men and dogs was formed and we advanced through the scrub with the horsemen behind and Michael Clarke in the centre with his hunting horn.

If guinea fowl or partridge were flushed they had to fly the gauntlet of a shower of throwing sticks, but if four footed game was put up such as hares, jackals, wild cats or gazelle, the dogs raced after the quarry with wild yelps taking their chance through a hail of trombash, while Michael Clarke, bending low over the saddle and 'doubling' his horn would gallop forward at full speed putting the dogs on to the quarry.

After the first salvo of throwing sticks had been discharged it was comparatively safe for the rest of the mounted hunt to follow, although the young Sudanese officers took no such precautions; they raced at top speed through the scrub regardless of flying sticks, water courses, boulders, and blind going. We seldom killed anything but it was all very much enjoyed. When the sun got high we used to retire to a tree and have an enormous Sudanese breakfast which had come out on the back of my truck, and then return to Fasher for a bath and a drink. On some Sundays we organised paper chases and again the pace was fast and furious with many spills and much competitive rivalry. Amongst some who will remember those pleasant mornings is General Jaffer Numeiri, until recently President of the Sudan. He was then a dashing young Mulazim in the Western Arab Corps and was usually at or near the head of the hunt.

One day a young Arab askari came to my office in the fort with a rather unusual request. His uncle was a Sheik who lived in the bush about a hundred miles to the south and who had just returned from Mecca to find that his herd of valuable camels was being depleted by lions. Would I bring my rifle and shoot one and at the same time appraise the beautiful carpets he had brought back from his pilgrimage.

Once more I experienced the feelings of happy hypocrisy which I had known in the south, and my resolution never again to shoot big game in the name of sport was assailed by doubts; it was my duty to rid the old boy of his persecutors and if that involved an exciting little hunt, so much the better. 'Yes, certainly I will shoot one of these troublesome lions, come to me on Saturday morning and you can guide me to your rich and generous uncle who will no doubt reward you.' The boy departed smiling.

We were delayed starting on Saturday and did not arrive at the Sheik's house until after the evening star had set; this star is known in Arabic as the negmat ed deif, the guest star; after it has gone down, an Arab host is under no obligation to provide food for an unexpected guest, only accommodation; however, enormous bowls of rice and liver were pressed upon me by my elderly host and I was made comfortable in his grass guest house. Next morning I got up at dawn to prepare for the hunt, but where were the trackers? Where were the beaters? And above all where were the lions? My host came to me with morning greetings, his jutting henna-dyed beard proclaiming his recent sacred pilgrimage. I put these questions to him.

'Inshallah, the hunt is tonight,' he said. 'The lions live far far away in dense bush but tonight they will drink at my waterhole, and you will shoot one from a tree; today I will prepare everything while you, my guest, will rest and see my carpets.'

This was boring news; I had no wish to hang about all day, thwarted of the hunt I had visualized, neither did I want to sit up all night in a tree to murder a thirsty lion; it sounded a little too like the game which visiting 'sportsmen' paid large sums of money to play. But I was trapped and would have to make the best of it.

I accepted an invitation to a midday meal and spent the morning with a book; the old Sheik appeared again later and took me off to see his horses and carpets both of which were of high quality. There followed an enormous feast of mutton and rice in the Sheik's house, then a good sleep. At three o'clock guides arrived and we set off on camels jogging through thick thorn scrub and sparse woodland for an hour; at last we came to a grove of haraz trees in a cleared depression covering a few acres; in the middle of the area was a well from which water was drawn by an ancient pulley and poured into a series of neat round mud pans where the camels drank; thorn bushes had been put over all the pans but one, twenty yards from which was a spreading haraz tree with a platform in the branches. I hoisted myself on to the platform and the camels trotted away leaving me to my rather unwanted vigil. It proved however to be more interesting than I had anticipated. In the late afternoon many different kinds of birds came to drink; at first a swarm of Sudan dioch appeared in a little black cloud, thousands crowded into the trees around me twittering, their droppings falling like rain; when they had drunk and departed a noisy flock of starlings came to drink and roost in my tree, then some guinea fowl came warily out of the bush and having visited the pan proceeded to dust themselves and chase one another in circles below me; as the light faded a flight of Lichtenstein's sand grouse flew in, stopping for a brief moment to drink and then clatter away into the gathering dusk.

Darkness came on quickly, but it was a starry night and when the bright moon rose it cast shadows across the sand and glittered in the water hole. I strained my ears to hear the noises of the night above the singing cicadas; fireflies began to dance among the trees; a striped hyena shuffled down to the water and began to lap, peering guiltily around. The light improved with the rising moon and it soon became bitterly cold; I wished I had brought another blanket, but at least I had not forgotten to bring some inner warmth and feeling for my flask I matched the hyena's lapping with my own discreet gurgle. During the next few hours a pair of honey badgers came to the water, squeaking and grunting as they trotted along side by side; I watched through my field glasses as they played on the moonlit sand, recalling that although they make affectionate and attractive pets, these little creatures, the size of an English badger, are perhaps the most feared animal in the African bush; they will make unprovoked attacks on men or game up to the size of buffalo and their courage is matchless. When they had gone I must have dozed off, for the next thing I knew was that a series of unearthly yells penetrated my mist of sleep; by now the moon was high and from under the trees trotted a pair of jackals stopping every few seconds to peer behind them and utter their querulous cry. It was an unusual noise, obsequious and fawning, but their behaviour told me what to expect next and I slipped off my safety-catch; a moment later a lioness was crouching at the water lapping slowly. Her great tongue threw ripples of silver across the pool and her black tail tip twitched in the sand behind; I raised my rifle and for minutes covered her hoping that she would be followed by her mate. Then, as she rose to go, I fired; it was an easy shot and the poor beast fell forward on to the sand. My mission was completed and my obligation as a guest fulfilled but it was with feelings near to disgust that I reached for my flask again and then settled down for the rest of an uncomfortable night of disturbed dreams.

I awoke at dawn to a far away cry of 'Asad fi maiyit wa madrub – Is the lion dead or wounded?' 'Maiyit' I shouted back, 'Asad maiyit, halas', and a short while later the camels trotted into view, their riders chattering excitedly.

I climbed stiff and cold out of the branches to inspect the victim of my atrocity and tried to join in the general rejoicings, around the old dead lioness. 'Mabruk,' they shouted; 'Mabruk ya sath el Bey'; 'Walahi, she stole my best camel Bijli in Ramadan'; 'See the scar where Abdul Rahman's spear struck her last year'; 'Ya salaam, she will have no more of my goats.'

They drew their arm knives and squatted down to remove the skin while my orderly brewed a mug of tea, and I listened to a saga of lion hunts and the wonderful properties to be derived from a dead lion. The fat would cure rheumatism and a thousand other complaints, the ground down whiskers taken in a brew of coffee would turn white hairs black; claws and hair from the tip of the tail had magic properties.

We trotted back towards the village through the chill morning air, savouring the rising sun on our backs and stopping to shoot some guinea fowl for my host.

I presented the old man with the lion skin and listened to more tales of its late occupant's iniquities, also a great deal of congratulations and gratitude from the assembled village. As I was packing the truck to leave, the old Sheik signalled to one of his minions who came forward with a rolled up carpet which he piled on to the top of my baggage, then the usual mutual courtesies were exchanged in Arabic. 'It is still early – stay.'

'We ask leave to go – the world is business.'

'God willing you shall return in safety.'

'We have been much honoured.'

'Then go in peace, go with peace and God protect you.'

At last I drove away, pressing on in haste to be in time for polo in Fasher. That evening I unrolled the carpet in my bungalow. It was black with dirt and there was almost no colour or pattern visible. I thought no more about it; however when I returned from parade next day my orderly was standing beside a bucket of soapy water and there, drying in the sunshine was one of the most lovely and colourful Persian rugs I had ever seen. The 'pay off' for murder most foul.

The winter weather at El Fasher was delightful, the mornings were clear and sparkling with dew on the desert's face; the air was dry and cool with the faint tang of the night's camel dung fires; horses were lively on the early morning rides and migrating duck were flying in from the north to the surrounding lakes. The days were sunny and warm ending in colourful sunsets and cold nights with the sky a dazzle of stars. As Christmas approached, DCs from outlying stations and visiting polo teams appeared; a race meeting was organised and picnic shoots were arranged for duck and sand grouse.

The big Christmas party was by tradition given by the governor in Ali Dinar's palace on Christmas night, where the entire Christian community of the town and most of the province gathered in carnival spirits to romp and skylark, to the astonishment of their dignified Muslim brothers. It was a good party and the test of the evening was the 'trial for the blue shirt'. This had been started many years before by bored officers of the Western Arab Corps. The qualifications for a blue shirt were threefold; the candidate had to have shot a Darfur lion (in more heroic circumstances than mine I think); to have acquired a local

polo handicap of over four goals, and finally, at midnight on
Christmas Day to swarm up the centre pole of Ali Dinar's assembly
room, over the main rafters and slide or fall down the far side. Gus
Powell and his charming wife came to drinks before we went on to the
party. 'I take it you are going to try the pole tonight,' he said. 'You'll
never make it; the Governor has had the thing polished like glass and is
laying odds against anyone getting up it – however I have backed you
for rather more than I would care to lose, so please don't get tight
before midnight and here's a little something which might help us
both.' Surreptitiously and without his wife seeing he pressed a little
ball of resin into my hand and helped himself confidently to another
drink.

It was a merry evening with corks popping, and although I do not
remember consciously observing all of Gus Powell's admonitions,
when midnight sounded I advanced well-resined upon the glistening
pole, having arranged to back myself handsomely. Thanks entirely to
Gus Powell's 'foresight' the climb proved perfectly simple and after
negotiating the rafters I landed at the feet of my benefactor who was
delightedly stuffing notes into his pocket. The party broke up as the
eastern sky lightened, and I returned to my bungalow to change into a
blue shirt and drive out to a meet of the Fasher hounds.

The early part of the New Year was spent in manoeuvres and
patrols; I travelled over Darfur visiting companies and watching exer-
cises conducted in delightful weather and usually in the proximity of a
good duck shoot. Gus Powell went on three months' leave to England
during which time the command of the Western Arab Corps devolved
on me.

The big forthcoming event was the horse show in southern Darfur
where the Rizegat tribe led by their Nazir would parade past Governor
Henderson. For this we drove south for two hundred and fifty miles
through Nyala and on to the southeast entering a country of large
sparse trees and scrub with occasional fulas where duck swarmed. We
finally arrived at the mud-hutted village of Sibdu on the edge of a large
fula surrounded by trees where grass houses had been made for our accommodation. John Clarke had already arrived with his mounted
infantry company and his trick ride; presents from the Nazir of milk,
chickens and eggs were in every guest house. We had an evening duck
shoot and dined under the stars together with a number of visitors
from Khartoum; drums from surrounding encampments beat late into
the night and the camp fires of the gathering tribesmen flickered in the

distance. Next morning the Governor and I with a mounted escort rode out preceded by the great bandera (flag) of the Western Arab Corps, a purple background with an upright crusader's sword.*

We rode to a mound a few miles from the village where we halted with our escort. Clouds of dust rose from the trees half a mile away where the tribe was mustering and then came the throb of the 'nahas', the copper war drums which had rung out before the Kalifa's battles to summon the faithful to die; the drumming came in a deep resonant boom above the roar of thousands of Rizegat warriors. At last the gathering moved out of the trees in a column of horsemen four abreast. In the front of the column, side by side on caparisoned camels, came two black giants beating the enormous copper drums which hung on either side of their mounts; behind them rode Nazir Ibrahim Musa, the head of the tribe, mounted on a grey horse. He was a big man, very dark with a white beard and piercing wide-set eyes; as he passed in his scarlet robes of honour he raised his sword in salute to the Governor and then left the column and came up to us. Behind the Nazir came his bodyguard of fifty mounted men clad in crusader chain mail and each carrying the shovel-headed spear of the Baggara which they raised and shook as they passed by. After the bodyguard came the mounted warriors of the tribe in phalanxes of four, through swirling dust, each man shaking his spear with a savage shout and making his horse rear and cavort against the 'thorn' bit. For what seemed like hours they came, dressed in white gibbas and turbans, their knives strapped to their upper arms, white teeth gleaming in black faces as they shouted. It was an impressive sight and served to remind one that the fighting flower of the Khalifa's army had been drawn from these fierce Baggara horsemen of Darfur. After six or seven thousand men had passed by the Governor, the column came to an end and John Clarke and I rode round the encampments chatting with the horse dealers and choosing remounts for the mounted company. It was then I had my first experience of the Darfur habit of 'daffering'. As we were riding over the plain, three horsemen appeared in the distance galloping abreast towards us at full speed their spears held high. 'This is a daffer,' said John. 'We just sit tight and do nothing but return their greetings.' We reined in and sat waiting as the horsemen bore down upon us with wild cries; just when a nasty collision seemed certain the horsemen

---

* This was the badge of the Western Arab Corps. It was taken from the traditional Dervish pattern sword which allegedly came to the Sudan from captured crusader's swords shaped in the form of a cross.

hooked up their mounts in a cloud of dust a few yards from us, and shaking their spears shouted greetings. 'Ahlan wa sahlan,' they shouted in welcome, 'shid a haylak ya Gharbiya – Greetings to the Western Arab Corps.'

'Allah yusallum ak wa yubarik fik,' we replied, 'God save you and bless you.' Out of the corner of my eye I saw another cloud of dust approaching at full gallop, sunlight gleaming on the spear heads, white robes flying, to come to an abrupt halt of rearing heads and waving hooves a spear's length away. Perhaps ones' nerve improved with each performance; anyway it was apparent that our hosts were enjoying themselves.

In the evening John put on his trick ride which produced loud Arab applause, particularly when a rider's girth broke decanting him at full gallop on top of the handkerchief he was reaching to pick up from the ground – quick as a flash another rider appeared at full gallop and sweeping the running man on to the back of his saddle careered in to the distance picking up handkerchiefs while he shouted his garbled war cry. The antics of the pantomime 'donkey' which concealed two askaris were perhaps the highlight of the show, they were unequivocal and coarse and appealed greatly to the Rabelaisian Arab sense of humour.

Feasts were given, robes of honour were presented and after another duck shoot the party eventually broke up and we returned to El Fasher.

Spring turned to summer and the heat increased. Gus Powell returned from leave, and at last came the joyous day when my wife and I boarded an aeroplane for Khartoum, and from there flew to Kenya for three months' holiday in that lovely land. The Mau Mau rising was in full swing and wherever we stayed nasty incidents were being reported; loyal servants were under terrible pressure from threats and atrocities committed on their families, cattle were being slashed and gangs of terrorists raided farms from the security of the Aberdare and Mount Kenya forests. The land was unhappy and all white men went armed; however it seemed to me that there was no trace of panic, elderly retired people stayed doggedly on their farms; social life went on as usual, except that everyone sat down to dinner with their pistol within reach. It was a sad time for Africans and Europeans alike. For a month we rented a tiny house on the coast at Malindi which in those days was unspoilt by tourism. The glorious Indian ocean rolled its breakers over the coral reef and up the white beach which stretched into the distance, the sun sparkled on blue water all day long, and a cool on-shore breeze kept the palm trees rustling. Crabs, oysters and prawns were a welcome change from the dry mutton and scraggy chickens of the Sudan; we luxuriated in sea water, sunshine and sloth and then went up country again to cool mountain air, cedar log fires in the evenings, and views of perpetual snow on the peaks of Mount Kenya.

After two months of pleasant leave in these lovely surroundings we flew back to Khartoum and on to El Fasher, with two dwarf mongooses from Kenya hidden in a pocket, and the resolve that one day when our wanderings were over and peace had come back to that Garden of Eden we would return to Kenya and live there.

I settled into the same routine of work and play for my last year of attachment to the Sudan Defence Force; the hot weather passed, the rains came and with them arrived a new commander for the Western Arab Corps; to my delight it proved to be a friend from my own regiment, Delmé Seymour Evans, who had served with Arabs in the Transjordan Frontier Force some years before. After a series of farewell parties and parades an aeroplane bore Gus Powell back to his Royal Marines in England; he had been a popular commander.

The rains that year were particularly heavy; thunderstorms crashed over the ironstone ridge of El Fasher, drumming on the tin roof of our bungalow; several people in the province were killed by lightning and the normally dry water courses became brown impassable torrents; the sunsets were of extraordinary beauty, the sky ablaze with scarlet and gold; grass grew in the desert, forming almost overnight a green carpet on the land; mushrooms sprouted and the Fasher hunt flourished. Soon after the rains had finished the cool weather came and with it the trekking and training season; tracks became passable, duck flew in from the north, polo started again and teams practiced for the Christmas tournaments.

My tour of attachment drew to an end; a letter came from the War Office ordering me to return to my regiment which was currently in Germany, standing by to sail to Hong Kong in the New Year. A round of farewell visits to outstations, a final polo tournament, and leave takings from Sudanese officers and men; another day of farewells in Khartoum, and as a broad silver Nile stretched below us again I recalled General Whistler's words in London four and a half years ago, 'You will enjoy the Sudan and the Sudanese' – he had been right, and now my affections lay both north and south of the Bahr el Gazal river.

7

Honey and Onions

THE LATE '50s AND EARLY '60s

———————◆———————

It was very pleasant to be back with my regiment again, after an absence of over five years; there were many new names and faces to learn; spirits were high at the prospect of going to Hong Kong, although personally I was apprehensive of being cooped up with no elbow room or sport for a period of three years, but the company would be good and I would have the opportunity for the first time since boyhood to indulge my love of sailing.

We returned to England and after a few weeks leave, sailed out of Liverpool early in 1954 with the whole regiment on board a new and luxurious troopship.

I took much vicarious pleasure in the wonderment and surprise of the young officers and troopers viewing the route that I now knew so well and had first sailed almost seventeen years before. The war did not seem to have altered things much; the same bumboats of cheap merchandise at every port, the pimps and panders of Port Said and the stifling heat of the Red Sea. Again as we cleared Cape Guardafui the monsoon struck us on the bow and the dining room stewards had less work to do. At Singapore my naval brother, Stafford, unexpectedly came aboard and together we sampled some of the bright lights of that oppressive sweat bath, then we sailed on for a few days until we entered the beautiful busy harbour of Hong Kong. The island peak rose into the clouds above us while junks, ferry boats and shipping of all kinds scurried backwards and forwards across the waterway; it was a colourful scene of commerce and the struggle for survival. We disembarked at Kowloon on the mainland and travelled through its noisy overcrowded streets, then over high hills and down into the Sekong valley beyond, where we prepared to settle in for three years, surrounded by paddy fields, our tank guns pointing into Red China.

Almost my first act on arriving in Hong Kong was to join the yacht club and charter a 'Dragon'; there were a number of these beautiful thirty foot yachts in Hong Kong and every weekend we raced through sparkling sunlit seas, either round a course in the harbour where the wind and currents were tricky, or offshore where a steady breeze came over the Pacific ocean. My boat was well named *Ecstasy*, and I had much pleasure in introducing other officers of my regiment to a craft which had come back to me over the years. On some weekends we went cruising to distant islands, where we would anchor off a sandy beach and swim in the warm clear sea, sleeping the night aboard with a shotgun handy to receive pirates who still operated with motorised junks amongst the remote islands; then on Sunday we would sail back to Hong Kong with the evening offshore breeze.

Despite the pleasant company of my regiment, the hospitality of the civilians, and the strange beauty of the place, I never felt a liking for Hong Kong; poverty and opulence lived side by side in overcrowded conditions, it was frustrating not to be able to speak the language and the social life of the island was rather more than I could happily digest; above all, the sense of being confined was oppressive. However good fortune was on the way.

About half way through our tour in Hong Kong, a friend of mine in the regiment, Caledon Alexander, who shared my feelings for the place, said to me: 'Let's get out of here. We'll take two months' leave and go shooting to your old haunts in India, a tiger skin would look nice in the mess, and as I've had a bit of luck on the stock exchange re-cently, all expenses are on me if you will help me catch a tiger.' Here was an offer indeed; although I no longer had any desire to shoot a tiger, it would give me pleasure to hunt for a friend and a chance to visit again the Indian jungles which I had loved so much.

I wrote immediately to my friend Henry Dunn who was Defence adviser in Delhi, and a keen hunter. He replied that he would arrange everything from obtaining a scheduled list of man-eaters and cattle kil-lers to booking the best area, borrowing rifles, and arranging trans-port. Bets entered in the mess Betting book laid heavy odds against success, but Caledon who was reading everything he could find on the subject of tiger shooting backed himself to win, and just before Christmas we flew to Delhi.

For a week we struggled with permits and a bureaucracy which was more testing to Caledon than to me, who remembered the form from days gone by. At last our permits were in order and we took the train to Jubblepore where we met and talked to the local Forest officer about our jungle, then, piling our belongings on to a hired truck, we set off on a hundred miles of rough road for the Saristal jungle.

News had gone ahead and on arrival we were met at the rest house by a small deputation which included the forest guard, two trackers, and the local head man with a few half grown bull buffalo for us to buy as bait; news was encouraging, there were several tigers in the area, one of which was an inveterate cattle killer.

We bought four young buffalo and, having carefully studied the map and sought local advice, ordered them to be tied at night each in a strategic place where a tiger might pass on a nightly prowl, such as cross jungle tracks or intersecting dry water courses.

Each morning at dawn, Caledon and I set off to visit two of the baits, sending a tracker and a villager to check on the others. It was delightful to walk quietly through the jungle as dawn came up, when the air was crisp and full of bird song, game was on the move and signs of the night's activities were still fresh; grey langur monkeys called to one another from the tree tops, peacocks scuttled across the path ahead; sometimes we caught a glimpse of spotted cheetle deer or heard the bell-like alarm note of a sambhur stag from across the ravines. Dew drenched us to the knees as we moved silently through the grass searching and listening for any evidence of a tiger's movements; the call of monkeys, deer, or birds usually had some significance, and a collection of vultures in the sky or in trees might mean a kill; as we approached our tied-up bait we moved with extreme caution in case a tiger which had killed in the night was still feeding and might present a shot. We carefully studied the area of each tie up planning which way a beat would go and where we would place the 'stops'.

For a week we returned empty handed from our morning stalks; the baits were driven back to be watered and fed at the bungalow while we lunched and read through the hot afternoon, waiting to go out again in the evening; we had seen the tracks of two different tigers in soft sand; each time our Ghond tracker had knelt down and gently touched the rim of the print to test its age, or point out an insect mark or fallen leaf which indicated that the tracks were stale. One morning we came upon a pack of wild dogs and the tracker shook his head ruefully. 'When the golden dogs move in the game moves out, followed by the tiger,' he said, and we returned to the bungalow to learn that the other two baits were still untouched.

That day the village head man came to see us. He squatted on the verandah sharing a tiny earthenware bowl of tobacco with the two trackers. 'Your luck is not good,' he said. 'Perhaps the spirits are not pleased.' I agreed with him and for a while we discussed moving the baits to different places and other ways of out-witting tigers, then the old man returned to his theme.

'If the spirits were pleased your luck might change,' he said. 'We have ways of bringing luck but they cost money; for example if we have a feast and money to buy drink and a goat we could make a sacrifice and please the spirits.'

I interpreted the conversation to Caledon. 'For God's sake,' he said, pulling out rupee notes, 'here's the money, tell them to get as tight as owls. If that makes the spirits happy we might try the same thing ourselves.'

I passed the money to the head man with Caledon's comments but avoiding the word owl which in Hindustani is an insult; the three little men rose beaming and disappeared towards the village; that night distant chanting and the throb of tom toms went on into the small hours, while Caledon and I sat under a full moon toasting good fortune in our own way.

Next morning as we returned from another blank inspection of our two tie ups we saw men collecting at the bungalow; the head man approached: 'Gara hogia,' he said, 'there's been a kill,' and pointing with his axe handle, 'the bait we tied where the footpath crosses the nullah four miles away. I am collecting the beaters now.'

We waited until about a hundred men had gathered and having chosen fifty to be stops, set off with the trackers to inspect the kill and make final plans for the beat. As we had hoped, the tiger had dragged the kill into a thick patch of jungle near a rock pool. It would almost certainly be lying up nearby and the outline plan we had made for this beat could go ahead unaltered; the plan was made on the principle that a tiger is obviously best driven in the direction he would choose to go. We returned to bring up the beaters who were sitting quietly in the forest two miles away; I explained the beat and put out the stops in a V formation with Caledon sitting on a village bed tied in a tree at the point of the V; the plan was to drive the tiger into the bottleneck which was situated on his most favourable line of retreat; if he turned to right or left, a stop in a tree would gently tap in an attempt to turn the tiger back on the chosen course; a well conducted beat would bring a tiger at walking pace directly under the gun. When all was ready, I climbed into a tree near Caledon and we heard the beat start with a loud shout to raise the tiger; it then moved forward with a tapping of sticks; a few peacocks rose screaming from the jungle or ran underneath us with a patter of leaves which brought our rifles to the ready, then, after what seemed like an interminable delay, the stops on our right started tapping; seconds later came the sound of an animal galloping towards us and a large tiger streaked across the open space on Caledon's left, giving him just time for one shot from his double-barrelled rifle; the tiger hunched and crashed on into the forest. I called to the beaters to take to the trees and joined Caledon on the ground. Very cautiously the trackers came through the bushes and we walked over to where the tiger had been hit.

'I'm fairly confident it was a good heart shot,' said Caledon. 'What's the plan now?'

'We'll follow him for a few hundred yards,' I replied, 'and if he's gone on we'll give him a couple of hours to die or stiffen up, then we send for some village buffalo and drive them ahead of us, they will rout him out quick enough.'

We picked up the tracks and followed them slowly, Caledon and I side by side with our eyes ahead, the trackers slightly to one side, their eyes on the ground; after a short way I motioned a tracker into a tree to scan the ground in front but he saw nothing; a little farther on we came upon blood smears on a leaf at a height from the ground which indicated a good shot; again the tracker climbed into a tree. Hardly had he reached the top when he was beside us again on the ground with the agility of a monkey and pointing with his axe. 'He's there, fifty paces away under those bushes,' he whispered; I motioned both men into the trees and we crept forward until a shadowy pattern of stripes appeared under the bushes ahead. I tossed a stone towards it, there was no movement and we walked up to the dead tiger; it had been an exciting few minutes.

Our return to the bungalow was triumphant, the tiger was slung on a pole and the beaters danced ahead of us waving their axes; children came running to see the dead 'cattle thief' and we had much fun placing small coins on the tiger's nose and watching little girls creep up to snatch them off. I marked in charcoal on the tiger's skin where the village skinner was to cut, then having carefully removed the whiskers, which would otherwise 'disappear', we composed a cable to the regimental Betting book in Hong Kong.

Next day our truck appeared at the bungalow; Caledon had decided to go back to Jubblepore for a night to collect stores, pick up and post our mail and despatch the cable; I wanted to investigate and if possible photograph a herd of bison reported to live in the distant hills. I took a tracker and a man to carry my sleeping bag, a few tins of bully beef and a canvas water bottle; we walked until evening, then made a fire and went to sleep listening to the night noises of the Indian jungle; we were on the move again with the first pink streaks of dawn, walking along a forested hillside from where we could see the jungle rolling away into the distance below us. Tracks of bison were frequent but the little Ghond tracker ignored them as stale; at last he pointed to a cow pat in the grass. Raising his eyes in thought he stood on one leg, slowly poking the toes of his other foot into it: 'The one who left this is close', he whispered. We picked up the tracks of a lone bull and for the next half hour I was treated to a wonderful example of Ghond fieldcraft and tracking; constantly testing the wind and with the certainty of a blood hound he followed signs which were all but invisible to me. They led us over sheet rock down to a muddy pool poached and criss-crossed by a hundred other bison tracks and over baked, stony earth. Every so often he climbed a tree and searched ahead; at last he stopped and pointed across the valley to a clump of bamboo: 'He's feeding there, Sahib, watch the tops of the branches'. I searched with my field glasses and after a while noticed a slightly unnatural movement in the branches; we crossed the valley and stalked carefully up wind: 'Now, Sahib, can you not smell him.' I shook my head and all at once the big bull walked into view forty yards away, the largest and most handsome of all the ox tribe.

The word 'bison' is a misnomer, the correct word is gaur (to rhyme with flower); they are true wild oxen, a mature bull standing six feet four inches at the shoulder and weighing some two thousand pounds; this lone bull stood in full sunlight, his dark brown coat gleaming, in contrast to his white-stockinged legs, curved horns surmounted the massive head, which he thrust upwards amongst the bamboo shoots. For five minutes we lay in the grass watching, then I gingerly reached for my movie camera; at the first sound of the whirring the bull's head came up and he swung towards us, then with a melodious bellow of alarm he crashed into the bushes and was gone, clattering over the stony hillside. 'Why didn't you shoot, Sahib?' said my tracker. 'Think of all that meat, we can't eat your photographs.' He was clearly as disappointed as I was elated by the incident.

At last our month's lease of the area came to an end; we gave the village another 'binge' to thank the jungle spirits, said goodbye to all concerned and motored off to Jubblepore. We had been remarkably lucky, won our bet, and still had a few more weeks to enjoy ourselves in India.

From Jubblepore we went by train to Jhansi where we were met by a smart young officer of the Deccan Horse and driven the thirty miles south to Babina where the regiment was stationed; I was back on familiar ground, but as I walked into the mess that I used to know so well, I had a feeling that I would find things much altered. I was quite wrong, it was like walking back into a long abandoned home; all the regimental possessions which had been so familiar to me and which we had packed away in the early days of the war, were here; the silver, the pictures, the carpets, bronze statuettes, trophies, even the painted miniatures of British officers who had commanded the regiment which could trace its history back to the eighteenth century; they were in the same glass cabinets on the wall; servants in the same livery brought drinks in the same silver goblets; the only apparent change was that the inmates of the mess were now all Indian, and I who would once have been a host was now a guest. The colonel introduced us to all the officers, most of whom seemed to have family connections with the regiment, and we sat down to an excellent lunch. In the evening I was taken round the regiment to meet old soldiers who might remember me; this was a wholly delightful experience. I had to answer many questions about British officers who had left India and been scattered the world over. Fortunately I had kept in touch with most of them and I listened with great amusement to semi-mythical but always affectionate anecdotes about my friends. That night a formal dinner party was given in the officers' mess, candlelight illuminated the silver on the table, and a band played the tunes of Gilbert and Sullivan and *South Pacific*; at the end of dinner the port was passed and the Queen's health was drunk; then a speech was required of me for which I was not prepared. Clearly some things had not changed much since independence, particularly, so it seemed, an enduring fund of good will.

At the weekend a tiger beat was arranged for us; I prayed that no tiger would appear, one was enough; I sat with my camera determined that if a tiger came to me I would first get a picture and then put a 'diplomatic' shot into the ground under his tail to speed him on his way; fortunately only a few startled cheetle and sambhur stags sped by; a tiger had broken out between the stops, the demands of hospitality were satisfied.

Our last appointment in India was a week's visit to Bundi state. His highness Bahadur Bundi, the Maharajah, was a friend of mine; he had joined Probyn's Horse as a young officer and, being a Rajput prince was posted to Bernard Loraine Smith's Rajput squadron where I got to know him well. During the battles in Burma he had been awarded the Military Cross for gallantry; then came a signal from the government of India to say that his father had died and he was to be ordered out of the firing line and return to rule his state; Indian princes were not expendable items. Bahadur's reply had been that Rajputs do not behave like that; he refused to leave and fought on until the intervention of the Viceroy forced him reluctantly back to his state. After the war he had become ADC to King George VI in London, a place not unfamiliar to him and where he had once been old Queen Mary's page. Bahadur was a handsome, somewhat dilettante bon viveur; we had kept in touch and our post war encounters usually resulted in a suitable celebration; at last I was able to take up his long standing invitation to visit Bundi.

Caledon and I took the train from Delhi to Kotah in Rajasthan from where Bahadur's car drove us some twenty miles to the newly built Phoolsagar palace a few miles outside the city of Bundi; the old palace was a large medieval Rajput fort in the centre of the city, but Bahadur had built a new one between two hills on the site of a shooting lodge; he had spared neither skill nor expense and the result was imposing; the dazzling white walls and domes surrounded a lily pond and swimming pool, the upper storey was a series of luxurious self-contained apartments each with its own verandah; below were large rooms containing a strange mixture of treasures and interesting bric-à-brac; one wing of the palace contained a squash court and a night club; from every window there was a vista of bright flowers between well kept lawns, beyond was forest and tigerland.

For the next week Caledon and I enjoyed a pleasant sybaritic life in some contrast to the month we had just spent in the jungles of Saristal; we rose late; sometimes Bahadur took us for a duck or sand grouse shoot, after which we would drive to a shady place in the forest to find iced champagne, chairs, tables and silver laid for a sumptuous curry lunch; we toured the old city of Bundi which half surrounded a lake and contained temples, forts and much fine architecture; we visited the state rest house on the lake where Kipling used to write, and we wandered over the ramparts of the old palace amongst engraved Rajput cannons covered in the rust of centuries. After dinner, and perhaps somewhat lulled by good living, we sometimes motored round drives in the Bundi forests, watching game with the spotlights on Bahadur's Landrover. Occasionally 'Kitten', Bahadur's beautiful seventeen-year-old daughter would escape from her lessons and come to chat and play; my last act at Bundi was to give her a baby tortoise. 'Oh, I shall call it Hilary,' she said, 'it looks so like you.' I often wonder if Hilary still browses amongst the flowers of Phoolsagar palace where Caledon and I spent that last enjoyable week in India.

At last the happy day came when the regiment boarded a troop ship bound for England; the Suez canal was closed and we crossed the Indian ocean, calling at Cape Town to refuel. Bad news came when we were on the high seas again; a signal from the War Office announced that we were to be amalgamated with another regiment at the end of the summer. It was the bitter blow which we had been half expecting since the government's decision to cut the armed forces. As our troop ship drove through the seas of the south Atlantic, Tim Llewellen Palmer, the commanding officer, and I leant over the rail discussing the administrative implications of amalgamation; after a while he changed the subject abruptly. 'As a regiment we have about six months to live,' he said. 'Tidworth is a good polo station and we have money in the polo fund. As soon as we get to England we will buy the ponies we need, put a team together and win the inter regimental polo tournament at the end of the summer.'

The inter-regimental polo tournament was open to all regiments of the army, the Royal Navy and the Royal Air Force. We had not played during our tour in Hong Kong, and we had a formidable task ahead of us. For the rest of the voyage, the conversation frequently turned from the gloomy subject of amalgamation to the more congenial one of plans to win the coveted cup.

Tidworth was, in those days, a pleasant little station on the edge of Salisbury plain; there were several polo grounds and always enough players to ensure regular games. We chose our regimental team and every moment of spare time during that summer of 1958 was spent in practice and play; at weekends we travelled to Cirencester, Windsor or Cowdray to play matches; slowly our team began to take shape and when at last the inter-regimental tournament took place, we won each round by a narrow margin to reach the final and beat our opponents by a single goal. Then amalgamation swept over the regiment and the 7th Queen's Own Hussars ceased to exist after two hundred and seventy years of a history rich in battle honours.

Fortunately I remained at Tidworth in a staff job, and for the two years, the longest period of time I had spent in England since leaving

Sandhurst, I enjoyed all that England and the Wiltshire countryside had to offer; I lived remote from my office, and daily escaped back to the small village of Great Durnford in the Avon valley; trout swam in the river which ran at the bottom of the garden; the hillsides were clothed in woodlands where pheasants and pigeons called and where, in early spring, appeared a carpet of aconites and snowdrops. The tempo of village life and the beauty of the changing seasons, each bringing its different pursuits delighted me; the English birds and butterflies, once so familiar, the flowers and fruit of English gardens, the foliage of summer, the frost of winter, and all the sounds and scents of the countryside stirred half forgotten memories of my childhood. The part of Devon where I had grown up was suffering the sad overcrowded fate of many other once wild and beautiful places; Wiltshire now became my favourite county, and it has remained so ever since.

My job in Tidworth was coming to a close, my sojourn in Wiltshire had been all too short, but towards the end of it I had good news; I had been appointed Military attaché in Khartoum; it was a pleasant prospect of better pay, promotion, and diplomatic privilege in a land which I liked; I was summoned to the War Office to see a staff officer who dealt with such matters. The officer in question was a friend of mine and I was in a buoyant mood; I filled in the normal form, and in the paragraph headed 'Purpose of visit' I wrote, 'To be instructed on how to bite an ostrich in the arse without getting a mouthful of feathers.' A messenger took the form away and after a long wait returned to usher me into the office of an affronted and angry looking general who rose from behind his desk; he looked from me to the piece of paper in his hand and then said sternly: 'It's actually top secret, but I think you do it like this.' Then puffing out his cheeks he blew into the air and his great front 'snappers' clanged together. 'Quite easy but you must be damn quick, what else can I do for you?'

'I came to see Colonel Hugh.'

'Next office,' said the General. I apologized and withdrew.

Hugh chuckled over the incident. 'The general has most of the answers,' he said, 'but I fear I have dull news for you. The Ambassador in Khartoum refuses to have you on his staff on the grounds that you served in the Sudan before Independence and presumably represent the worst of brutal imperialism – the man is a nuisance; apart from being sorry to have raised your hopes, we now have to find someone else who does not know the country and who will be of little use to us until he does.'

'And in the meantime?' I asked.

'You are to command the armoured cars in the Aden Protectorate Levies. Now let's go and drink damnation to that bloody ambassador.'

I returned to Wiltshire crestfallen and disappointed; I had wanted that job; the Sudan government was a military one; the President was my old friend Abboud Bey and I had known most of the Cabinet ministers with whom I would have had dealings; besides, I liked the Sudan. From what little I had seen of Aden, I did not particularly want to spend eighteen months there.

However 'Yom asal, yom basal'*, a day of honey, a day of onions; I rather suspected that my days of honey were numbered.

> Be'old a cloude upon the beam
> And 'umped above the sea appears
> Old Aden like a barrick stove
> That no-one's lit for years and years
>
> Kipling: *For to Admire*

The port of Aden lies on the south western tip of Arabia. It became important to Britain as a coaling station when the Suez canal was opened in 1869, shortening the sailing distance to India by nearly four thousand miles. Aden guarded the southern entry to the Red Sea. The hinterland to the north was known as the Aden Protectorate and covered an area rather larger than the British Isles; it is a grim country of arid mountain and desert.

The Aden Protectorate Levies had been in existence for some years; they were recruited from the Arab tribes of the Protectorate and officered by British officers seconded from their regiments; the Levies' role was to keep order amongst the warring tribes of the interior. There were several battalions of infantry, and a squadron of small 'Ferret' armoured cars, sixteen in all; the headquarters of my squadron was across the bay from Aden at Khormakser, but the 'troops', each of three cars, were dispersed in the mountainous interior, attached to various infantry battalions; communication was by air and if the cars had to be switched from one trouble spot to another, two of them could drive into the great belly of a Beverley troop carrier and fly over the mountains to where they were needed.

There was constant trouble in the Protectorate, where the situation and terrain was not unlike the old north-west frontier of India; every tribesman carried a rifle, a bandolier, and the big curved Arabian

* Arab proverb.

dagger known as a djambia; every able-bodied man was a warrior whose object, it seemed, was to raid, steal camels, carry on tribal blood feuds, and ambush civilian and government convoys going on their lawful occasions. The game was, on the whole, a fairly friendly one, and as with the Pathan tribes of the north-west frontier, the British political agent was, to a certain extent, regarded as a referee who could move with a degree of immunity between dissident and warring factions, drinking coffee and negotiating with sheiks who were raiding each other and ambushing government forces of law and order. It was a way of life which had been passed down through the ages; the rugged and harsh nature of the country had shaped the men who inhabited it; their trade was fighting. Some tribes received an annual allotment of cash to keep them quiet and help them develop their villages; the money was paid in Maria Theresa dollars, minted in England and transported in sacks on heavily guarded camels; if the tribe misbehaved, the payment was withheld; to disarm a recalcitrant tribe would not only have been an immensely difficult task, it would also leave them defenceless against the malevolence of their neighbours.

My second-in-command and troop leaders were British when I arrived, but it would be my charter to watch over their replacement by Arab officers; in eighteen months' time I would hand over to the last British squadron leader who, at the end of his tour, would hand over to an Arab; independence was on the way. In the meantime we had a few more or less non dangerous little wars on our hands.

By reason of the dispersal of my troops, I spent much of my time in the heart of the Protectorate flying from place to place. It was pleasant to soar into the mountains away from the heat of Aden and stay in some 'Beau Geste' fort for a day or two; I usually took my shot gun because rock pigeons flew up and down the steep ravines in the morning and evenings, and sand grouse came to drink at the scarce water holes.

One of the toughest and most troublesome tribes were the Shamshi Rabizy who lived in a remote area guarded by high barren mountain ranges; several years before, the Shamshi Rabizy had ambushed a company of the Levies as they passed through a defile in the mountains. They had lain concealed and attacked at close quarters with a murderous fire before closing in with their knives; a number of Levies and two British officers had been killed in the fight; a punitive force had been sent, driving the tribesmen back into their mountain vastnesses; now they were on the rampage again and it was decided to teach them a lesson and reopen a long disused road through their country.

Consequently within a short while of leaving the peaceful Avon valley, I found myself high on a barren plateau of Arabia, watching a battalion of Arab soldiers attack a wall of mountains ahead. My armoured cars with their battalions were converging on the centre of Rabizy country; a column would be formed to open the old road to Aden where the ambush had occurred, I would then fly in to take over the column which was to be officially known as Hook col.; at present I had nothing to do but sit and listen to the occasional crackle of musketry ahead. During the afternoon a strange little entourage appeared; it was a section of Levies escorting three blue-painted figures stripped to the waist; they were Shamshi Rabizy prisoners; they still wore their bandoliers of ammunition but the Levies carried their rifles and djambias. I had never seen one of the so called 'blue boys' before, and I couldn't help wondering whether their blue dye was the same as the woad with which our ancestors confronted Julius Caesar in 55 BC; the section commander handed me a note from their Company Commander: 'Please look after our chums, get them back to HQ for questioning and let me have my section back, we're a bit short handed.' Here was quite a problem; I only had a few British gunners and storemen available and no facilities for guarding prisoners. One thing I did have was a very resourceful 'old sweat' of a British sergeant with many years of service; I called him over: 'How the hell do we look after these blokes tonight,' I said. 'We've no proper means of guarding prisoners and they are valuable items.'

'Easy, Sir,' he replied. 'I'll dig 'em a nice sandy 'ole, about ten feet long and two feet deep, and wide enough to lie down in, then I'll get the lads cutting thorn to make a big 'igh fence. With a man on guard they'll be snug and safe for the night. Another thing sir, these wogs is fastidious like. If thy wants to pump ship we get an army belt and buckles it on 'em back to front, then we lets 'em out on a long rope; they'll be safe with an army belt buckle.'

As the work proceeded, I went to talk to the prisoners; they were handsome lithe young men painted blue from head to foot, their only clothing was a coloured cloth, or 'futur' round their waists held up by a studded leather belt; round their necks suspended on twisted leather thongs hung the little silver caskets containing texts from the Holy Koran; they stood up as I approached and we passed the normal Arab courtesies, as we talked they stared wide eyed at the digging tommies; it was probable that they had never seen white men before, and I was not surprised at the interest they were showing. Then one of them said, 'You are making our graves; please bury us facing that way,' and he pointed towards Mecca. I assured them that provided they did not try making a bolt for it, no harm would come to them. 'In fact,' I said, 'if you behave yourselves you'll have a ride in a motor car, then in an aeroplane and perhaps a sight of the big city. When this fighting is finished you will be given back your djambias and returned to your country. It's just that you're out of the game for the time being.'

They looked a little more relaxed. I inspected their rifles which, of course came from behind the iron curtain; the djambias were ancient and beautifully made heirlooms worked in silver, and studded with semi-precious stones.

In the evening I watched the incongruous scene of an armed tommy standing somewhat embarrassed guard over three blue figures who bowed towards Mecca, and were then led out one by one to squat in the desert on the end of a rope. They were given a blanket each, a box of rations and cigarettes, then they were ushered through the thorn zariba for the night. Next day, a ration aircraft flew them out of my ken; by the time they climbed aboard they were chatting happily with their captors in the universal language known only to Tommy Atkins abroad.

On that afternoon a tremendous storm broke over the mountains ahead, lightning crackled in the dense black clouds which hung over the massif, thunder echoed from peak to peak as I watched from under a clear sky; half an hour later I heard a rumbling coming from the valley below, where a few three ton lorries were parked on the sand; the rumbling increased to a roar, as round the bend came a twelve foot high wave of muddy water sweeping with it large boulders, which shattered and rebounded against the cliffs; I stood well above the tumult wondering whether the little party below would escape; men were running and one by one the lorries began churning across the sand to safety – all but one, a single reluctant starter; I saw the driver leap from his cab, open the bonnet and work furiously at the engine, he jumped back into the driving seat, but I could hear nothing above the roar of the flood; an NCO was waving from the far bank and just as I calculated that he had left it too late, the driver abandoned the lorry to its fate and sprinted for his life, climbing the far bank as the rising brown tide enveloped him to the waist; then I watched the torrent hit the loaded three ton lorry, bowling it over and over round the bend and down the mountain-side never to be seen again. It had been a dramatic few moments, and since that day have I have never pitched camp in a dry water course anywhere near high mountains. In an hour the flood in the valley had subsided to a trickle.

In the morning I was called to the wireless; Hook col. was assembling, a helicopter would pick me up at mid-day and fly me in to take command; I told my young Arab servant to pack my bag, we were flying into Rabizy country. At twelve o'clock, I heard the hum of a helicopter in the distance and walked out to the improvised strip. The pilot landed and opening the door, signalled us to get in; I turned to beckon my servant, but all I saw was my bag on the sand, and a small cloud of dust in the distance where the boy was bolting – he was due a month's wages but had apparently decided to get his priorities right. I never saw him again.

We took off and soared over a landscape of crags and ravines; here and there a tiny green strip of cultivation came into view in the valleys, or a string of camels moved on a precipitous path. After a twenty minute flight the pilot pointed, and I saw below us the Levies' zariba with my armoured cars; we landed amongst them in a billow of dust.

The next twenty-four hours were spent putting the column together and studying the aerial maps of my route. I had on call a flight of jet aircraft which I could summon from base in Aden at ten minute's notice; this was in case I met opposition in the narrow defile where the ambush had occurred. I was determined to call it up even if there was no opposition just for the hell of it, and to give the 'blue boys' an air show. The Levies were hoping for some action, some of them had old scores to pay off against the Shamshi Rabizy. Personally, I rather hoped that the blue boys would have enough sense not to take us on, I had no wish to knock them about, my charter was to open the road; if, however, they blew up one of my cars, or tried an ambush, I would have to think differently.

Finally I gave the order to move and we set out along the old disused road, armoured cars leading, then infantry in trucks, and armoured cars at the rear; the country through which we passed was ideal for an ambush, and we moved with caution, covering the infantry as they dragged boulders from the rough track or worked on the crossing of sandy 'wadis'; for two days we wound through bleak rocky scenery without seeing a man or a camel; sometimes we passed a cluster of mud huts where a few women and some stray dogs moved. The Shamshi Rabizy had faded into the hills with their camels and goats, or were they watching our movements from an ambush in the hills? On the

The house on the hill: Kiserian.

H.H. at Kiserian.

Lion cubs in the Mara.

Denis Zaphiro, Game Warden, Lokorono, with a Nile perch
caught in Lake Rudolf.

With The Hon. Rosie Pearson in the Aberdare forest, 1982.

Technical adviser for The Flame Trees of Thika. On location with Elspeth Huxley.

Home from the hill: H.H. Wiltshire, 1987.
(*Photograph by Molly Dineen*).

third day we approached the defile where I intended to call up air support; it was a gap in the mountains through which some great flood must have burst in the dawn of time; black granite cliffs rose on either hand, and the white sanded wadi beckoned us through its gloomy door in the mountains. I halted the column and scanned the peaks through my field glasses; nothing moved but the ravens which circled croaking over the gorge; my soldiers searched the wadi for foot prints: there were none. I picked up the microphone to RAF headquarters: 'No opposition seen,' I said. 'Entering defile in minutes, figures, ten. Bring on cabaret now.' 'Roger' came the reply, and we moved on again towards what seemed to be the bowels of a mountain range. As we drove between the perpendicular cliffs of the pass, there was a devastating roar and three jet fighter planes passed over, flying between the crags, then they swept up into the sky ahead to circle behind us and come again and again; I wondered whether any blue boys were attending the show; the walls of the canyon echoed back the thunder of the planes as we drove through deep shade into sunlight a few miles beyond; then the voice of the flight commander came on the air: 'That's it, we're getting a bit short of fuel, I think we'll get home to our tea.' I thanked him, and the column moved on to bivouac in the open surrounded by a thorn zariba. Next morning after a few hours driving we topped a rise and looked down on the waves of the Arabian Sea; soon we were swimming in the surf, and waiting for low tide, to start the long journey through glittering moonlight down the wet beach to our headquarters at Khormakser.

Leisure time in Aden was taken up with polo which we played on grounds of baked desert. When the time came round for annual leave, the RAF flew an Aden team of which I was a member to play a series of matches against the polo clubs in the Kenya highlands. It was a delight to be surrounded again by greenery, and play on well-mown grass in sight of the snows of Mount Kenya; but coming from sea level to the rarefied air of eight thousand feet was something of a physical test, particularly as the demands of hospitality had to be met between games. When not playing polo I spent as much time as I could fishing the mountain streams for rainbow trout. This took me to where torrents cascaded down through the forest, spreading here and there into pools at the tail of which were 'runs' of deep water where rainbow trout took a wet fly with all the vigour of their kind, fighting and jumping in diamonds of spray. Scrambling through the forest was energetic work, but the fishing brought that sense of peace and concentration which comes to one beside a trout stream; except perhaps that here tracks of game and an occasional crash of undergrowth above the sound of fast water served as a reminder that behind my back were elephant, buffalo and rhino, against which a light trout rod would be of less defence than an ability to climb swiftly into the trees.

We called our polo team the 'Arabians', and although I still have a few small silver objects to commemorate that very pleasant tour, I think that they should be classed as mementos of Kenya hospitality rather than trophies; we were not a very formidable team but we enjoyed ourselves in those cool uplands, for a month during which time the barren rocks of Aden seemed happily remote.

Shortly after my return to Khormakser, a letter came telling me that my next appointment was to be Military attaché in the Sudan; the information was accompanied by a letter from my friend in the War Office ensuring me that this time it was 'in the bag' and I could make my plans accordingly.

The job in Aden had been, on the whole, rather a depressing one; 'Arabisation' necessarily meant a lowering of standards; officer material was scarce; loyalties were strained, and it was difficult to see what was to become of the country after independence. It seemed that only a British presence in the dreadful place made the country financially viable; I was bored by the usual clap trap talk of the politicians which, of course added up to the understandable attitude that, 'self rule however bad is preferable to alien rule however good'. The Arabisation programme had brought me slightly in touch with politics and confirmed my view that most emergent politicans were mendacious and fluent liars, flaunting patriotism as a refuge for self interest. I left Aden and flew to England with few regrets and high hopes for the future.

A few weeks of late English summer, part of which I spent in London receiving instructions – then as the woods and hedgerows of Wiltshire began to take on autumn colours, I found myself back on the old trail again boarding a cargo steamer outward bound from Liverpool. There were about ten other passengers on the ship, Kenya settlers, South Africans, and some Somali students returning from London; the Captain was a witty old Scot with a penchant for good food and wine; at his table I sat next to a beautiful Somali girl, who flirted prettily in the cockney accents which she had acquired as a nursing student; I think she enjoyed being the only girl on board, and her company added much to the pleasure of the long sea voyage to Port Sudan where I left the ship.

After a night in the Red Sea hotel, I caught a plane for Khartoum and that evening went to a party given by my American opposite number, to meet the military attachés of other foreign embassies; it was a hospitable gesture which launched me straight into the cloud cuckoo land of diplomatic life.

Within a few days of my arrival, our Ambassador took me to meet the President, General Ibrahim Abboud, who I had last met when he had examined me in Arabic a number of years before; he was the same shrewd and urbane man, of infinite courtesy who I had known as Senior Sudanese staff officer in the Defence Force; we talked briefly of days gone by and of mutual friends and he welcomed me back to his country. For the next week I visited each minister of the military government in turn, swapping reminiscences with those I knew and trying to remember the points they had raised between cup after cup of scented black coffee.

My predecessor had left me a good deal of reading matter compiled over the years concerning projects, problems, and personalities of importance; with that and other embassy files I slowly read my way into my none too onerous duties. The Head of Chancery humorously guided me into the pantomime methods of diplomacy when dealing with friendly, less friendly, and unfriendly foreign missions. With the aid of my assistant military attaché, an efficient Arabic-speaking major, I began to understand the ways of the world into which I had stepped from regimental soldiering and I decided that I was going to enjoy the job.

The Khartoum which I had known was not much altered in appearance except that it was larger, dirtier, and every big building seemed now to be occupied by a foreign embassy. It was difficult to understand what business some of the remote and bankrupt countries had in maintaining expensive missions in Khartoum, but it appeared that an up-to-date world atlas was fully represented in multicoloured flags and brass plaques behind which a certain amount of mischief was, no doubt, planned. The Sudan had been independent for a number of years and a faint communist voice could be heard in the larger towns, for which listening posts were provided within the gloomy iron curtain embassies, most of which boasted their country's name under the banner 'The People's Democratic' somewhere or other, presumably proclaiming that Western governments have a lesser regard for either 'the people' or 'democracy'.

The reason behind the assiduous courting of Sudanese diplomatic favour was that, apart from its size, the country took its tone partly from the Middle East and partly from emergent Black Africa; it could talk with the ambivalent voice of either or both persuasions; Khartoum and the northern Sudan had all the flavour of Arab culture but to the south and west the borders touched on five different Black African countries; Sudanese politicians could with some truth, but probably more cynicism, say either, 'We Arabs' or 'We Africans' whichever suited their purpose best. But whatever they did say was zealously noted down by foreign embassy secretaries and reported in a multitude of languages to distant capitals who were scrambling for political or material preferment in the country. It was a situation which must have appealed greatly to the Sudanese sense of fun.

As time went on I got to know the other military attachés well; we developed into a kind of club, meeting fairly regularly and swapping such information as we considered prudent to pass on. I formed quite a friendship with the senior of the two Russian colonels; naturally we rarely talked 'shop' but I found him a humorous, affable, man. He had been in a British hospital during the war and professed, I think genuinely, a liking for the English who, he said, had saved his life; perhaps his friendliness was assumed in the course of duty, but I suspected that that was not altogether the case and I liked him. His movements were, I think, considerably more restricted than mine and when I returned from a tour of some place of special interest to the Russians such as a Red Sea port, I knew I could shortly expect an invitation to his embassy where, after caviar and vodka he would show me beautiful films of the Russian ballet; unhappily these were always followed by a none too short viewing of a worker's paradise on the Black Sea or the Baltic; then with more vodka he would turn to the subject of my recent trip; if I was trapped into making a comment I would recommend that he make the tour himself, and we would both laugh in the knowledge that he would probably seek permission in vain. After several such occasions I decided to pay him in his own coin and I arranged a film show for him in my garden; I knew he liked horses and sport and I had chosen from the British Council library the Grand National, the Wimbledon tennis championships and other sporting events, leaving to the last one which I suggested to my friend might be of some 'travel interest'; it was the film of the Queen and the Duke of Edinburgh's tumultuously enthusiastic welcome to India, an event probably not much publicised in Russia. After the show he came to me laughing: 'Beautiful, beautiful,' he said, 'but perhaps you make a "leetle" propaganda for me?'

'Well,' I said, 'let's make a pact. You keep on showing me those lovely ballet films and cut out the worker's playtime stuff, and I will show you a catalogue of what films I can get and you may choose.' He agreed, laughing; thereafter I was able to enjoy his caviar and the ballet without the subsequent contrasting spectacle of overweight female factory workers romping in the waves.

I spent as much time as I could on tour, visiting the military out stations which I had known before independence. It was my charter to liaise with the Sudan army seeing what help Britain could be with their military problems in such various matters as the supply of equipment or the setting up of a Staff college under a lecturer from the British army. It was interesting enough work but since the government was a military one, it behoved me to try and understand the intricacies of Sudanese politics which had their roots in both regional and religious sectarianism; sometimes it was a rather baffling exercise.

Another reason that encouraged me to spend as much time outside Khartoum as possible was that I found the high pressure diplomatic entertaining somewhat irksome; there was a ceaseless round of embassy cocktail parties to celebrate arrivals, departures, national days, birthdays and other significant occasions which had sprung up with the shifts of modern history. My desk was piled with invitations and my diary dotted with notes of times and places and whether uniform or civilian clothes were demanded; sometimes there were two or more parties to contend with in an evening which might require a quick change of clothes in between. At these 'pentecostal' gatherings, where the word 'Excellency' was heard on every side, one was initially presented with a glass containing too little whisky and too much warm soda, then having scanned the company in vain for the sight of a pretty face to lessen the ennui of the occasion, I would seek the genial companionship of the American or French military attachés and we would swop news and scandal, not always unconnected with our work, until the guest of honour departed and we were free to go home; however, the supply of news and scandal never really caught up with the frequency of these tedious occasions.

For light relief I sought the company of the Khartoum civilians, mostly Greek or Lebanese families with business interests in the country; they were a small compact society of 'Alexandrine' quality about whom Lawrence Durrell might have chosen to write; charming, witty and mostly wealthy, they provided a refreshing change from the formal company of most of my diplomatic colleagues; whenever I felt the need of sybaritic relaxation I could move from one 'Alice in Wonderland' existence to another of more mirth and entertainment, where one's only duty was the pursuit of laughter and pleasure. I greatly enjoyed the hospitality of this attractive community.

When I was not on tour, my house always seemed to be full of guests; Khartoum was a convenient stopping off place for south bound or north bound travellers in Africa; parties of young officers driving from England to join their regiment in Kenya would arrive travel worn and thirsty having come through the Libyan desert via Kufra oasis; visiting officials, military and naval attachés from the Middle East, and, in the cold weather, a stream of friends travelling to and from England fill the pages of my visitor's book for those happy three years. Sometimes duty took me to Addis Ababa, Kampala or Nairobi for a few days, then it was pleasant to soar out of the blazing heat of a Khartoum summer and breath cool upland air again. Whilst in Khartoum I off-set the torpor of a sedentary office life by playing polo with the Sudan army or flighting sand grouse on the battle field of Omdurman; if ever I had a guest sufficiently interested in military history we would climb Jebel Surgham after the sand grouse flight was finished and, with the aid of the maps in Winston Churchill's *River War*, pick out exactly the positions and movements of both Kitchener's and the Khalifa's army on that fateful September day in 1898.

Towards the end of my tour in Khartoum, President Abboud was invited to England by the Queen for a State Visit; he was to bring some of his ministers with him. Our Ambassador, Sir Ian Scott, and myself were commanded to accompany the party throughout the visit which would start in late May 1964. It sounded an amusing prospect and required a fairly lengthy correspondence with London who were preparing a crowded fortnight's programme of entertainment for the President. When the time came, Sir Ian and I flew home ahead to brief, and be briefed, by the Foreign Office and other dignitaries concerned with the visit. At last every detail was arranged, and we found ourselves in London on Victoria station, where the Queen and most of the Royal Family waited on a red carpet for the special train from the airport bringing the President and his party. I surreptitiously took a last look at the programme in my pocket which assured me that in the State drive through London to Buckingham Palace, my carriage was number six; I had only to meet the Sudanese dignitaries allotted to me, guide them to carriage number six and be swept down the Mall behind an escort of Household Cavalry through waving crowds. It was a simple, novel, and rather pleasing prospect. The train drew up, the guests stepped out, the band played and the Queen greeted President Abboud, then we moved to where the carriages were coming forward; I watched carriage number four and five arrive and depart but to my dismay the next to come and go were numbers seven, eight and nine; there was no number six; the procession departed leaving my Sudanese friends and I, uniformed in full fig, standing disconsolately on the pavement with no transport and an appointment with my monarch in twenty minutes time. My only salvation would be a London bobby, and as if in answer to my prayer one strode forward; I quickly explained our predicament; the only hope of being in time for the reception was to beat the Royal procession to Buckingham Palace and lurk there until it arrived. 'Leave it to me, sir,' said the bobby. He made a magic sign down the street and a taxi appeared from nowhere; after a rapid conversation with the driver the bobby jumped in beside us and we sped away shooting through lights and past traffic police; in no time Buckingham Palace loomed above us and we entered a side door just in time to watch the procession arriving. An official led us stealthily from hiding to join the little throng mounting the steps to be greeted by the Queen. My Sudanese friends were delighted with their adventure, but I was somewhat crest-fallen.

Later that day I had tea with a girl friend. 'You lied to me' she said. 'I stood in the Mall exactly where we had arranged, cheering like mad and you were never in that procession, I suppose some lesser folk had to go by taxi.' 'As a matter of fact, they did,' I said. It was rather disappointing and I have wondered to this day what did happen to carriage number six.

There followed a very entertaining fortnight of pomp and VIP treatment for the President and his entourage of which Sir Ian and myself were lucky members; banquets, receptions, and dinner parties followed one another in bewildering confusion; we toured the sights and historical places of London, most of which I had never seen before; we were whisked up to Scotland by special train for a tattoo at Edinburgh Castle and to see the building of the Forth bridge; on return to London the President was able to indulge his love of roses at the Chelsea Flower

Show, and his love of horses at the Derby, where from the Queen's box he watched 'Santa Claus', the horse he had backed, gallop in a winner; we visited Westminster Abbey and banqueted at the Guildhall, and during that fortnight we were served with so much cold salmon and mayonnaise that I have never been able to face it since. During what little spare time we could find I was constantly asked to perform some task not on the official programme: the Foreign Minister wanted to visit a London pub, the Minister of Health wanted to see Bart's hospital, someone wanted a tour of London on the top of a bus; it was a busy and amusing time in perfect summer weather.

One of the President's entourage was a tribal leader from the western Sudan, a giant of a man, very impressive in his robes and the only member of the party who spoke no English; he expressed a wish for a London made suit and a pair of shoes. Accordingly I took him to be measured, first to Gieves in Bond Street where the little tailor glanced upwards for a puzzled moment, then calling for a step ladder climbed up to measure the massive shoulders which were shaking with mirth; we then visited a boot maker where assistants came hurrying to gaze with admiration at the biggest pair of feet ever displayed in their ancient establishment. It amused my good natured Sudanese friend greatly and he declared that the finished products would delight his tribe.

One event which caused the Sudanese great pleasure happened after we had been visiting an RAF station in Oxfordshire; something delayed us and as we were due at a reception for Royalty in London that evening, the traffic police were alerted and there followed a most impressive circus display of driving and motor bicycle riding. Our fleet of Daimlers sped back to London at eighty miles an hour, shepherded by police motor cycles who shot past us to crossroads to hold up traffic and overtook us again and again as we swept through red lights all the way to our hotel in London; it was a wonderful tour de force which delighted the Sudanese but terrified me.

One incident occurred which might have marred an otherwise successful state visit, and even that had its humorous aspect. It was arranged that the President should visit a certain university in Scotland where a number of Sudanese students were studying, not all of whom were of the same political persuasion as their government. On the morning of the visit Sir Ian Scott sent for me and told me that there had been an anonymous telephone call threatening the President's life that day. Only the President had been told and he demanded that the visit go ahead, he had faith in the British police. 'Just watch your step,' said Sir Ian, 'and I expect we will see a lot of rather funny looking dons at the reception.' He proved right; as the President moved amongst the African students in the crowded hall, I looked around and noticed a number of 'professors' of more military than scholastic bearing, their close cut hair and shiny black boots proclaiming their true calling; behind the President there towered a 'don' whose sub fusc suit failed to disguise a wrestler's frame, his right hand was thrust forward in his coat pocket and his eyes searched restlessly over the crowd. Fortunately nothing untoward happened, but we breathed more freely when we finally drove out through the gates of the university.

'After the Lord Mayor's Show comes the dust cart' and I returned to Khartoum to contemplate my 'in' tray pregnant with files over which I bowed a head recently extracted from the clouds.

It was at about this time that a curious little incident occurred, the final outcome of which I would dearly like to know. I was sitting in my office one morning when my clerk ushered in someone who I took to be a Sudanese; I rose and greeted him in Arabic to which he replied in English. I thought this was rather odd and then I noticed that the man was trembling in a state of desperate agitation; I called for coffee and when the door was closed my visitor made an unusual request: 'Have you a Bible here?' he asked, fixing me with staring eyes; I pointed to one on my desk in which, by coincidence I had just been looking up the lesson I was to read in the cathedral on Sunday. He seized it and thrust it towards me saying, 'Swear – swear that you will not betray me.'

'No,' I replied, 'I will swear nothing. You must first calm down and tell me what this is all about.'

'I am a fugitive,' he said. 'I am an officer of the Ethiopian Royal guard and with the Emperor's relative we tried to make a coup, but we failed; the other officers are killed but I escaped and fled here.'

'Why do you come to me?'

'Because we are both officers and Christians.'

'What do you face if you return to your country?'

'I would be tortured to reveal my friends and then put in the lion dens; I need your help to get out of this country, if the Sudanese find me they will send me back.'

'Very well, you will not be revealed but I must speak to our Ambassador about you.'

I rose and walked to the door but he was there before me with his back to it and thrusting the Bible at me. 'Swear', he said.

'That is not necessary, I have told you, you will not be revealed, wait here until I return,' I said, and leaving the door open so that my assistant could watch him I went to the Ambassador's office.

'You must have absolutely nothing to do with it,' he said. 'There would be the hell of a diplomatic row if it was known that he had come here, please get him out of the Embassy at once.' I returned to my office wondering what to do; I suspected that the man was not exaggerating the reception he would receive back in Addis Ababa; he was running the gauntlet for his life in a strange country where he didn't know the language; I did not know the details of his crime, but it sounded a common enough one for modern Africa and to refuse him even a sporting chance of survival would be distasteful to say the least; I was in a quandary.

He leaped up as I returned still clutching the Bible. 'There is absolutely no way I can help you,' I said, 'but I will show you where you are on the map; come over here and listen carefully.' Five minutes later as my office door closed behind him I quickly stuffed some bank notes into an envelope and calling my clerk said, 'Follow that man and when he is out of the Embassy – and not before, hand him this and say he left it in Colonel Hook's chair.' It was with a guilty feeling that I returned to the lesson for next Sunday, and the words I read were 'A certain man went down from Jerusalem to Jericho'. I was less than pleased with myself and I have often wondered what did become of the hunted man.

I was determined to visit my old haunts in the southern Sudan from where the muffled rumblings of discontent could occasionally be heard. My masters in London required a report on the matter and I set about seeking permission from the Sudanese government who were somewhat sensitive about the 'goings on' in the south of their country. At last I got clearance to make a three week tour of Equatoria and Bahr el Ghazal Provinces, where I intended to look up any of my old soldiers that I could trace, and to talk to what missionaries, merchants, and government staff were left after the 'troubles' which came with independence; I also looked forward to trying out my new fishing tackle on Nile perch in the rivers of the South.

I set out by Landrover in late March for the long drive over sandy tracks, south westwards to the Bahr el Arab river beyond which lay the southern provinces; after four days of gruelling driving we splashed across the river and entered the land of the Dinkas. Tall naked herdsmen leaning on their spears stood on one leg watching the Landrover go by; thatched huts built on stilts dotted the boundless plain; beautiful bare-breasted girls waved from the road side, and in the shimmering distance herd upon herd of cattle grazed.

In Wau I stopped for two days to seek out old acquaintances and fish the pool below the bungalow which I had occupied as a bimbashi; then I moved on towards the Congo border, making a detour to the village where, I had been told I might find my old bash shawish Sambiri Belal; I drew up at a cluster of mud huts and sent some little boys to look for him; after a short wait I saw the old man striding towards the Landrover; grizzled and lined with the same grim unsmiling face that I remembered so well from a dozen or more years ago. He halted, saluted and greeted me as though we had met yesterday; two chairs were put under the village council tree, tea was brought, and for an hour he told me what had passed in the turbulent years during and since the mutiny of the Equatorial Corps against the new independent government in Khartoum. It was a heart breaking story and as he recounted it, I could not help a feeling of guilt for the way that the British government had behaved. I made no excuses by trying to explain the bigger concept of independence; in his eyes, the masters he had served so loyally had walked out leaving him at the mercy of his ancient enemies; it had happened before in the break up of Empires. As I sought news of individuals in our old company my feeling of guilt turned to something akin to shame and I switched the conversation to the present and the future. Finally I gave him an English pipe and a stock of the tobacco that he used to like and I departed with a heavy heart.

At the Congo border I turned east through green forested country and pursued a leisurely three day journey back to the Nile at Juba where I was entertained by the small Greek community; then south to the Uganda border and the Fola rapids where the Nile plunges through a narrow gorge three hundred yards long and perch wait for wounded fish in the big pool below the torrent of white water. After a day's fishing and a visit to the Nimule game reserve, I doubled back to Torit and then headed east for Teratania and the Kidepo valley; by now, early rain clouds were beginning to gather in the sky; dense black cumuli were looming over the Ethiopian hills and the night sky flashed. I had no wish to be caught by early rain in this remote area where roads would flood and bridges be swept away; however, I was determined to try for one of the big elephants which cross over the border from Uganda in search of dom palm nuts in the Kidepo valley.

After a long hot hunt, I bagged a bull with good ivory and as I sat waiting for the tusks to be removed rain storms began to appear overhead; I sent my driver Ahmed back to bring up the Landrover as quickly as possible over the rough burnt plain; an hour later I heard it approaching and when it was a hundred yards away there were two loud reports and it stopped; fearing the worst I walked over to where Ahmed was contemplating the front wheels which had run over a cluster of burnt stakes; both tyres were so badly ripped that they would have to be repaired with 'gaiters',* and I knew that we had used our last gaiter two days before. Adopting a policy of non interference in mechanical matters, I walked away and lighting a cigarette contemplated the dismal future while I waited for Ahmed to report the worst news possible. As far as I could see we were probably facing a very long walk and the abandonment of our possessions including my ivory; even supposing we could effect some form of running repair, if the rain caught us now we would bog down in the black cotton soil of this great plain; I cursed my cupidity for ivory as I listened to the mocking sound of thunder drawing closer, like the war drums of an enemy moving in to the attack. Then I noticed that Ahmed was running backwards and forwards between the Landrover and the dead elephant and I went over to see what was happening; he was skilfully manufacturing gaiters out of the elephant's ear; in no time the tyres were pumped up and we were bumping gingerly over the plain as the first big drops of rain spattered on the wind screen.

Two days later we loaded the Landrover on to a Nile steamer at Juba and I flew back to Khartoum to write my report.

When my three year tour as military attaché was drawing to a close, I wrote to the War Office to enquire what further mischief they had in store for me; their reply was rather what I suspected it might be – I was to go back to Aden in a staff job; that idea did not appeal to me in the least; clearly the Arabic language which had afforded me so much pleasure in the past was now threatening to haunt me with postings to the least attractive places in the dying Empire. Aden was on the brink of independence and the British would shortly be making yet another 'dignified withdrawal' leaving a government which would inevitably be overtaken by coup and counter coup and a land which would seethe with bankrupt turmoil in no time. It was a depressing prospect, and I

---

* A tough rubber disc placed between the inner tube and the wall of the damaged tyre.

was beginning to suspect that I had extracted all the pleasure I could reasonably expect from an army life.

A few days after this gloomy news, and as if in answer to my forbodings, a telegram came from a friend in Kenya. Would I consider leaving the army and taking the job of hunter in charge at Treetops, a game viewing lodge in the Aberdare forest; I made up my mind at once and flew to Nairobi to clinch the matter. On return to Khartoum I wrote to the War Office and a few months later, having bade farewell to my Sudanese friends, I returned to England for my final leave.

The process of leaving the army is simpler and more peaceful than the process of entering it, and I gratefully bowed my way out of a profession which had provided me with time and opportunity to indulge in plenty of fairly unmilitary activity – or as one of my friends put it 'scope for the artful abuse of Her Majesty's time'.

A month later, in October 1964 I stepped out of an aeroplane on to Kenya soil to begin the life of a civilian.

8

Safari Seasons

KENYA: 1964 TO 1984

The small township of Nyeri is a hundred miles north of Nairobi, lying on the eastern slopes of the Aberdare mountains which rise steeply behind it; dense forest and grassy glades give way to bamboo on the higher slopes and then to moorland which rolls upwards to a height of fourteen thousand feet. On the edge of the lower forest, some ten miles from Nyeri is a water hole and salt lick much frequented by big game. Treetops is a wooden house built on stilts overlooking the pool where tourists can spend a night game watching; it was my job to escort parties of game watchers through the forest and to spend the night at Treetops, answering questions about the game. I had two other hunters to help me which meant we were each on duty for one night in three, an arrangement which provided plenty of spare time for the pleasures and pastimes of Kenya of which there are many. I have always liked watching game and I now found myself being paid to do so on a two year contract. Elephant, buffalo and rhino came to the salt lick on most nights together with a host of smaller game such as waterbuck, bushbuck and warthog; sometimes a leopard would appear, or that rare forest antelope the bongo; it was an impressive sight to see a hundred or more elephants move silently out of the forest in daylight to drink and dig with their tusks for the salt, the babies gambolling about in play and the big tuskers placid and aloof from the herd.

It was a pleasant enough life but I felt confined and was impatient to see more of East Africa and the game parks which were within reach of central Kenya; consequently a friend and neighbour of mine, Digby Tatham Warter and I devised a plan over many decanters of port of starting a non-shooting safari business, camping with our clients in the game areas and National Parks of East Africa. When my contract at Treetops was finished we explored through Kenya, Tanzania and Uganda seeking out remote camp sites, finding river crossings and making tracks where few if any vehicles had ever passed before. We had brochures printed and distributed and at last we were each ready to receive up to six clients and drive into the blue with hunting cars and a lorry to carry the camp and staff.

It is surely a duty to oneself to strive against the pessimistic axiom that in life one cannot 'have one's cake and eat it'; more often than not an endeavour to do so is thwarted, but when one triumphs in a small degree then life can be sweet indeed. To me, life in the African bush surrounded by animals and birds has always been a *dolce vita*, and in the mid 1960s became my means of livelihood and profession; the abundance and variety of birds and game to be seen on a safari in East Africa is remarkable but it is not only this that holds a newcomer to the country in thrall, it is the ambience of the great plains, the forests and distant mountain snows and a quality of light and sky which have always evaded both description and the artist's brush.

Our safari season started at about Christmas time and went on until the threatening of the long rains in early April, when it was prudent to get our heavy lorries out of the bush. We started again in late July and went on until the advent of the short rains in November.

The parks and reserves of Kenya, Tanzania and Uganda cover some forty-three thousand square miles, but there were also many unscheduled wild parts of Africa available to us for safari – in all, an area of about the size of England.

My favourite safari country was the area on the Kenya/Tanzania border comprising the Mara Masai game reserve in Kenya and the Serengeti National Park and Ngorongoro crater in Tanzania. This is in fact all one natural game area, but the artificial international boundary divides it. However, in the early days of our safaris, the border could be crossed with no trouble.

This whole magnificent sweep of country, covering over eight thousand square miles, consists of great open plains broken sometimes by rocky outcrops and intersected by rivers, the banks of which are clothed with fine timber and dense bush. High escarpments rise out of the plain and herds of game are always in sight.

Thanks to my old friend John Owen, the director of Tanzania National Parks (and he for whom I had collected rodents in the Southern Sudan), we were allowed to camp where we liked in the Serengeti. In the Kenya Mara we could also camp anywhere we chose.

It was always a special and rewarding delight to take children on safari; they entered a fairy land of animals, birds and butterflies which they may never have dreamt of. I liked to think that the sight of a pride of lions with their cubs playing fifteen yards away or a herd of fifty elephants feeding through the trees would provide a thrill which would stay with them through life, to days when such sights may be rare in changing Africa.

On several occasions I spent a children's Christmas safari in the bush, with a decorated thorn Christmas tree, turkey and plum pudding. My old African cook, appropriately bearded and scarlet cloaked, would hand out presents, with the nightly carols provided by lions arrogantly proclaiming 'This land is mine, mine, mine.'

In the Kenya Mara there were a number of Masai villages and these red-cloaked cattle-owning wanderers added to the scene of Africa as it probably was hundreds of years ago. They would stand leaning on their spears and wave as our hunting cars drove by, and then turn back, whistling and singing to their tightly packed herds. Sometimes a few young men would stride into our camp and squat by the kitchen fire, much to the annoyance of our old Kikuyu cook, who objected not only to his hereditary enemies, but also to the swarms of flies which always followed these young Masai.

Masai boys are put through a rigorous commando-style training before they can claim to be full scale warriors. Their lives, like those of all small boys, are a succession of mischievous 'dares'. One exciting game they used to play involved finding a sleeping rhino, when a strong wind was blowing. One little Masai boy would creep stealthily upwind and place a stick or small pebble on the slumbering creature's back, and the next would creep up and remove it. No doubt this often ended in a scene similar to that of the little English boys fleeing from an irate farmer's orchard.

During one of our first safaris, two young Masai came loping into our camp. The story they told was this: a lion had been taking their cattle and four warriors had set out to hunt it with spears. They found the lion in some bushes which they surrounded; then they moved in. The trapped lion charged, and severely mauled one of the men. The lion was then speared to death, and the wounded man was left with a comrade while the two others came for help.

Fortunately, one of my clients had been a trained nurse during the war so, piling the medicine chest into a car, we headed across country for fifteen miles, guided by the Masai. The wounded man, lying beside an old dead lioness, was in a bad way, with deep claw and puncture wounds all over his body. Our nurse, Mary Colman, decided that he should be got back to camp, where there was warmth, hot water and tea.

On our return, Mary went to work on him with professional skill. His wounds had already scabbed over, and we knew that these must immediately be opened and cleaned to prevent septicaemia. While Mary worked on his head and neck, he opened the wounds on his body with a thorn. Never for a second did he flinch, but continued joking and boasting with his friends despite a badly crushed shoulder and broken arm. When the work was finished, we drove him to the little hospital at Narok. A year later, we returned to the same camp, and in strode our Masai friend, fit and well, still boasting and with scars to show. He was also, no doubt, a hero with the village girls.

As if to prove the Arabic adage which says 'Once you have drunk of the waters of the Nile, you are sure to return and drink again,' many of our clients returned to us for a second or third time. To provide variety, we used to take them to other parts of East Africa: the Aberdare mountains which rise through fine forests to moorland peaks of fourteen thousand feet; the dry Samburu country in the north of Kenya where the colourful and varied bird life was a special attraction; the great rivers, lakes and waterfalls of the Ugandan parks, where we could fish for Nile perch in the swirling rapids with one eye cocked for the huge crocodiles which infest the waters there.

It was in the Samburu country that we had a nasty experience with one of these sinister creatures; we were resting in our tents after lunch when a hubbub arose from across the Uaso Nyiro river, where a little Samburu boy watering his goats had been seized by a crocodile. His young friends flew to the rescue and tried to pull his arm from its jaws, while others gallantly attacked the creature with their spears until, well perforated it let go and slid into the depths.

The little boy was brought into camp with no flesh on his left arm. We patched him up as well as we could and sped for a small bush dressing station an hour's drive away. As with our Masai friend, the little boy appeared at my tent a year later, proudly bearing my spotted Jermyn Street handkerchiefs which had been his tourniquet and sling, now washed and neatly folded by his mum. He seemed none the worse, and gave us the present of a goat.

Those of our clients to whom Africa was a new continent initially wanted to be shown the well-known and commoner big game of the country: elephant, lion, buffalo, leopard and rhino, often called the Big

Five. During our early years on safari, we learned how these animals were likely to behave when watched from a motor car.

In all British colonies, shooting from a car had been strictly illegal, and this law paid a very good dividend when national parks and game reserves were planned. Perhaps the animals considered the rare sight of a motor car as merely another strange creature on the plain, and ignored them accordingly. Other colonial powers, who permitted shooting from cars, found that in their newly formed national parks the sight of a car, or even the sound of an engine in the distance, would send the Big Five high-tailing over the horizon – behaviour which is taking years to eradicate.

However, in the case of elephants, which not only have long memories, but are also prolific travellers, we had to move warily if a herd came into our area from a hunting or poaching district. We were frequently chased by elephants, usually by cows protecting their calves, but these charges were mostly brief demonstrations to see us off the premises.

On one occasion, however, the situation appeared to be somewhat different. I was driving slowly along a riverine forest line with a charming Peruvian couple, when we encountered a large mixed herd of elephants, with their babies, entering the forest. The last baby was safely concealed when out of the forest popped an enraged old cow in full pursuit of our hunting car. I turned away into the open plain, allowing the old thing to come quite close at full charge, and expecting her to give up after a few hundred yards. She didn't, but continued to hunt us, screaming with rage, to the accompaniment of my Peruvian friend's shouts of 'Caramba' and other Spanish expletives; he was enjoying himself enormously.

After the best part of a mile, we were abruptly confronted by an uncrossable water course so, trusting to luck and the generally forgiving nature of elephants, I swung the car round to meet her and, flicking my headlights and blowing my horn, I advanced upon her at the pace of a sharp cavalry trot. This was too much for the old cow, and she turned away to the forest, having done her duty by her nephews and nieces. Somewhat relieved, we spread a table in the shade, opened a thermos of dry martini, and addressed ourselves to the picnic basket.

Watching lions is usually a leisurely occupation. At midday, a pride is likely to be lying in the shade, the only activity being the untiring play of the cubs, both amongst themselves and with their parents' twitching tails. It seems that lions are entirely oblivious of motor cars, even at a few yards' range. But this can be misleading, for if a man should appear on his feet to a pride of lions, the reaction is likely to be a scene of angry panic, lashing tails and instant flight.

If we encountered a pride of lions in the early evening, we usually stayed with them for a while to see whether they were inclined to hunt before nightfall. As the heat goes out of the sun, the pride stirs itself, stretches and gazes about the plain. Then the lionesses, who do most of the hunting and killing, move off towards the grazing herds in the distance. One lioness always remains with the cubs to protect them not only from hyenas and leopards, but also against their father, whose interest in his offspring is often gastronomic as well as paternal.

The hunt is sometimes a cleverly arranged exercise with a skilfully planned downwind ambush, and sometimes an inefficient and haphazard affair, ending in failure. The kill is not a sight for the squeamish. The old story, 'With one blow of her mighty paw,' etc., is, I think, a myth: I have never witnessed such a clean blow out of the many lion kills that I have seen. When a quarry is caught it is pulled to the ground and bitten to death in an apparently casual fashion.

I have watched a pair of lions tackle an old bull buffalo and take nearly an hour to pull him down and kill him, which the male eventually achieved by engulfing the buffalo's muzzle in his jaws to prevent breathing. The lioness started to feed off their victim before his life was extinct. On this occasion, the children in my second hunting car returned to camp while the battle raged, somewhat disillusioned by the behaviour of the King of Beasts.

Lions frequently take terrible punishment from their more formidable prey; the forward kick from a big bull giraffe has been known to maim and even kill a lion, but it is from buffalo that they are likely to meet the most opposition, and sometimes death. My clients and I were once following a herd of a dozen old bull buffalo through belly-deep grass when a pride of lions sprang up and attacked the last buffalo in the line. His comrades galloped away, and the lions soon had their victim on the ground, and were attempting to kill him. Suddenly, the rest of the herd halted, turned around and bore down upon the lions in wrath. Their charge was a formidable sight, and one which the lions did not dally to contest; they fled with all speed, pursued out of our ken by the grunting bulls.

A few minutes later, the bulls trotted back to their wounded comrade. Nosing and horning him to his feet, they walked him away, supporting his tottering frame on either side. We slowly followed this procession into the open plain, where the herd stopped and, encircling the wounded beast, performed a sort of macabre gambol around him, lowing as they sniffed and nudged his wounds, and mounting him from behind. I knew that elephant would bear away a wounded comrade like this, but I had never heard of it being done by buffalo. Indeed, to this day I have not heard of another incident of this kind. But, as Pliny said, 'Ex Africa semper aliquid novi.'*

Lions are sometimes driven off their kills by hyenas, particularly in the Ngorongoro crater in Tanzania, where large and formidable packs of hyenas hunt. I remember watching three lionesses kill a wildebeest in the crater; then, decorously lapping the blood of their kill, they waited for the male to finish his snooze and come for his meal. The scene was then invaded by a hooligan mob of hyenas, chattering and caterwauling with obscene laughter; they jostled and insulted the lionesses who disdainfully retreated to the large tree which shaded their lord and master. He strode forward through the howling pack and, seizing a large hyena by the scruff of the neck, shook the delinquent as a terrier shakes a rat, and finally threw him high in the air after his demoralised friends. Then all four lions returned quietly to the feast.

In the Mara we sometimes encountered herds of buffalo up to eight hundred or a thousand strong in the open plain; as we drove slowly through the herd, the young bulls would position themselves facing the cars while the cows and calves remained in the background; sometimes, when the wind was unfavourable, the herd would panic and charge towards us, only to split to either side of the cars and thunder past in a cloud of dust; there was no menace in this, only a wish to seek cover and be rid of us. I was once told by an old buffalo hunter in the Sudan that if a herd charges a man on foot, the best policy is to mount an anthill and, waving both hat and rifle, shout, sing and dance an Irish jig; the herd will then divide, leaving him unarmed. The one time I put this advice into practice, I found that it worked – but I badly needed a cigarette when the herd had passed.

The only menace from buffalo might come from an old lone bull who is cornered or perhaps has been wounded by lion or poachers. If ever I encountered such a one who looked truculent, I would present him with my rear bumper and plan an escape route, because once a bull buffalo charges he will never give up. Several of my acquaintances have not lived to pass on this advice.

* There is always something new from Africa.

When Digby and I started our safaris, the Game Department esti-
mated that there were over twenty thousand rhino in Kenya. There are
now thought to be about four hundred left. This appalling reduction is
the result of indiscriminate butchery carried out by poachers both from
inside and outside Kenya. The poachers, once armed with poisoned
arrows, now operate with sophisticated and sometimes automatic
weapons, and they will not hesitate to do battle with the law. The
reason for this poaching is that the price of rhino horn has recently risen
to over five hundred dollars a kilo; it is smuggled to the Far East in the
primitive belief that it acts as an aphrodisiac, and to the Arab countries
to provide handles for their curved djambia daggers. When we started our safaris, we usually saw several different rhino in the course of
a day's game watching in rhino country. Now they are a rare sight indeed.

Nervous, irascible, irresolute and shortsighted, it is difficult not to
consider the rhino a clown of the African bush. It is easily approached
from downwind and can be induced to wander towards the car by a
good mimic making a series of high whining calls followed by a few
short snorts. However, it is as well to have a getaway in mind as the
distance decreases between that formidable horn and the car. I admit
to having misjudged that distance on several occasions and once, with
my clients' curiosity satisfied and their cameras empty, I turned
towards camp and was starting a dissertation on the habits of a rhino,
when there was a cry from my game spotter followed by a tremendous
thump on the back of the car, which was lifted a foot off the ground. I
sped for home to contemplate the damage. This was further proof that
no wild animals are totally predictable.

For me, the greatest charm of African wild life was the charm of
birds; if there was a keen ornithologist amongst my clients, as was
often the case, my pleasure was heightened. I kept notes, and corre-
sponded with ornithologists both in Kenya and England, with careful
observations of bird migration during each month of the year.

Continual safari was a rewarding way of life amidst great beauty and,
almost always, congenial company. But it also involved long hours and
quite hard work; if my clients, after a dawn start, decided to sit late
into the night beside the camp fire, I had to stay with them until the last
tent was zipped up and the camp given over to the noises of the African
night. It was therefore with some relief that, after several months of
safari, I welcomed the thunder which announced the coming of the
rains. I could then drive with my staff the long road to my home,

Kiserian, on the slopes of Mount Kenya, and my garden, already refreshed by the first few showers and starting to burst with colour.

My friend Sylvia Richardson, who farmed a few miles away, had dealt with everything in my absence, so I would be free to sit on my verandah writing my bird notes and listening to my collection of classical music. Sometimes I would go down the hill with my trout rod to one of the fast running streams which came from the glaciers of the mountain. Then, in the evening, I would drive over to Sylvia with a basket of rainbow trout to watch the colours decay in her well kept garden.

The rains brought snipe into Digby's swamp some twenty miles away, and at a word from him, I would put my labradors in the car and be off to his ranch for two days' shooting and desultory evening discussions on the past and future of 'Hook and Tatham Warter safaris' as we feasted on the delicious little birds.

During the school holidays my sons would fly out to Kenya and we would go to the coast at Lamu, where we had a house on the beach. It was a paradise for small boys, where they could run wild, goggling, water-skiing, going fishing in the Arab dhows, returning to school in England as brown as berries. When they were with me at Kiserian, the boys could enjoy camping in the mountain forests with fishing rods and air guns, usually surrounded by a gang of little African boys who taught them the ways of the bush.

During the 'off duty period', I had time to visit friends and clients in America and England. Back in Kenya, I had a constant flow of visitors: friends from England, globe-trotters and young people with letters of introduction. This was a welcome relief from solitude (by this time, sadly, my marriage had come to an end). My African house staff also enjoyed these visits; they indulged their traditional African hospitality and took a genuine interest in the guests, whom they considered as much theirs as mine.

One of our favourite guests was my old friend from the Sudan, Denis Zaphiro. He usually arrived unannounced on his way to some remote area where his Game Department duties were taking him. At the sight of his Landrover my butler would automatically bring in more logs for the fire and top up the whisky decanter in preparation for a late night.

After one particularly exhausting safari season, Denis appeared at my door with his Game Department staff and Landrovers. 'I'm taking you on a busman's holiday,' he said. 'After thirty years as a Game Warden, I'm retiring, and this is to be my last long patrol. We start tomorrow and are heading for Lake Rudolf and beyond.' And so, next morning, we set off northwards, I with neither clients, responsibilities nor plans, but only my fishing tackle, my bird books and my African game spotter, David, who refused to be left behind.

We picked up a mutual rancher friend on the way, and took the rough road north again towards the southern tip of the lake, which stretches for a hundred and forty miles to the borders of Ethiopia. We camped on the way under shady trees and, as the heat went out of the day, we wandered into the bush with our shotguns to where guinea fowl and francolins were calling. The guinea fowl here in the north were 'vulturine': good to eat and carrying a 'cape' of feathers much valued by salmon fishermen for making the elver fly. I soon had a good supply of these capes, salted and dried and ready for my friends in Scotland who would perhaps respond with an invitation for me to visit their bright waters on my next trip home.

After two days' driving, we reached the high bluff which looked down on the 'jade green sea' below us. It was a moonscape of desolate beauty, which we paused briefly to admire before descending the rocky track down to the lake shore. For the next week or so, we drove slowly northwards along the east bank of the lake, using remote tracks known to Denis and his Turkana game scouts. We started at dawn and drove until about ten o'clock, when the heat had become oppressive and we sought the shade of trees or rigged a tarpaulin for protection, rest and iced lager. Many parts of the coast were infested with large crocodiles; they lay shoulder to shoulder in hundreds, and as we aproached, it seemed that the whole foreshore would rise and waddle into the lake.

We decided that the presence of crocodiles would probably mean the presence of their prey: the shoals of Nile perch which feed near the lake shore. We would therefore cast about for somewhere to camp, then, as the sun tilted towards the west, blow up our rubber dinghy, attach the outboard motor and go fishing, usually with some success.

We followed this procedure for several days, until disaster nearly overcame us. We were in the dinghy, cruising slowly along some two hundred yards from the shore, when Denis struck a big fish. It took control for about twenty minutes before coming alongside, but it was still not ready for the gaff. Tom Bower (our rancher friend) made a gallant lunge at it, but in vain, and the gaff tore a sizeable gash in the rubber hull. Denis, attending to his fish, failed to realise what had happened until the bubbling and whistling of the now flabby dinghy made the situation apparent. Tom reached out and put his hand over the gash; it was only partly effective. At this moment the outboard engine cut out, leaving us with a strong offshore wind and a sinking dinghy. I tugged and tugged at the engine, cursing it and the Japanese who had made the infernal thing, while the wind drove us slowly away from the shore. At last I gave the engine a despairing thump with my fist, followed by a savage tug; it spluttered, coughed and burst into song. We headed for the shallows, where Denis landed his 60lb perch, and the dinghy sank in a last flurry of bubbles.

On every night of that safari, as we lay on our beds under the stars, Denis would produce a small black suitcase containing his classical records, of which he had quite a collection and considerable knowledge. I had never before listened to music under such idyllic, if somewhat eerie conditions. The moonlit lake, the faint lapping of the waves and the occasional grunting of crocodiles seemed to add magic to the clear tones of Handel's *Messiah* on the night air.

Thus we continued northwards until we came to the ill-defined Ethiopian border. We were determined to see something of the wild country which lay beyond so, leaving most of our transport behind, we crossed the border with six armed game scouts in the back of a Landrover, and continued north across country. The area seemed quite deserted, and we stopped to eat our sandwiches in the dappled shade of a thorn tree: three white faces apparently alone, perhaps lost, and armed with nothing but a picnic basket.

Suddenly Denis's roving eye detected a movement in the hills above us. I peered through my field glasses and saw a posse of men, naked to the waist and armed with rifles, moving towards us through the rocks. The leading figure halted and levelled his rifle at us. 'Bandits,' said Denis, grabbing his rifle and shouting to his scouts, who piled out of the Landrover and took up defensive positions. All movement stopped and a period of uneasy silence followed. Then Denis gave further orders in Swahili: 'I want you each to show yourselves briefly and wave your rifles at our friends over there.' This little drama was enacted with laughter and enthusiasm and resulted in the sulky withdrawal of our would-be guests.

We then returned across the border into Kenya for a last evening's fishing, before turning our backs on the lake and driving eastwards. We followed the border for fifty miles to the frontier post of Sabarei, and then drove south through dramatic wooded hill country towards North Horr and the great white Chalbi desert.

We finally came to the edge of the desert and, having filled all our water containers, we set off, following the wheels of the last lorry to cross. The glare from the white saline surface was blinding, but the going was fast and by late afternoon we had reached a little oasis with palm trees and clean standing water: an ideal place for a camp. Folding chairs were produced and, with a bottle of iced lager each, we contemplated our beautiful surroundings while the camp was set up around us.

I was wearing shorts and sandals, and gradually I became aware that my bare legs were crawling with large camel ticks, some of which were already bloated with my blood to the size of small grapes. Denis and Tom were also infested with the beastly creatures, which were marching in droves towards us across the sand. We shook and pulled them off as best we could, and then sprayed insecticide and sprinkled paraffin on a large tarpaulin which we put under our feet. These ticks are the curse of camel country: they are large, active and dangerous and, in Arabia, they are known to cause temporary blindness within a few hours. We had obviously taken over our little paradise from a recent camel caravan, and we were glad to leave next morning. My tick bites lasted for another two months and finally landed me in Nairobi hospital.

We drove on south to Marsabit – a wooded, mountainous oasis of some 800 square miles, surrounded by bleak desert on all sides. We camped here for a day or two, photographing greater kudu and elephants with outsize ivory, while we searched for rare birds. It was a pleasant change to sleep under blankets again and enjoy the cool mountain air. Then we rolled down the hillside and headed south once more.

After some forty miles, Denis turned west along a rough track into the Ndoto mountains, where the seasonally dry Milgis watercourse winds between the peaks. Here we cut down our baggage and took to ponies and camels belonging to the Game Department, and for two nights our evening concert from the Albert Hall was replaced by the roaring and grunting of lions trying to stampede our animals.

Game was scarce in that rugged wilderness; many tracks of poachers suggested the reason for this. Denis showed us a place where he and his scouts had had a pitched battle with a group of poachers a few years earlier; there lay the empty cartridge cases and a few chips of bleached bone left from the hyenas' and vultures' meal.

We made a detour into the hills and returned to our motor transport. Then, sending the lorry back to Maralal by an easy route, we took the

Landrovers to open an old track which led us to the main road south to Maralal. From there, it was an easy hundred and seventy miles to Kiserian, home and comfort. It had been a good safari.

In spite of many years of pleasure and interest in far away places, I had always cherished a wish to return to my first love, England. I had left at an early age, but memories of the English countryside and the changing seasons each bringing its own delights and activities, had always stayed with me, and grown stronger with time.

During my last few years in Kenya, the conditions for our safaris had deteriorated sadly. The Tanzanian border was closed; Uganda was in turmoil and inaccessible; and the Kenyan reserves were becoming overcrowded. New safari firms were springing up, catering for package tours in permanent tented camps; zebra-striped minibuses followed one another across the plains, harassing the game and scattering their refuse behind them, and the air was frequently filled with the hideous drone of aircraft landing on new airstrips to disgorge their pentecostal passengers for a twenty-four hour safari in the bush.

All this of course was progress – but it was not to my liking. When my sons left their schools and universities and based themselves in England, my mind turned more and more to thoughts of a little house in Wiltshire. Perhaps I would never have made the decision on my own but, while I was away in England in 1984, my African landlord, with whom I had enjoyed a long and happy rapport, sold Kiserian to a rich Kikuyu businessman, who demanded vacant possession. I had no inclination to look for another house and so, encouraged by my sons, I packed up after some twenty years in Kenya. Having found jobs for my staff and said goodbye to my friends, I turned my back on that good life forever.

Epilogue: Home from the Hill

The President of the Shikar Club rose in the Savoy hotel, after that august body's annual dinner.

'I have a few sad things to report,' he said, 'before I turn to more cheerful subjects. Firstly, one of our oldest members, Colonel Hilary Hook, has died in Kenya.'

A few bald-headed members nodded contentedly and picked up their glasses of port, but my friend Maurice Coreth slipped away to the telephone to ring the hall porter of the Muthaiga Club in Nairobi.

'Is Bawana Hook dead?' he asked over the crackling line.

'I don't think so,' came the indistinct reply. 'I helped him to bed last night.'

Perhaps it *was* time that I appeared in the flesh to my English friends.

My sons met me at the airport and we drove down to Wiltshire in spring sunshine to stay with friends and look for a house. One day, as we drove from village to village over the broad expanse of the Wiltshire downs with their wooded valleys and streams, I remarked that I was reminded of a Kenya landscape.

'Yes,' replied Simon. 'It is just as beautiful under a foot of snow in February, but you may take a little time to appreciate that.'

At last we found a small house, and I started struggling to master those elements of domestic science which had eluded me in the past. After I had established myself, I made a sentimental pilgrimage to South Devon to stay with my brother Ivan, who had returned to live there. Together we walked again the rugged cliffs over which I had dangled as a boy collecting birds' eggs, and we looked out to sea at the offshore rocks which had been our happy fishing grounds. Brixham harbour was still a place of beauty; sail had given way to motor trawlers, but the tang of the sea and the fish market filled me with nostalgia, as did the broad Devon tones we heard in the old harbour pub where an aged and almost familiar cat slept in the same chimney corner as his ancestor had over half a century before.

On the last day of my stay, my brother and I went to tea with the Prowse family, many of whom had worked for my mother. Ninety-year-old Edith Prowse, who had looked after me as a child, was sitting by the fire knitting. She looked up as I entered, and with a sly smile said:

'You baint Master 'Illery – you were a pretty little boy you were, I used to bath 'ee. Where d'you get all them wrinkles?'

'Long years in bad stations,' I replied. I was indeed 'home from the hill'.

Appendix 1

Many years later, in 1984, the sequel to this story came into my hands. It had been republished in *Sudan Notes and Records* in 1940 and was given to me by Mr K. D. D. Henderson, a one-time governor of Darfur province and editor of *Sudan Notes and Records*. It is reprinted below in its entirety.   H.H.

ESCAPE IN THE GRASS

By Capt. Greenwood (Highland Light Infantry)

The following is reprinted from THE MESSENGER. *It is not possible at present to contact the author but we have made bold to assume his permission.*

The incident to which it refers is recorded briefly in an Intelligence Report dated February, 1909. Sheikh Musa Madibbo later sent a message to say that he 'had not come to fight the Government but to drive the Dinkas from the Bahr el Arab.' He had fallen foul of the Sultan of Darfur as this time and was later compelled to take refuge in Sudan territory. EDITOR.

I always did like the Dinkas. Happy, idle, contented people, with few wants and no cares, singing to their cattle in the sun.

Stark naked and free by the river banks and singing to their cattle in the sun.

All they wanted was to be left alone.

Just like everybody else.

Until trouble came, and then they clamoured for assistance. Just like everybody else. 'Not till the fire is dying in the grate...' and all that.

And so they were left to look after themselves, chiefly because there weren't enough people to go round and we couldn't cover all the ground.

That was twenty-five years ago.

Nobody had ever been to see what happened to the north of the Post, between the Post and the River, which ran in a wrongly dotted line on a 'provisional' map.

We vaguely knew that great plains stretched for miles in all directions and that there the Dinkas roamed about over the new-burnt pastures when the rains were over, driving their great flocks and herds northwards across the Lol up to the Bahr el Arab River. They gave no trouble to speak of and paid a 'token' cattle tax yearly to the Government which had never found time to go up and count their cattle.

All very easy and everybody was quite happy.

Then the Arabs started coming down from beyond the River to the north, and panic spread and grew with every raid over the plains, and the Dinkas fled before the Arab horsemen thundering over the hard burnt soil and took refuge on the fringe of the forest to the south.

Poor, gentle, timid Dinkas, they just ran and ran till where the plains met the forest. The Arabs used to ride down like lightning from their country beyond the River, spearing anyone they met on their road who offered resistance, and recrossing the river with a mob of raided cattle driven before them and lithe naked Dinka girls strapped on to their great saddles behind them.

So it went on. Something had to be done.

So I was sent up to the Bahr el Arab, across the River Lol north of the Post. I and Shawish Kapsur, Almaz, Selim and Yambios – to meet Musa Madibo, the Sheikh of the Arabs. He lived in unadministered country and beyond reach of the law.

Slatin arranged the meeting on the river. So I went up to the River and the shadow that was over the plains lifted and the Dinkas came forth again out of the protecting forest and drove their great bellowing herds back to pasture over the plains; singing to them by the rivers and lying in the sun.

We stood and looked at the River. There was no sign of anybody on the banks. I said, 'He ought to be here by now. We've had much further to go than he has.'

Kapsur said: 'You never can depend on Arabs.'

I said: 'But the Pasha himself wrote to him and fixed the date.'

'You can't depend on Arabs.'

I said, 'Well, we can't waste all day looking at the river waiting.'

'It's always waste of time to make a date with Arabs.'

That was Shawish Kapsur. He was a black heathen from somewhere or other – I forgot where. Some of our police came from the other side of Africa – kidnapped as children by Fellata pilgrims up Sokotu way and set free by us (with luck) in the Bahr el Ghazal.

Shawish Kapsur was very brave. He once charged a charging elephant, shouting and waving his straw hat, and turned it. I watched him as I lay (exhausted) in the mud. All very long ago. But for Kapsur and his fantastic charge, I suppose I should still be under the mud, down Meshra way.

So we turned back from the River and started to cross the two miles of high grass that bordered it.

It was very high grass. Once you left the track you could see nothing. The grass was high over your head.

A roan antelope showed up somewhere – it must have been standing on a mound in the grass. I shot it. Not for its head – I was through with all that. I wanted food for my police and porters. There was no grain to be had in the

Dinka country that year – it wasn't worth sowing any crops with the Arabs coming down like that, grazing their horses in the standing corn and pillaging the grain stores.

We went to cut up the dead roan, but couldn't find it. The grass was very thick. The roan had dropped stone dead – I shot dead true in those days.

For all that, we couldn't find it.

The sun had got very hot and we went back to camp.

Rhin came along in the evening – he'd been out to look for his wife and family out with the cattle on the plains somewhere.

He brought some milk but couldn't get any grain.

He said there was no news of any Arabs.

Next day we found the roan. It had dropped stone dead, just where we'd been looking for it. Afterwards I remembered that.

Then we went up to the River again – there was nothing else to do and one might as well wait there and watch the water running.

I gave my mule to Selim to hold and wandered up the bank. Almaz and Yambios were fishing. Shawish Kapsur came along with me.

I was wondering how long I ought to stay waiting for a man who might never come, who lived beyond reach of the law, whom nobody had ever seen, except perhaps Slatin in the old Mahdi days. And then there was a thunder of galloping hoofs and I was in the middle of a crowd of Arab horsemen who'd suddenly appeared from nowhere.

I said: 'Peace be upon you.' I thought this was Sheikh Musa arriving with the usual Arab bluster and fantasia.

But there was no reply. 'And upon you the peace' and nobody dismounted to greet the Governor's representative on the river. All the Arabs carried the long dervish spear and a few of them had old Remington rifles. Then I noticed the leaf-shaped spear heads and some of them were red.

Again I said, *El Salaam aleikum*' and still there was no response.

I said, 'I have come as arranged by the Pasha to make peace on the border. Where is Sheikh Musa?'

Pax Britanica and all that.

How fantastic!

What should Arabs want with the peace when the finest sport in the world was to be had at the expense of the unbelieving dogs of Dinkas? Infidel and uncircumcised Dinkas, flaunting their shame before the pious Moslems. The ride through the night – the fording of the boundary river – the mad gallop over the plains – the chase of the slim, shrieking Dinka and the long spear piercing his shining naked back. . . .

The slender naked black girls lifted from the cattle posts and strapped, struggling, to the great saddles.

The mob of cattle driven bellowing to the north. . . . The boasting of great deeds done that day, in the safety of the camp fires fifty miles away . . .

There it was. They looked on it all from a slightly different angle.

It was to them as one who might propose a *modus vivendi* between pig and the Kadir Cup people, or the fox and Craven Lodge.

I might have thought of that before.

Everybody was shouting at once and crowding round me and the horses all steaming and fretting.

Kapsur had got separated, and I never saw him.

Then somebody said, 'You've got no business to be on our river – you're our prisoner and you're coming along with us.'

I went on talking and nobody listened.

The Arabs grew impatient. They were in a hurry. They were on a raid and had been killing. The long grass surrounding us was no place for coffee-housing, for it would soon be full of Dinka spearmen gathered like kites out of the blue. The Dinkas are terrified out in the open, but they are brave in the long grass, moving naked and swiftly, like snakes. So the Arabs were in a hurry to get on. Delay in the grass meant death. I went on talking and talking and the Arabs went on shouting and shouting, becoming more and more ex-cited and truculent. I wondered if they would just spear me and gallop away and if so whether I might as well not kill some of them first. And whether they might not bolt if I emptied my magazine into them.

On the whole I thought that wouldn't do.

Finally, with a lot of brandishing of red-tipped spear I was bundled and shoved along, all among the horses.

I wondered what had happened to Kapsur – he was not far wrong in saying you can't depend on Arabs.

The cavalcade moved on – I was somewhere in the middle. We were on the edge of the long grass. For some reason it was quite open between that and the river.

Everybody got spread out all over the place and two Arabs rode close to me. We went along like that.

It was terribly hot and black dust got beaten up by the horses' feet where the grass had been burnt.

The cavalcade made a huge cloud of dust. I was very angry.

Then I thought of the dead roan. After all, I was much smaller than the roan. So I made a rush and dived into the long grass and curled up and lay still.

The Arabs rode up and down, up and down looking for me. I saw their bearded faces. I saw and heard their long spears prodding the ground for me. I remembered that the fox enjoyed being hunted, but all the same I was very frightened.

A horse trod on my ankle, but it didn't hurt. I was thinking of the beaten fox lying in the hedgerow. I don't know how long this went on. I was very fright-ened but, after all, if I couldn't find the roan...?

Suddenly the Arabs all rode off, still shouting and cursing. I lay still for a long time. Perhaps they might come back again. I was parched with the thirst of fear and choked with black dust, and it was terribly hot.

I stood up and saw no sign of Arabs and crept slowly away, guessing my direction by the sun.

Something else was moving through the grass. I could hear it.

When I moved, it moved, and when I stopped, it stopped. Apparently some-body or something was stalking me.

But I had to go on and always it came on, too. I don't know how long this went on. If only I could see it and shoot it! But I could see nothing but high grass.

I went on. There was nothing else to do. The noise came closer and closer and we both kept stopping and listening.

Our paths were clearly converging and we finally both stopped a yard apart.

I saw the grass move at last and put up my rifle, and a voice, said 'Don't shoot!'

It was Shawish Kapsur. He'd been captured, too, and like me had dived into the long grass.

He was very brave, but he thought *something* had been stalking him and he was frightened.

Thousands of acres of high grass and the paths of two fugitives must converge to the same point in it.

So together we returned to camp and drank a lot of water. Then we went and looked for Almaz, Selim and Yambios, but couldn't find them.

Rhin went to see if his wife and children were all right, but they'd gone.

Everybody had gone.

Once more panic was upon the plains and all the people were pouring south again, back to the Lol and the forest where the Arabs dared not come. The experiment had failed: The mission was a frost.

There was nothing to be done except go back to the Post and write a report.

We marched all through the night. The night was full of lowing cattle all on the move.

You could feel something wrong with the night.

I dare say something or other happens when the whole night is crowded with thousands of people all driven onwards by fear.

During the night Almaz and Yambios turned up. They'd been stripped and disarmed and had a bad time. Selim got back next day. I was glad they were all right.

Panic had travelled ahead of us and the country of Malwal and Gok was deserted. We recrossed the Lol River where a precipice falls into it from the south and there we made a camp and a zariba, for here the forest met the plain and so there was wood.

Old Sultan Chakchak and Akot and Yatong were there, his son and daughter. They'd heard all about the raid – it had been a very bad one and one of old Chakchak's sons was said to be dead.

Next day rumours came that the Arabs were coming right down to the Lol, and the Dinkas kept pouring down from all directions. Angyou of Fett, Wulerim Jok from Otocto, Dow Niol, Abdel Rahman of Kurok, all claiming protection and all their people crowded up on the Lol banks where there wasn't grazing for all that mob of cattle.

Old Chakchak sent Akot and some of the less timid Dinkas away north to look for his missing son and get news.

Rhin, my Dinka interpreter, went, too, to try and find his wife and children.

So Yatong interpreted for me.

She was very intelligent. I liked Yatong. Old Chakchak was drunk most of the time, but Yatong knew everything, and so it didn't matter. She was a wonderful girl. A day or so later some Sudanese soldiers arrived and we made a Post.

Yatong said the precipice place was called Nyamlell, so we called the Post Nyamlell.

That was all twenty-five years ago, and I'd forgotten all about the silly, timid, helpless Dinkas and the disgusting Arabs and the long grass and tall slender Yatong. They'd all faded away into the haze of pre-war limbo long ago.

But the other day I happened to meet Rogers in the Club and asked him where he'd come from.

He said, 'Place called Nyamlell, if you've ever heard of it.'

Oh, God!

Appendix 2

————————◆————————

MILITARY AND GOVERNMENT TITLES AND TERMS

INDIA
Jemadar Indian army: as used, it refers to the rank of Viceroy's commissioned officer, i.e. not commissioned by the monarch but by the viceroy. A rank unknown in British service. A Jemadar was promoted from the ranks on merit and wore one pip (his senior, a Risaldar, wore two). He called you 'Smith Sahib' and you called him 'Jemadar Ahmed Khan Sahib'. They had their own mess and were the backbone of the old Indian Army.

THE SUDAN
The more senior ranks of the Sudan Defence Force were officers seconded on attachment from the British Army. The ranks used were Turkish and the historical background to this is as follows: Turkey was once the suzerain of Egypt and all ranks, civil and military, were Turkish (not Arabic, which creeps into Turkish). Britain took over the administration of the Egyptian Army in 1882 after the battle of Tel el Kabir, and it was officered in the middle and senior ranks by British officers with Turkish rank seconded to the Egyptian army with higher rank and pay; this was inherited by the Sudan Defence Force.

Askari (Arabic)   A private soldier.
Bash Shawish   Sergeant-Major.
Bey   A title used after a surname as a mark of respect. See *Kaimakam*.
Bimbashi   (Turkish, meaning 'Leader of a thousand')   A company commander with the insignia of one pip and a Turkish crown.
Buluk (Turkish)   A company of soldiers.
Buluk amin   Quartermaster sergeant.
Hajana   Local word for the Camel Corps, one of the four Corps in the Sudan Defence Force.
Hukuma   Government.
Janabuk   A term of respect founded on rank, when referred to someone of the correct rank. The affix 'uk' means you or your, hence Janabuk means

'Your excellency'. If referred to a third person it would be 'Janab el Bimbashi' – 'His Excellency the Bimbashi'. See *Kaimakam*.

Kaid   The senior soldier in the Sudan was a general, known as the Kaid. The title Pasha was used after the name as a term of respect.

Kaimakam   The rank above Bimbashi (two pips and a Turkish crown as opposed to a Bimbashi's one pip and a Turkish crown). Kaimakam's automatically took the title 'Bey' – Kaimakam Smith Bey etc. – as a term of respect.

Miralai   Rank commanding one of the four Corps in the Sudan Defence Force.

Mulazim   Lieutenant.

Onbashi   Full corporal – two stripes.

Pasha   A term of respect used after a name. See *Kaid*.

Sagh   Major, held by Sudanese.

Shawish   Sergeant.

Wakil Onbashi   Lance-corporal – first stripe.

Index

203